LAND SLIDING:
IMAGINING SPACE, PRESENCE, AND POWER IN
CANADIAN WRITING

Why have so many of this century's prominent political and literary critics wanted to find a single metaphor to describe the character of Canada? Why have so many used land-based metaphors in reference to the divisions between centre and margin, colony and empire, wealth and power? W.H. New, in *Land Sliding: Imagining Space, Presence, and Power in Canadian Writing*, investigates this established paradigm by examining why so many writers have accepted the land as a comprehensive image of nationhood. Is there in fact, he questions, a landscape that is 'natural,' unmediated by social values and literary representation?

Asking what 'land' as an abstract concept and a physical site has to do with writing, representation, and power, New looks at the 'sliding' relationship by which people associate their surroundings with their position in society. New's study of land in literature is a commentary on the way a culture produces values by transforming the 'natural' into literary idiom and, in turn, making literary convention seem natural. *Land Sliding* develops not as a history of uniformity or progress, but as a series of dialogues between past and present, between paradigms and disciplines. It draws on a wide range of texts, including First Nations narratives, contemporary poetry and fiction, government documents, and real estate ads, as well as artwork and photographs, to illustrate the complex associations that link place, power, and language in Canada today.

W.H. New invites readers to look again at Canada's changing cultural character by rereading both the landscape and the people who have interpreted it. *Land Sliding* will have an important place in many disciplines, among them literary studies, geography, fine arts, and Canadian studies.

W.H. NEW is a professor of English at the University of British Columbia. He has written more than thirty books, which include literary history and criticism as well as poetry.

W.H. NEW

Land Sliding: Imagining Space, Presence, and Power in Canadian Writing

UNIVERSITY OF TORONTO PRESS
Toronto Buffalo London

ISBN 0-8020-4119-1 (cloth)
ISBN 0-8020-7962-8 (paper)

Printed on acid-free paper

Canadian Cataloguing in Publication Data

New, W. H. (William Herbert), 1938–
Land sliding : imagining space, presence, and power
in Canadian writing

Includes bibliographical references and index.
ISBN 0-8020-4119-1 (bound)   ISBN 0-8020-7962-8 (pbk.)

1. Canadian literature (English) – History and criticism.*
2. Land use in literature.   3. Canada in literature.
I. Title.

PS8101.L3N48 1997   C810.9   C96-932283-6
PR9185.5.L3N48 1997

University of Toronto Press acknowledges the assistance to its publishing
program of the Canada Council and the Ontario Arts Council.

This book has been published with the help of a grant from the Humanities
and Social Sciences Federation of Canada, using funds provided by the Social
Sciences and Humanities Research Council of Canada.

For Peggy, David, and Peter

land.slide (land'slid) *n.* **1.** A reconfiguring of land formations, particularly of unstable material (rock, soil, and the like), as, e.g., following glaciation. **2.** An overwhelming electoral plurality.

Canada: such a cold, cold country ...
a wide land that must be shouted across with electrons.

Douglas Coupland, *Microserfs*

Contents

List of Plates

Acknowledgments

I would like first of all to thank Giovanni Bonanno, of the University of Messina, and his Italian colleagues for setting this book in motion, and for their generous hospitality and cordial enthusiasm; and Gerald Friesen, of the History Department at the University of Manitoba, whose conversations with me on the subject of 'land in Canada' have invaluably helped shape the text that follows.

I would also like to thank my colleagues at the University of British Columbia, especially Margery Fee, Jane Flick, Sherrill Grace, and Iain Higgins, who read early drafts of chapters and made many constructive suggestions, and Leslie Arnovick, Richard Cavell, Pete Chamberlain, John O'Brian, Mava Jo Powell, and Graeme Wynn, who generously answered a variety of questions; my students Noel Elizabeth Currie, Dorothy Seaton, Graham Huggan, Anne Rayner, and Richard Phillips, whose research in related areas stimulated further thought on the subject of land, and the students in English 505, 545, and 546 at the University of British Columbia, for their spirited discussions of literature; the staff of the Humanities and Fine Arts Divisions of the University of British Columbia Library, and of the Public Archives of Canada; students and colleagues at McGill University, the University of Ottawa, and Shaanxi Normal University in Xi'an, where portions of these chapters were presented as lectures; Daniel Clayton, Amanda Goldrick-Jones, David English, James Doyle, David New, and Ronald Rees, all of whom provided leads that helped resolve particular problems; Irene Ho, who answered questions about Mandarin terminology; and the many owners of prints and texts in copyright, whose cooperation has helped make this publication possible. Gerald Hallowell, Karen Boersma, Darlene Zeleney, Emily Andrew, and Beverley Beetham Endersby provided careful and thoughtful editorial advice at the University of Toronto Press. Douglas Killam generously permitted the reprint, in revised form, of a section of chapter 3 that was first published in *WLWE*. Special thanks, as always, go to Peggy New, for her critical sensitivity and loving support.

Sources and Permissions

Permission to quote from writings in copyright has been granted as follows:

D.G. Alexander, from 'Canadian Regionalism,' in *Atlantic Canada and Confederation*, courtesy of University of Toronto Press

Margaret Atwood, from *The Journals of Susanna Moodie* (1970), by permission of the Oxford University Press

Margaret Atwood, from *Surfacing* by Margaret Atwood. Used by permission of the Canadian Publishers, McClelland & Stewart, Toronto

Irene Baird, from *Waste Heritage*, courtesy of Ronald D. Baird

Earle Birney, from *Collected Poems of Earle Birney* by Earle Birney. Used by permission of the Canadian Publishers, McClelland & Stewart, Toronto

George Bowering, from *Burning Water*, courtesy of Stoddart Publishing Co. Limited

George Bowering, from *Urban Snow*, courtesy of Karl H. Siegler, for Talonbooks

John Buchan, from *Sick Heart River*, courtesy of A.P. Watt Ltd

Ernest Buckler, from *Oxbells & Fireflies* by Ernest Buckler. Used by permission of the Canadian Publishers, McClelland & Stewart, Toronto

Lovell Clark, from 'Regionalism? or Irrationalism?' courtesy of *Journal of Canadian Studies*

Dennis Cooley, from *The Vernacular Muse*, courtesy of Turnstone Press

Douglas Coupland, from *Microserfs*, courtesy of HarperCollins Canada Ltd

Kateri Damm, from 'i lose track of the land,' original version in *Gatherings II*, courtesy of Theytus Books; revised version from *my heart is a stray bullet* (1993), courtesy of the author and Kegedonce Press

Knut R. Fladmark, excerpts from *British Columbia Prehistory* are reproduced by permission of the Canadian Museum of Civilization

Dave Godfrey, from *Dark Must Yield*, courtesy of Press Porcépic

F.P. Grove, from *Over Prairie Trails* by F.P. Grove. Used by permission of the
Canadian Publishers, McClelland & Stewart, Toronto

F.P. Grove, from *A Search for America* by F.P. Grove. Used by permission of the
Canadian Publishers, McClelland & Stewart, Toronto

Claire Harris, from *Drawing Down a Daughter*, courtesy of Goose Lane Editions

Cole Harris, from 'The Emotional Structure of Canadian Regionalism,' courtesy
of the author

Daryl Hine, from 'Point Grey,' courtesy of the author

Jack Hodgins, from *Innocent Cities* by Jack Hodgins. Used by permission of the
Canadian Publishers, McClelland & Stewart, Toronto

Jack Hodgins, from *The Invention of the World*, courtesy of Macmillan Canada

Harold Horwood, from 'Men Like Summer Snow,' courtesy of the author

Hugh Kenner, from 'The Case of the Missing Face,' courtesy of the author

A.M. Klein, from 'Portrait of the Poet as Landscape,' from *Complete Poems, Part 2*,
courtesy of University of Toronto Press

Henry Kreisel, from 'The Broken Globe,' courtesy of NeWest Publishers Ltd

Robert Kroetsch, from *Completed Field Notes*, courtesy of the author and Sterling
Lord Associates (Canada) Ltd

Gatien Lapointe, from *Ode au Saint Laurent*, courtesy of Claude Lapointe

Margaret Laurence, from *A Bird in the House* by Margaret Laurence. Used by
permission of the Canadian Publishers, McClelland & Stewart, Toronto

Margaret Laurence, from *The Diviners* by Margaret Laurence. Used by permission
of the Canadian Publishers, McClelland & Stewart, Toronto

Douglas LePan, from 'A Country without a Mythology,' from *Weathering It* by
Douglas LePan. Used by permission of the Canadian Publishers, McClelland &
Stewart, Toronto, and the author

Hugh MacLennan, from *Two Solitudes*, courtesy of Macmillan Canada

Eli Mandel, excerpts from *Another Time, Stony Plain*, and *Life Sentence*, courtesy of
Press Porcépic

Daphne Marlatt, from *Ana Historic*, courtesy of Coach House Press

W.O. Mitchell, from *Who Has Seen the Wind*, courtesy of Macmillan Canada

Elsie Moore, as quoted by Pauline Greenhill in *True Poetry*, courtesy of McGill–
Queen's University Press

Alice Munro, from 'Thanks for the Ride,' courtesy of McGraw-Hill Ryerson
Limited

V.S. Naipaul, from *The Enigma of Arrival*, courtesy of Aitken, Stone & Wylie Ltd

Lucy Ng, from 'The Sullen Shapes of Poems,' courtesy of the author

E.J. Pratt, from 'Towards the Last Spike,' from *Complete Poems, part 2*, courtesy of
University of Toronto Press

Bill Reid & Robert Bringhurst, from *The Raven Steals the Light*, courtesy of Douglas & McIntyre Ltd

Charles G.D. Roberts, from *The Last Barrier and Other Stories* by Charles G.D. Roberts. Used by permission of the Canadian Publishers, McClelland & Stewart, Toronto

Sinclair Ross, from *As for Me and My House* by Sinclair Ross. Used by permission of the Canadian Publishers, McClelland & Stewart, Toronto

F.R. Scott, from 'Mackenzie River,' 'Old Song,' and 'Laurentian Shield,' from *Selected Poems of F.R. Scott* by F.R. Scott. Used by permission of the Canadian Publishers, McClelland & Stewart, Toronto

Wilfred Watson, from 'Laurentian Man,' courtesy of the author

Tom Wayman, from 'The Ecology of Place,' courtesy of the author

Rudy Wiebe, from *My Lovely Enemy*, courtesy of the author

Ethel Wilson, from *Swamp Angel* by Ethel Wilson ©1954. Reprinted by permission of Macmillan Canada

LAND SLIDING

Land-Forms: An Introduction

Reading Images of Land

The striking cover of the 1993 reprint of *National Fictions*, Graeme Turner's analysis of film and narrative in Australia, shows a 1990 oil painting by Julia Ciccarone. The painting is called *Blanket*. In the foreground, the upper torso of a man can be seen. He is lying on his back on a tessellated floor and, with both hands, is clutching at the plateau that occupies the visual background; he has apparently even grasped the edge of the land, and is sliding it towards him, pulling the landscape over him (and towards the observer), like a blanket. At least, that's what it looks like. But this painting, while it can perhaps be seen simply as figurative play, seems insistently to *mean more*, to call for more 'interpretation.' Why the land-shapes? Why the blanket? Why a man? Why the chequered floor?

Possibly the observer should be seeking a 'symbolic' connection between the male desire for cover and post-Edenic knowledge; or a literary, 'intertextual' link between the seemingly domestic tiles and, say, the 'chequer'd scene' of Alexander Pope's 'Windsor Forest' (1704), where 'waving groves ... part admit, and part exclude the day.' Perhaps a 'metonymic' association of some sort is in order; if a chessboard seems an unlikely parallel with the patio tiles in the painting (though the association with the masculinity of combat is possibly relevant), a more likely association might be the piazzas of European classical and court painting, or the configurations of seventeenth-century Dutch interiors, for then a 'metatextual' reading becomes possible. As Victor Burgin points out, in 'The City in Pieces' – an essay, written as part of a tribute to the theorist Walter Benjamin, on the relation between city and body, and on the power of the conventions of visual 'perspective' –

Perspective provided, quite literally, the 'common ground' on which the identification of architectural space with corporeal space could 'take place'. In
the Renaissance, the inaugural act in constructing a painting was to lay out the
horizontal plane which united the illusory space of the image with the real space
of the viewer. This is the familiar grid of receding squares, accelerating towards
a vanishing point, which in many paintings rises to the finished surface thinly
disguised as a tiled floor. (35)[*]

The tiles in Ciccarone's painting, however, dispute rather than confirm
Renaissance 'distance.' They question the validity of traditional representations of 'perspective' – for while they set up a border between 'natural'
and 'constructed,' the landscape, as depicted, transgresses it – and hence
(by extension) the tiles call into question the conventional perspectives
that are used to interpret the relations between human beings and the
land. (Who shall have authority here? who shall have power? the man?
history? the artist? Nature? Truth?) Perhaps, that is, the man in the
painting (apparently of European extraction) is not pulling the landscape
towards himself; perhaps the land is pulling the man, pulling him out of
the frame of traditional design (the parterre mind-set, or substructure)
and releasing him into local truth. Or is there a third option? Is the man
just hanging on to whatever edge he can, in the face of whatever goes by
the name of experience, only to inhabit the half-world of fiction, with
'truth' or 'reality,' always imagined, nowhere to be seen?
    Still there is the land itself, and the striking attraction to it, which
insistently remains at the centre of *Blanket.* Why is it, a viewer is encouraged to ask, that people treat the land as protector, or as cloak, or as

---

[*]   Burgin earlier establishes a relation between body and space by alluding to the 'widely-
    known drawing by Leonardo da Vinci' (of a man with limbs outstretched, touching the
    perimeter of a circle and the edges of a square) which articulates 'the harmonious
    relation of parts to whole as Vitruvius found in the human form. We may moreover
    recall that the circle and the square are the diagrams of, respectively, the *orbis terrarum*
    and the *castrum* – the subject territories of the Roman Empire and the Roman military
    camp. The body is not simply that which is to be contained by a building, the body
    contains the very generating principle of the building' (34).
        The Leonardo drawing likely also picks up on – and secularizes – medieval drawings of
    Christ-on-the-Cross (God in human form) as the *orbis terrarum* or microcosm of the uni-
    verse – as, for example, in the Ebsdorf *mappa mundi* (lit. 'cloth of the world'), which places
    the head, hands, and feet of Christ at the cardinal points of a map of the world (Christ's
    head at the top, pointing to the east, associated with Paradise), and Jerusalem at the navel.
    For the Ebsdorf map, see Woodward 310, or (more clearly) P.D.A. Harvey 28.

comforter? Why and in what ways do they consider it theirs? When do they identify with a particular land, and what (if anything) causes them to find other lands and land-shapes alien, or alienating, or downright oppositional? How, moreover, do they communicate their degree of identification? What words and signs do they use? What assumptions does the 'language' make about the 'natural' character of the relations between people and environment? What, in short, does *land* have to do with *writing*, with *representation*, and with *power*? These questions, and the connections and associations that they ask about – specifically in the English-language writing of Canada – constitute the subject of this book.

One set of conventions that for many decades governed interpretation suggested that we think of artistic landscapes as representational: designs, perhaps, but delineations of what could, by visiting the place of painting (or place of 'origin'), be replicated in sensory experience. But as the Ciccarone painting makes clear, the act of representation is by no means simple. The observer and the observation interact to shape what is seen (in the sense of 'understood'); representation gives way to conceptualization. Moreover, while those who represent and those who interpret both draw on the physical reality of the object observed, they also invoke additional filters as they 'read the land.' They draw on overt associations (at once personal and political, cultural and historical) that derive from experience and training; they draw directly on an aesthetics of arrangement; and they draw indirectly on the numerous sets of socialized assumptions (about knowledge, about nature) that – simply because they have been so wholly absorbed – are unlikely even to have been consciously examined. I am concerned in this book, then, not so much to explain what 'land' is – to tabulate the dimensions of Canada, the statistics of ownership, the chronology of expansion – as to explain how various *configurations of land* function in literature (and so in Canadian culture at large) to question or confirm configurations of power.

Reading Space, Place, Land

'Land,' in consequence, has to be seen as a verbal trope in Canadian writing, not simply as a neutral referent. But complications attend this understanding. While the word *land* often functions as a familiar synonym for *dirt* or *earth* or *ground* or *loam* (and can be emotionally charged even in this context), it sometimes also resonates with notions of ownership or social attachment (*territory, home, property, estate, plot, yard, grounds, region, nation, world*). In such conditions the constructed or customary relations between land and class, land and gender, land and ethnicity, land and capital, all become more apparent than if *land* is construed as a neutral or objective term.* Yet *land* can also function not just as the revelation of the status quo, but also as the *space* or *place* or *site* of challenge to the accustomed borders of power. It shifts, in this context, from a designation of locality to a (perhaps more abstract) designation of activity. Land functions in cultural discourse, therefore (and in other cultural practices: mining, farming, real estate sales), both as an icon of stability and as a medium of change. Fixity vies recurrently with fluidity, position with positionality, the place of social residence with the condition of being there.

One's attitude to estate occupancy, for example, will vary in part with one's role in the managerial system that uses property as an arbiter of privilege: take the plantation system as a particular kind of paradigm. An owner might love the land for what the very possession of it states to the world more than for itself; an agricultural worker might gain little of the owner's social status but nevertheless love the land for its beauty or fertility; a woman, if social convention has consigned her to a domestic interior, might well perceive the land as an alien territory, or alternatively construe it as the site of freedom; a slave on the same estate (designated as part of the property) might construe even the interior domestic space as a site of others' privilege, and hence as a further demarcation of (unequally distributed) power. All might speak in land-based metaphors – about their place in the world – and in this way express their satisfaction or dissatisfaction with the established system of authority. All might emphasize the arbitrariness of the boundary lines, or 'maps,' that demarcate their particular sphere – all, that is, except the most privileged, who

---

* Seeking to differentiate among these words by examining root derivations does not prove entirely successful. The word *dirt* derives from an Old Norse word for 'excrement,' and *ground* from the Old Norse for 'grassy plain'; but *earth* derives from the Gothic for 'earth,' *field* from the Old Norse *fold* or 'open ground,' and *land* from the Gothic for 'land' (though it is apparently related, paradoxically, both to the Irish Celtic for 'enclosure' and to the Cornish for 'open space'). The word *place* has Greek roots, meaning 'broad way'; *soil* has Latin roots, though whether from *solium* ('seat') or *solum* ('ground') remains conjectural; *place*, too, derives from Latin (*spatium*, or 'extent of distance'). Contemporary shades of meaning do, of course, distinguish these words in modern English, both referentially and metaphorically. *Land* to a farmer might in one context mean the physical extent of fields, or acreage, and in another mean the dirt or earth itself, the consistency and fertility of loam or podzol or gumbo. The word *plot*, moreover, can refer both to a kitchen garden (a 'vegetable plot') and to funerary customs.

might well regard their position as 'earned' and the demarcations as 'natural.' But as a group they will likely divide in how they interpret the land: they might find in it a confirmation or encoding of a fixed system (whether governed by class, wealth, gender, or race); alternatively, they might read it for some revelation or sign of the fluidity of social change.

As the extensive body of theory concerning space and spatial relationships makes clear, *land, place,* and *space,* though related terms, are not equivalent. In particular, geographic and sociological theory argues that place and space are relational notions: *place* (as the most influential theorist of the subject, Henri Lefebvre, anatomizes the term) designating a particular use of space, and *space* designating the set of (epistemological, political, sensory, and imaginative) assumptions governing a people's attitudes towards social production, social distance, and hence social power (11–12, 16). ('Space,' that is, is not a given; it is culturally constructed or *produced.*) Lefebvre's 'space' incorporates temporal change, even insists on it,* in order to resist the fixity of assumed norms of distance; at the same time, it acknowledges the force that all conditioned responses to spatial convention can exert within a given society. By way of example, it might be helpful to think of the question that a familiar Leo Tolstoy short story title asks: 'How much land does a man need?' In the story, the phlegmatic answer is a six-foot plot to bury him in. But the question 'How much *space* does a person need?' calls for a different kind of answer entirely, and these answers will vary with 'positionality,' depending on the values attached to distance and independence, closeness and collectivity. 'Distance,' that is, is less empirical than systems of measurement might imply, for 'acceptable nearness' varies from culture to culture, and even within cultures varies with circumstance. What is congenial space for one set of people might be confrontative for another; what is communal or collaborative space to one group might be competitive to another. And roles alter. Is the person who 'needs space' young or old? in urban, suburban, or rural conditions? impelled by the public credos of individual freedom or governed more by the proximities of an extended family? in a 'close' relationship or in a 'distant' one? at the 'centre' of activity and power or situated (whether passively or by desire)

---

* For example: 'In space, what came earlier continues to underpin what follows ... The preconditions of social space have their own particular way of enduring and remaining actual within that space ... The task of *architectonics* is to describe, analyse and explain this persistence, which is often evoked in the metaphorical shorthand of strata, periods, sedimentary layers, and so on' (229).

at a 'margin,' on a 'perimeter,' or at a 'leading edge'? The language of
relationship here is spatial, and the temptation is to read relationship as
a sociological abstraction – but underlying all the abstract questions about
social relations are the specificities of empirical experience. What, in
short, does the person want or need space for? (a hayfield, a workshop,
a cell, a private chamber, a podium, an exercise yard, a psychic room, a
social reputation?) Lefebvre asks how 'space' has come to constitute a
social *commodity* in the transactions of power that relationships represent.
Acknowledging these contextual dimensions, I wish also to ask how spatial
metaphors – in particular, in the *language of land* – function in literature
as part of the process of constructing, questioning, and confirming assumptions about social reality.

Lefebvre devises a tripartite schema to support his analysis, dividing his
subject into *spatial practice, representations of space,* and *representational spaces*
(33, 245). In the first category he places such spatial structures as roads
and houses, which express certain social expectations about physical
needs and economic transactions. The second category refers to geomet-
ric configurations such as open arcs and closed circles, lines and squares,
grid systems and interlocking boxes, perspective conventions and *trompe
l'oeil*; the third category deals with the symbolic function of spatial allusion, as in the semiotic codes of any culture's art: these ask, for example,
not 'Where is "North"?,' but 'What is *meant* by "North"?' And what are
the conventional associations that accompany the words *town* and *country,
box* and *diamond, corner* and *centre,* or (more diffusely) *left* and *right, near*
and *far, too far* and *close enough?** The relevant contexts here are broadly
cultural, not just narrowly national; they relate to geography, but they
also configure a deeply ingrained social inheritance of attitudes to gender, race, class, power, role, responsibility, and play.[1] The language of
land – the terms *garden, valley, island, mountain,* to mention some of the
most obvious nouns – cannot, in these contexts, be construed simply as
references to physical phenomena. The language that alludes to gardens,
mountains, and so on constitutes, at the same time, an ongoing history
of a culture's relations with place and space.

---

*   For example: Henrietta Moore demonstrates the cultural relation between space,
    time, and gender in one tribal group; for the Marakwet, not only is land ownership
    linked with gender rights and responsibilities, but so also is the language of space
    and time. The words *tai* ('right') and *let* ('left'), for example, indicate spatial direc-
    tion; they also encode a particular cultural perspective, for they signify, respectively,
    front, past, coming, ancestors, and *behind, future, going, unborn.*

Only in the latter decades of the twentieth century have geographers begun to examine the way they read the land (Derek Gregory and David Livingstone, for example).[2] In the process, empirical accounts of products (including political boundaries and 'natural resource' management systems) have been giving way, at least to a degree, to analyses of methodology and of the politics of the discipline's own discourse. To call cultural geography an intellectual *site*,[3] and to call the landscape a *discursive terrain*,* is in some measure, that is, to draw on the extensive semiotic theory that sees *text* as a *ground* of contestation. To the degree that 'landscape' becomes a *text*, runs this argument, it can be 'read,' turning the exercise of geographical observation – metaphorically at least – into a theatrical activity.[†] If landscape is rendered as spectacle, moreover, the

---

* The term is used by Daniels and Cosgrove: 'Spectacle and text, image and word have always been dialectically related, not least in theatre itself, and this unity has been the site of an intense struggle for meaning ... [L]andscape is the discursive terrain across which the struggle between the different, often hostile, codes of meaning construction has been engaged' (59). In the rhetoric of this particular passage, of course, the dialectical relation is figured not as theatre, but as a form of military combat. See also Meinig, who studies landscape as a 'way of seeing,' an encoding of such phenomena as home, wealth, and travel; Cosgrove, who in *Social Formation* asserts that landscape is a social and cultural product, citing Palladianism, Virgilian eclogues, American religion, and industrial capitalism in support of the argument; and Zukin, who distinguishes between kinds of landscapes (urban, moral, industrial, suburban, etc.), acknowledging that contemporary landscapes are more likely sociological images than paintings; Zukin recognizes that spatial metaphors and symbolic geographies are cultural forms.

† Burgin notes that, in ancient Greece, rhetoric was an 'art of space' involving staging and gesture, as well as an 'art of speech,' and he uses this connection to elucidate the different social 'stages' on which contemporary spatial relationships are enacted (43).

    Importantly, Mary Carruthers, in *The Book of Memory*, has demonstrated that the medieval art of *memory* was also spatial. Medieval speakers and visual designers, that is, drew on Greek and Latin rhetorical conventions, using the technique of what Carruthers calls the 'architectural mnemonic' (71). Ornamented letters and pictures, for example, served temporally to permit people in the present to retrieve and meditate upon the voices and ideas of the past (so that the cathedral or the illuminated manuscript is intrinsically a literary form, a rhetorical activity [221–8, 253]). Just as the space in a drawing functions diagrammatically – 'The framework of the page provides a set of orderly *loci* ... [which] is also the manner of the page of memory' (249) – so do the spatial representations of speech (242 ff.). The visual associations which permit speakers to *position a sequence* of words has a parallel in such images as ladders and architectural forms in medieval design; for example, the triple-tiered *ark* is conventionally a mnemonic for the study of scripture; when it is also identified with the *apotheca*, or 'storehouse,' it becomes a metaphor for both *memory* and *book* (45).

geographer's role by extension turns into that of the observer/voyeur, who classifies and 'objectifies' phenomena not according to some intrinsic and eternal paradigm of verities but in response to cultural training and immediate stimulus. The *reading of the land* is less a fixed science, then, than a social process.

What then about the reading of the *language of land* (that is, the words that express the idea of 'land' and attempt to represent it, as distinct from the idea of reading-the-landscape, or treating the land itself as kind of language, or word)? Lefebvre is circuitous on this issue. Drawing directly on Marxist principles, he recognizes the role that land plays within modes of production (involving rent, profit, and wages [323–5]);[*] land, that is, functions as a commodity in class structure, in capital exchange, in resource control, and in territorial (hence national or political) assertion. But how the language works – as a code of what he calls 'representational spaces' – remains (except inferentially) largely unexamined.

For their part, the editors of *The Post-colonial Studies Reader* (Bill Ashcroft, Gareth Griffiths, and Helen Tiffin) eschew the term *land* in favour of *place*; they associate the word *land* with 'landscape,' in fact, and define the more specific term *landscape* in relation to the philosophic tradition that separates 'objective world' from 'viewing subject' (391).[†] While 'land' does not equate solely with 'landscape,' by substituting 'place' they foreground yet another issue: the 'complex interaction of language, history and environment' that they identify with a 'gap' between an imported language and a lived environment. Place can be text, that is, and text place. Post-colonial *textual place* is a 'discourse in process,' in which the language that negotiates the distance between words and experience

---

The mental search for data, or to make sense of data, emphasizes a further boundary between mind and nature: the Latin word *silva* ('forest'), by common metaphorical extension, meant 'a mass of unrelated and disordered material' (62) which the trained student of rhetoric could, like a trained hunter, learn to read. See also Carruthers's *The Witness*, which discusses the 'habit of allegory' (17) in their own culture that led medieval European travellers to read Other worlds as they did.

[*]   One geographer who does raise linguistic questions about his discipline is Gunnar Olsson, especially in *Lines of Power/Limits of Language*, where he argues that the 'primary data' and 'proper place of geography' lie in words rather than in 'empirical observations of the conventional kind' (154).

[†]   The word *landscape*, Simon Schama observes (10), derives from *landskip*, a colloquial English rendering of the Dutch *landschap*, which, like its German root, *Landschaft*, indicated a 'jurisdiction,' a unit of engineered habitation – which Schama considers a narrative in its own right – as distinct from a background to narrative or a land painting.

serves concurrently as a 'metonym of the continual process of [cultural] reclamation' (391). Put another way, 'place' exists both in the empirical environment (which words can be used to 'read') and on the page, in the language that is being used to do the reading.[4] But if a language (together with the values it encodes) has been brought from somewhere else, and is being used to describe a new environment and to voice another culture's inevitably changing values, the old terms might no longer conventionally apply. 'Commonly understood meanings' can break down. Under these conditions, the language is at once an impediment to communication and the very means of communication, a site of paradox, a ground at once of exhaustion and creativity.

Reading the Language of (Canadian) Land

The (primarily English-language) Canadian textual examples to which *Land Sliding* refers can thus be seen as representing larger social issues than, say, cultural nationalism. Clearly, there is a set of specific local terms that does describe or contrive to represent Canadian land – 'The Prairies,' 'The Canadian Shield,' 'muskeg,' 'hoodoos' – though the latter two terms are not limited to Canadian usage. But even if these and related terms do reflect the particulars of local geography and local vocabulary, that does not mean that they will be uniformly understood; nor does it mean that allusions to Canadian land will necessarily use the local terms or adopt Canadian values or get 'right' (that is, according to Canadian perspectives) the semiotics of dimension, distance, or what Lefebvre calls 'representational space.' Representations of 'Canadian land' consequently illustrate many of the sociocultural and socioeconomic issues raised by post-colonial theory: the issues of colony and empire, wealth and power, centre and margin, the opportunity to speak and the likelihood of being heard. The particular and local,[5] that is, do not exist in a cultural and historical vacuum; they derive from conventions – and while they can and do often re-record these conventions, whether for good or ill, they also counter and contend with them, reclaiming continuously the power of reality from the presumptions of knowledge.

Two sets of examples will illustrate how an imperial discourse involving land in Canada – in which the conventions are crafted about *but outside* Canadian experience – sets up this paradigm, articulating a conditioned sensibility. Sustained over many decades, this discourse for a long time shaped how people perceived Canadian landforms and Canadian realities (and in some quarters it continues to do so); by extension, it also conditioned what these people thought to be propriety and acceptability in language and art. 'Reality' existed in one form in local experience, in another on the conventional page; hence the imperial discourse led, obliquely perhaps, and over time, to various political, social, and verbal forms of post-colonial resistance, but along the way it gave rise to a number of long-lived and oddly fixed misapprehensions and assumptions about what a Canadian experience of space, place, and land might mean.

The first set of three examples comes from *Through Canada with a Kodak*, the 1890–1 travel journal (first published in 1893) by Lady Aberdeen (Ishbel Gordon, Marchioness of Aberdeen and Temair). The second set of three examples comes from *Sick Heart River* (1941), the last novel written by John Buchan (Lord Tweedsmuir), who from 1935 to 1940 acted as Canada's thirty-fifth governor general. Both authors were British; both enjoyed the wealth and privilege of aristocratic status (though Buchan was not born to nobility); and both display an educated articulateness that serves a specific set of assumptions about appropriate social practice. These assumptions (relating language and propriety to space and land) came to be associated with Empire, power, and a particular British-based notion of class – which many Canadians emulated, and which many others, who weighed convention less approvingly against local experience, in varying degrees parodied, resisted, displaced, and dismissed.

Through Canada with a Kodak is not the work of a professional writer; but as a none the less deliberately crafted travel diary, it provides an instructive revelation of what one person thought worth observing about late Victorian Canada. The degree to which these observations also display culturally shaped expectations about beauty, utility, society, and race indicates, further, how the language of apparent description is also a language of coded evaluation. The Countess's cross-Canada journey (in a private Canadian Pacific Railway car) begins in Ontario, and heads west across the prairies, through the Rockies, to Vancouver, leading along the way to these comments:

We thought we had chosen quite the best time of year for our trip, ... for when we woke up the first morning after leaving Ottawa, we found ourselves passing through roads all flaming with the gorgeous autumnal tints of the maple ... I think, if I am to be truthful, I must admit that this scenery would have borne rather a forbidding aspect if it had not been for these rich colourings, and we can scarcely wonder if newly-arrived emigrants bound Westward feel rather depressed at passing through a stretch of such apparently sterile country... And yet this region has charms of its own – ... the geologist ... will tell you of the yet comparatively unexplored riches of silver and copper and other metals which are stored up for Canada's children beneath the unpromising looking surface, and the artist will revel in the wild grandeur of the mountain and lake scenery all along the coast of Lake Superior. A succession of magnificent promontories, frowning rocks and crags, surround the lovely bay of that vast expanse calling itself a lake, meets your eye as the train bears you along, and you lay down your pencil and brush in bewilderment as to which point to seize amidst so much beauty, and instead, you revert to the faithful rapid Kodak to record your memories ... (94–7)

[In the Rockies] we rush about from side to side, and from end to end of our car, attempting, if not to photograph or sketch, at least to imprint some memory of the magnificent panorama unrolling itself before our eyes. But all in vain! There is such a thing as being surfeited with fine scenery, and it is a transgression against nature to hurry, as we did through these glorious scenes. All that remains now is a remembrance of towering snow-capped peaks rearing themselves up in all their strength above us, and stretches of mountains changing in the varying light of sun and cloud, from palest blues and greys to rich tones of yellow and red and purple, ... as the autumn foliage shows itself blending with the deep browns and blueish-green colours of the waters foaming below. (131–4)

At Vancouver we were most hospitably entertained by the Mayor ... , and ... the Scotch and the Irish residents combined together to give us a most hearty and kindly reception ... In this way we heard much of all that was doing in the place, and of its wonderful growth since the disastrous fire which utterly annihilated it five years ago. Within three months after the fire four hundred houses had been erected, and the progress has since been so rapid that there is now a population of 13,000. This is the more remarkable when we reflect that the site on which the town stands was covered with a dense forest ... Their great roots have to be removed, and the heavy wood and dead timber have to be cleared at an enormous expense before the land can be utilised ...

We must tear ourselves away from Vancouver and its beautiful surroundings with regret, and embark in the 'Islander' for the five hours' crossing to Victoria ... Is it indeed Victoria and Vancouver Island where we have arrived? Has not the 'Islander' lost her way, and brought us by a short route back to England, and landed at Torquay? ... English voices and faces abound, and English customs predominate so largely that the illusion would be complete if we were not recalled to our whereabouts by the presence of the Chinese pigtail everywhere. (141–6)

Sick Heart River, Lord Tweedsmuir's saga of psychic trauma in the Arctic, presents a more deliberately organized set of images than does the Countess of Aberdeen's diary, but it records some of the same presumptions about wilderness and society. The novel constructs the North, for example, as attractive and magnetic, but manufactures psychic tension by refusing to allow the North to be a place in which anyone can reasonably live. The North is declared ultimately to be a place of death, decay, corruption, and despair – a place to be defeated (by dismissing the power of its attractions) lest it defeat the central character's hold on the powerful triumvirate of civilization, manliness, and corporate virtue. As Leithen, the central figure, travels north, the omniscient narrator provides a series of comparisons to spell out the nature of virtue and the potential of disaster:

Leithen led the way up the Clairefontaine [to a meadow]. There was something tonic in the air which gave him a temporary vigour ...

It was a cup in the hills, floored not with wild hay, but with short, crisp pasture like an English down ... The place was so green and gracious that all sense of the wilds was lost, and it seemed like a garden in a long-settled land, a garden made centuries ago by the very good and the very wise.

But it was a watch-tower as well as a sanctuary. Looking south, the hills opened to show *Le Fleuve*, the great river of Canada, like a pool of colourless light. North were higher mountains, which ... were sending the waters ... to untrodden Arctic wastes. That was the magic of the place. It was a frontier between the desert and the sown. (43)

The real trouble was that suddenly everything seemed to have become little and common. The mountains were shapeless, mere unfinished bits of earth; the forest of pine and spruce had neither form nor colour ... In coming into the wilderness he had found not the majesty of Nature, but the trivial, the infinitely small – an illiterate half-breed, a rabble of degenerate Indians, a priest with the mind of a child. The pettiness culminated in the chapel, which was as garish as a Noah's Ark from a cheap toyshop. (74–5)

For to Leithen it looked as if in this strange place he had got very near his journey's end. He toiled in the wake of the Hare for something less than a mile ... He tried to step in the Indian's prints, but found them too long for his enfeebled legs. He who had once had the stride of a mountaineer now teetered like an affected woman. (111; see also 173)

To catalogue the characteristics of these several observations might lead to comments about the surfeit of adjectives used to describe autumn colour, or to reflections on conscious or unconscious racism and the impersonality of the references to Indian characters. ('The Hare,' who labours hard for Buchan's British hero, is only once in the entire book referred to by name.) This commentary might suggest evidence for distinguishing between the sublime and the picturesque in art (the 'grandeur' of the one, and the fascination with 'promontories' that marks the other). Or it might lead to an analysis of the gender hierarchy implied by Buchan's definition of masculinity. But in both Buchan's text and Lady Aberdeen's, these observations are all informed by a conventional association between development, morality, and land. Within this paradigm, wild land equals animality (the Lake Superior crags 'frown,' the Rockies 'reared up'), together with superstition, childishness, weakness, the 'illiterate,' the 'degenerate,' the 'sterile,' the 'stunted,' and the 'unfinished'; civilized land, by contrast, equals the cleared, the 'utilized,' the resource-based, the 'formed,' the 'settled,' and (most especially) the 'green and gracious' garden shaped apparently by English wisdom. The wild might on occasion be magnificent, beautiful, or 'grand,' but the civilized observer (these texts warn) must be wary of identifying with it: far better to tame it in the conventions of art, to sketch it, or – better still? – to snap a photograph of 'scenes' and carry on, investing time and money in the familiar. Language, moreover, not the land itself, is a medium *of* the familiar. Hence these writers (both of them writing in and for their time, and out of the literary conventions of both their time and the society that trained them to speak and to see) resist the local language of the communities and places they seek to describe, and substitute their own (local) British idiom for it.* Lady Aberdeen's understanding

---

* It is clear, however, that 'their time' seems to persist into the 1990s for some readers, affecting editing and marketing policies as well as interpretation. Marjory Harper notes that Lady Aberdeen's diary provides valuable historical information, arguing that it reveals 'the positive image of Canada held by tourists and emigrants alike, and cultivated in the fervent Imperialist climate' of the Britain of the 1890s (lxxv); the power of Empire to shape what would or would not be accepted as 'positive' remains, however, unsaid. Buchan's book, marketed in Oxford's 'World's Classics' series, reveals a different style of editing. David Daniell provides eleven pages of 'explanatory notes' to the 1994 edition; while these notes do not translate all the Latin in Buchan's text, they do annotate all the specific Canadian references, yet these appear to be shaped by European training (and expectation) rather than to establish what the Canadian words mean in Canada (and, to give him credit, in Buchan's book). Hence *habitant* is translated as 'native to the area' (215), rather than (as a number of dictionaries, including Walter Avis's *A Concise Dictionary of Canadianisms*, indicate) a francophone 'farmer' of a previous generation; *mackinaw* is translated as 'a thick

of the word *lake* will not extend to 'vast expanse,' and Lord Tweedsmuir's affirmation of a green-garden norm leads him away from the Arctic until the landscape can seem approvable, 'like an English down.' The similes suggest a likeness. But specifying *difference*, not likeness, is the inherent model here; hierarchical *differentiation* is the social intent.

This language of land, that is, together with the implicit set of dimensions that accompanies and underscores it, at once conveys some particular political attitudes and appears to ratify them as 'natural.' But what is 'natural'? What, by contrast, is socially contrived? To what ends do writers and readers turn these language conventions? What happens when writers and readers in a society such as Canada's want to acknowledge established traditions yet to resist simply reinscribing them, or to parody tradition without necessarily rejecting it, or to devise variant forms of convention in the name of greater accuracy or greater freedom? And what in any event do these questions have directly to do with space, place, and land?

Reading Land Sliding

The four essays that follow focus on some of the land-forms (not physical, geomorphological *landforms*, but conceptual *land-forms*) that anglophone Canadian writing employs. In these essays I am not so much concerned with the ostensible accuracy of representing empirical landforms in Canada (eskers, cols, drumlins, monadnocks, and the like) as with the political implications of a series of aesthetic choices: those that involve *territoriality, property, region,* and *site.* The four essays are openly selective, not encyclopedic – they certainly do not mention every Canadian literary reference to land and landscape – and they are concerned with demon-

---

blanket, worn by Indians; also a large, flat-bottomed, sharp-ended boat' (215) rather than as a woollen coat or jacket, usually with a tartan pattern; *muskeg* is defined as a 'Cree Indian word for swamp' (216), though the word has been wholly absorbed into Canadian and American English; *arêtes* and *couloirs* are called 'terms in French Switzerland (as in Dauphine) for sharp ridges and gullies' (217), as indeed they are, though the terms have long been in use elsewhere as well, having become standard terms in geomorphology: the point is not that such terms are not Swiss, but that they don't have to be Swiss here to make sense of Buchan's text or to make sense of Canada. By trying to read the Canadian land through European language, such definitions distort what they purport to clarify, curiously reiterating, in a way, the mind-set, if not the precise observations, of Lord Tweedsmuir and Lady Aberdeen.

strating only some of the social functions of literary language in anglophone Canada: the way it embodies (and so reveals) social presumptions;
the way it works unconventionally to reject social presumptions; the way
it criticizes, validates, or sometimes seeks to be neutral; the way it resists
uniformity. Some of the examples are drawn from what might be called
a 'genteel' tradition in Canadian letters, some from 'popular culture';
some are 'experimental' in form, some 'radical' in politics. It is important
to emphasize that these terms – like 'neutrality' and 'objectivity' – are
inherently relative, manipulated by (and often manipulating, however
unintentionally) the agents and hence the paradigms of cultural power.
But that is the point. My intention here is not to produce a linear history
of a national culture or a new geography of social relations, but to provide a discontinuous analysis of some textual practices, to indicate how,
inside a social context, land-language *slides*.

Canadians, of course, have long thought of themselves in connection
with the land. As scores of writings indicate, they are fascinated by distance and scenery, park and farm, property and region, river system and
mountain range, 'cottage country,' religious codes involving nature, and
the staples they can produce from the land and use in trade – all this in
a largely urban society. It is no surprise that major ecological movements
(Greenpeace, for example) have developed in Canada, or that the nation
depends for its wealth largely on natural resources, or that the tourist
industry characteristically relies on images of wilderness beauty to represent local reality, or that in the 1980s one group of politicians wanted the
right to own property to be enshrined in the national constitution. But
it should also be no surprise that these positions are inconsistent. While
many influential commentators have in the past encapsulated a collective
Canadian identity in land-based metaphor – one thinks of the critic
Northrop Frye, in *The Bush Garden,* for example, talking of a 'garrison
mentality';[6] or of the politician Alexander Mackenzie and the poet E.J.
Pratt, alluding to Sir John A. Macdonald's National Dream as a problem
of building a railway across a 'sea of mountains'; or of the historian
Donald Creighton, conceptualizing Canada as the offspring of the 'empire of the St. Lawrence' – my purpose here is somewhat different, for I
do not assume that the land is a 'natural' image for a distinctive national
character, or that a national character is by definition fixed. Instead of
accepting the land as a concluding image of identity, in consequence, I
am interested in why it has so often been accepted as though it were, and
what this acceptance implies.

This book develops, therefore, not as a history of uniformity or progress, but in a series of dialogues, both explicit and implicit. There is a kind of dialogue with the past, for example, in the attempt to understand why previous commentators have characterized the land in Canada as they have, and what their systems of value – particularly their embrace of the hierarchical values of Empire – have to do with present social conditions.[7] The characterization of land as *female*, of Canada as the Empire's *child*, of wilderness as *savage*, of utility and domesticity as the only acceptable measures of the *beautiful*: such judgments, however questionable and in whatever measure repudiated, remain influential. These metaphors encode attitudes and expectations; they tell of what some people take to be true, whether they are or not, and hence they reveal the unstable ground of social norms. Hence 'dominant' and 'marginal' constitute two poles of another exchange, in that these essays also deal primarily with the schooled values that the dominant forms of culture in Canada have assumed to be standard and have celebrated; at the same time, they dispute the notion that a dominant culture is necessarily monolithic and uniform. 'Classes' or 'categories' cannot stand in for 'individuals,' though the reverse is often true: individuals frequently appeal for recognition through classes or categories, seek personal status or legal definition by identifying with some larger unit of power, and so in varying ways become 'representative' members of a group. But the group (which can be anarchic and can be tyrannical and can take on a variety of other characteristics) can never *typify* all individuals; it can function only as the product of negotiations among differences. So with 'dominance.' While dominant cultures, to their own detriment, frequently pay little attention to the values of the people they consider marginal, the cultures of the people on the margin (wherever the margin is placed) do not function completely without reference to the currents of thought that these people themselves are resisting. The act of resistance is an act of recognition – even, potentially, of ratification, which is one of the paradoxes of postcoloniality. But because the language of literature, among other kinds of communication, can be a medium of resistance as well as a medium that passively confirms the status quo, cultural values – and the particular forms through which these are expressed – do change.

Dialogues thus occur in this book within chapters, as paradigms interact, and between chapters. Each essay on anglophone Canadian writing points to some of the main trends involving the land that occur in parallel fashion in francophone Canadian writing. The footnotes, too, constitute a kind of running dialogue with the main text. They do not simply document sources; they allude to other literary and historical interpretations, to art history and anthropology, sociology and geography, suggesting ways in which cultural studies can draw on several forms of scholarship. The plates, likewise, are not mere decorations, but examples of how the principles and practices that are being discussed in relation to literature permeate other discourses also; they are tangible demonstrations of the degree to which those people who have worked in such media as painting, cartooning, lithography, and photography have also addressed the subject of land in Canada; how they have variously represented line, texture, and spatial relationships; and how they have used these visual designs to comment on cultural reality or to shape how such realities can be perceived.

Each of the following chapters deliberately *plays* with the 'language of land' in its title, creating metaphor in order in part to discuss metaphor, but also to emphasize the play – the manner, the fitful movement – of perception. Chapter 1, 'Landing,' is concerned with the language of *contact* and *territoriality* – with the constructions of 'self' and 'other' that create the categories 'Native' and 'European,' and with some of the writings that develop out of this distinction. For instance, it considers the literary form of Native tale-telling, and it considers the way contemporary First Nations literature functions as revisionary history; it also addresses the way so-called European writings (religious and documentary narratives, among other forms) observe the *new-found land* through the old land's eyes, acknowledging, of course, that the very idea of the 'novelty' of a 'new' land is a 'European' or 'old-world' phrasing. Such forms revise what they see in the process of seeing it. Both the Native and the European writings struggle with the disparity between a learned *idea* of landscape and an observed and observable *setting*. But this division between place and people – whether it is imposed upon a culture or taken as axiomatic within it – is not the only disparity to be interpreted. The character of oral and written practice, the politics of religious and documentary testimony, the conventions of 'art': each of these features of discourse is also a way of studying social organization and values, in place and over time, and of examining the relation between aesthetic conventions, the placing of authority, and social change.

The subsequent chapters pursue these questions further. 'Land-Office' (chapter 2) considers the literature of ownership, whereby 'land' is claimed for occupation in a variety of ways (*property* and *military advantage* are recurrent terms). 'Landed' (chapter 3) asks how notions of place, and particularly of *region*, become talismans of identity, associated with notions of *home*. By contrast, 'Landscape' (chapter 4) reaches after something that at first seems a little more intangible; it looks at ways in which 'land' and 'speech' become one, at ways in which utterance can be read as a *'field' of composition* and also as a *site* of cultural resistance and social reform.

Taken together, these chapters look at a range of works, from conventional to unconventional fiction and poetry, from 'scientific' commentary to real estate rhetoric, from 'newspaper verse' to autobiography and academic critique. Each deals with the complex interplay between place, power, and the English language. Each examines the force of metaphor within a social context. Each deals with the relation between literary language and the construction of social value. Together, they invite the reader to look again at Canada's changing cultural character, and to see it afresh, by rereading the land.

1

Landing: Literature, Contact, and the Natural World

Land and Power Codes

Conventional images illustrating the European arrival in North America usually depict a Renaissance courtier of some sort, in helmet and tights, or a sea captain, planting a flag on a deserted beach, with dense forest in the background. Why this image should have so long been accepted as realistic is not a mystery: it reflects the power relations in the society that concocted the image and so designed and perpetuated the social myths.[1] But the unreality of the image is easy to recognize. How representational, after all, are these configurations of nature and landscape – or, conversely, how artificial, how formulaic? The landing seems quiet, the bush constricting, the newcomers orderly: is this the way it was? After the rigours of the sea-crossing and the length of time the trip must have taken, how can it be that the 'explorers' in these pictures are so elegant, so neat, and so *clean?* And why is the new world construed as deserted when the Native peoples are already there, and have been there for generations?

In these illustrations, 'Indians' occasionally peer out of the bush at the strangers, and assorted European military men frequently stand around on the beach with muskets and trade goods, wearing expressions that range from numbing uncertainty to absolute faith in divine direction. Sometimes, instead of the flag, the newcomers hold a cross or kneel, though whether in thanks for the promise of fresh territory or in thanks for having survived the transatlantic journey remains unclear. Territory is the subject here. 'Territory' is a designation of claim over land, of *jurisdiction*, the power to *say the law*. Here on this beachhead, the figure with the power sign (flag, cross, musket, perhaps even sextant) is always

European; he uses a system of received authority (politics, religion, technology, economics, science, military might) to claim both the beach and the lands to which the beach is a threshold. And he (the power figure here always seems to be male, reflecting experience for the most part, but also representing the gendered hierarchy of European social organization) enacts this claim as though it were his *right* to do so. The visual images in these illustrations, in short, do not record events with what for a long time was considered photographic fidelity; instead they *encode* a prevailing set of power relations, of social assumptions about the character of authority and about the readiness with which various peoples would have access to it.

The land is one of these European visual codes, an indicator variously of nature and morality – one that, by differentiating between a paradisal earthly garden and a savage earthly wilderness, encoded what was taken to be the 'natural right' to territorial expansion. By the terms of this code, those who lived in the garden were manifestly good and deserved to acquire more territory; those who lived in the wilderness, if anyone lived there at all, deserved to give their territory up to those who were morally superior. Verbal structures – vocabulary choices, the formal arrangements of words – run parallel to these visual codes; for words, too, function as codifications of social values. *Nature, paradise, wilderness, garden, earthly, savage*: each of these words encapsulates a set of assumptions. In particular, as terms in a recurrent binary paradigm – garden vs wilderness, heavenly vs hellish, clean vs dirty, orderly vs chaotic, lawful vs lawless, mature vs childish, moral vs savage, natural vs unnatural – they emphasize the persistence of an existing hierarchy by constructing limits to social and intellectual options, as though these limits were given or 'natural' or axiomatic.

Language, that is, helps shape attitudes and judgments; it also embodies attitudes and judgments. Literary 'style' – by which I mean the effects achieved by the form and arrangement of words: the combination of sound, tempo, word choice, pitch, visual pattern, grammar, sequence, sentence structure, paragraphing, genre choice, and all such organizational features – at once derives from and contributes to a prevailing set of social and aesthetic values. It can therefore function as a very conservative force in society (and 'canonical' literature is always defined as that which serves the values of a dominant or prevailing group); it can also function to disrupt or question prevailing conventions – by refusing to use them, by resisting the borders of currently acceptable practice or genre distinction, and by renewing or designing alternative patterns of communication. This chapter comments first on 'Contact' literature, and on the filters that are imposed on interpretation when one set of cultural values confronts and (at least for a duration) subsumes another.

Those conventional images of explorers landing on an alien shore, and *taking over* – or of the successive waves of settlers landing on an alien dock, and *starting over* – hint at the ambiguities of contact and border-crossing. Threat and promise interact. Will the inevitable changes be better or worse? Will the encounter with new people and the access to new land destroy culture or facilitate it? Or do these binary questions falsify the options, and hence distort how history and experience affect individual peoples? Whose perspective is being looked at here, after all, and from what historical vantage point? Who is contacting whom?

Contact Language

The *language* of 'starting over' – even as in the phrases 'a second start' or 'a separate beginning' – is relevant here, for it affects the form of Contact literature. It is a way of putting a positive spin on cross-boundary encounters, of making physical confrontations and confrontations between systems of value seem potentially creative. As of course they can be – though not always, and will not seem so to everyone, as the language of 'foreign threat' and the 'end' or 'death' of culture makes clear; but this language, too, serves a particular social desire: it would read cultural change negatively, define the present in terms of purity, and claim power for whichever version of 'elite' could claim to be most 'pure.' *To start over, to begin again*: the language of recommencement, however, implies several separate kinds of premise – renewal, repetition, re-enactment, reconstitution. It perhaps suggests the possibility of a reclaimed innocence, but if so, it carries with it the knowledge of a preceding fall (or at least metaphorical fall) from grace. It perhaps also raises the prospect of an alternative, or of alternatives (in the plural). And while it promises no improvement, it behaves rather like a body of voters on the verge of electing a different party into power, for it tempers disillusion with expediency, likelihood with hope. The language of starting over, that is, codes a set of ingrained attitudes, and this chapter begins – or 'begins again' – *with* these attitudes because they affect both the history of European–Native relations in Canada, and the terms by which the people who came to assume power in the country – shaping the dominant culture – came to imagine them.

Terms such as *new world, savage wilderness*, and *virgin territory* at once derive from and impinge upon a perception of the land; by extension they also tell of a pattern of social relationships – a pattern that is, or has been, deemed to be 'natural.' Perceptions of a *natural world*, to generalize further, construct a paradigm of social order; at the same time, they assume that something called a *natural word* also exists: a language that 'naturally' – and therefore powerfully – conveys universal ('everywhere') norms of social practice and human behaviour. But obviously such language is not natural (meaning 'given' or 'unlearned'), not neutral, not value-free, and not without consequence. It is, by contrast, a set of conventions involving sound, sequence, structure, and 'correctness,' a set of conventions that through practice and over time has come to construct 'meaning' and to associate command over the word with civil and religious authority. 'Starting over' in an old world's old language might simply 'transplant' existing presumptions and prejudices, changing locale but not expectation. To examine the literature of *Contact*, therefore, is of necessity to probe the assumptions of language.

Immediately there is a problem. For an English-language vocabulary, with all its history of buried metaphor, is being used here in order to try to reconstruct a time in North America when English was not widely spoken, and when Native languages (at least fifty-four of them, in a dozen separate language groups) were the primary ones spoken in the northern half of the continent. Europe had not yet occupied this territory, and indeed had not yet 'found' what was already there. The 'finding,' however, would utterly change the course of culture to come.*

'Finding.' Herein lies the central metaphor of Contact literature, preceding 'occupation.' And the image of '*dis-covery*' (or 'unhiding')† – 'unhiding' that which is 'hidden' only to those who are unaware of it because, as Maritimers express it, they 'come from away') – makes several assumptions. The first of these assumptions involves the question of

---

* D.M.R. Bentley's *Gay/Grey Moose*, reflecting in numerous ways on 'nature' referents in English-Canadian writing, refers to the 'landmark case of *Johnson v. M'Intosh*' in United States jurisprudence, an 1823 decision 'still cited in American and, occasionally, Canadian land disputes involving native peoples,' wherein 'Chief Justice John Marshall held that, while "exclusive title" to a given area in North America had passed under the "fundamental principle" of "discovery" from its "original inhabitants" to the particular European nation that discovered it, the Indians remained "the rightful occupants of the soil, with a legal as well as just claim to retain possession of it ... "' (153).

† 'Unhiding the Hidden' is Robert Kroetsch's phrase, used to title an article about the writing process.

power. Those who claim to have done the 'discovering' presume authority over place, other persons, and value. They then translate what they have 'found' into their own terms; as they do so, they claim their authority to be *natural* (by which they mean 'reasonable,' a 'matter of course'), and it *seems* 'natural' because it derives from their own system of value. (While this is patently a closed argument, it seems in practice nevertheless to have been repeatedly effective.) In turn, their images of land constitute outward extensions of their determinations of 'natural' values (the world in nature somehow 'proving' the reasonableness of their judgment).

This language permeates commentary, for example, on empirical landscape, on memory, on music, and on art. In *The Idea of Landscape and the Sense of Place, 1730–1840,* John Barrell argues that 'it would have been very hard, in the second half of the eighteenth century, for anyone with an aesthetic interest in nature to describe a landscape without applying to it' the vocabulary of the sublime, the beautiful, and the picturesque, which encoded assumptions about 'natural' reality; he refers, for example, to the intentions and effects of landscape terminology: 'A "grove" in natural landscape was, no doubt, thought of as having ... been designed and planted by God; but more to the point ... is that the language of natural description in eighteenth-century poetry was well supplied with words – another example ... is "lawn" – whose tendency, like that of "grove," was to present a landscape as an orderly arrangement of objects – a *design*; and the words which did tend, in this way, to reveal a design in nature, were preferred by most writers to those which did not.' Other terms include *prospect* and *scene,* both implying the 'remoteness' of landscape from the observer, who (by means of this distancing) kept nature under control (42–3). Ann Bermingham, in *Landscape and Ideology,* argues the relation between such designs in nature and the designs of power in canonical art. Noting that beauty resides wherever power does (83), she observes that landscape painting emerges in England when a version of the rural comes to serve some dominant social value, as when Sir Joshua Reynolds praises, and thus canonizes, the paintings of Gainsborough. Bermingham also analyzes the effects of the Enclosure Acts on perceptions of place and space (and of paintings in which figures are depicted as owners of 'grounds' or 'estates'), which leads to comments on Constable's picturesque paintings (anti–industrial and nostalgic for a time when 'home' meant 'happiness' and a 'house' could be represented *in* rather than *apart from* a landscape), and to reflections on the 'allegorical landscapes' of the mid-nineteenth century, which endorsed diversity across class lines, as represented by the varied use of fields (192). Extend-

ing to music this commentary on the relation between landshapes and
memory, Charles Rosen's *The Romantic Generation* relates the study of
particular images, ideas, and words to Romantic musical composition.
Rosen cites, for example, the influence of picturesque sensation (images
of foliage, river, mountain, and floating islands) on song cycles (137), and
the analogies conventionally drawn between the force of water and anger
(139) and between mountains and ruins (143), respectively; yet he goes
on (159) to assert that (after Goethe) the Romantic artist was interested
not so much in the truth of Nature as in a method of arriving at the
truth, a method that required extended personal observation *and an
ordering* of the artist's experience of the external world. Hence in music
– Schumann is Rosen's example – composers were less satisfied by simply
using analogies between emotion and sound than by attempting to convey
through music the actual process of responding to the landscapes of sight
and memory.[2]

The images of 'garden' and 'wilderness,' therefore – which recur in
writing as well as in pictures of explorers traversing and taming savage
lands – are not simple, objective references to a neutral empirical reality.
They are *tropes,* or figurative ways of conveying attitudes and ideas. Such
terms describe *territory,* clearly, but they also embody expectations about
'nature,' and attitudes which over the course of time have come to express a complex set of relations between fertility (as in the phrase 'Mother Nature') and law (as in the phrase 'Natural Justice'). Because these
(acquired, inherited) attitudes affect literature in Canada, the initial
questions in this chapter deal with the distinction between images and
the 'real world' (empirical phenomena), and between two or more forms
of perception. What, for example, did the land *look like* before the Europeans 'found' it? What did they 'see' when they did arrive? And what
were the implications of their living *in* and *on* the land after that?

Aboriginal Lands and Natural Order

It is not simple to cross cultures, and for someone who is not aboriginal
to try to reconstruct the world of Native attitude before contact with
Europe[3] presents a variety of difficulties, for several reasons. Native cultures were oral; there were many of them; and in several ways they differed from each other as well as from written cultures. The character of
'evidence' and the ways in which any people interprets this evidence are
also culturally biased. For example, most modern 'records' of North
American Native history and mythology have been primarily shaped by

European eyes – translated, culturally interpreted, edited sometimes for the sake of English verbal or social propriety. These records, moreover, came into existence after Contact had already modified how Native cultures perceived. The term *Indian* itself tells of one kind of change, as does the recent revitalizing of words such as *Native, First Nations,* and *aboriginal.* Terms such as *Red Indian** or *Indian* (the terms by which Native peoples have customarily been described in historical, political, and literary documents) carry imperial connotations, and they demonstrate one of the most fundamental of mistaken European expectations of North America. This expectation historically proved divisive because it identified and consequently defined a disparate group of peoples in a single, exclusive, inaccurate, presumptive, and unquestionably powerful manner. *They* (even the pronoun draws a line, proves potentially divisive) had been *named* from *without.* Such European names shaped *them,* leaving them without active control (as far as the English language was concerned) over the character of their own culture. That 'Indians' in recent years have renamed themselves 'Native,' 'aboriginal,' 'First Nations' (in the plural, though the idea of 'nation' raises further questions about social models) – or rigorously insisted on tribal affiliations – serves as one way for the indigenous peoples to reclaim control, to reinterpret a disempowering past, to reattribute public value to the oral history, and thus to invest the future with renewed options. Relevant to the subject at hand, *renaming* is a verbal process, one that affects post-contact society and geographical nomenclature as well. The area that cartographers have long called the 'Northwest Territories,' for instance – a name redolent with claim-staking: two of the territories, Franklin and Mackenzie, are even named after European explorer/namers – is in 1995 well on the way to being renamed Nunavut and Denendeh. But the process of redefinition (which involves unlearning as well as learning) is politically slow.†

---

* A common explanation of this term is that it derives from the practice of the Beothuks in Newfoundland, who painted themselves in red ochre, an insect repellent.

† Connected with this process is the continuing history of treaty making, and its relation to notions of governance. The work of Jean Manore and S. Barry Cottam of the University of Ottawa, for example (reported at the Boundaries conference at the University of Edinburgh, 5 May 1996), examines the implications of Treaty 9 in Ontario. Briefly stated, one reading of history asserts that 'Indian lands' turned into 'Ontario–Quebec' lands when Ontario was extended north to the Albany River in 1889, and when Quebec in tandem was extended north to the Eastmain River in 1898; when the federal government, through the Boundary Extension Acts of 1912, subsequently extended the two provinces north to the sea coast, included in this transfer was the idea that the

This apparent aside illustrates a process and a principle. Naming shapes attitudes. Moreover, the *language* of naming shapes attitudes, and the language and attitudes of the namers – when they come from outside a local culture – are often at odds with the perceptions (and hence the 'realities') that the local cultures live with. The immediate result is a series of difficulties in cross-cultural comprehension. Beyond lie the subsequent difficulties facing literary expression, difficulties that result when the language of reality (in this case the language of 'land') has been occupied by foreign presumptions. Who determines what 'wilderness' is, for example, or what is 'natural,' or what in a landscape is 'beautiful'? This argument does not suggest that aboriginal cultures are somehow a 'truer' source than England is in which to find the working aesthetic criteria of English-Canadian literature; to do so would be to romanticize the past and falsify cultural practice. Nor does it deny the territoriality of Native societies – the practices of warfare and slavery, and the shifting occupation of land – prior to European contact. The point is that the names for land and people derive from presumptions about natural order, and that these presumptions are open to interpretation.

For example, definitions of the physical limits of nature are not universally fixed; they derive from separate cultural conventions. European convention read nature (of which land was one manifestation) as a separate space (God-given, though not always God-blessed) through which human beings moved. Applied to aesthetics, this assumption can be traced in part to Aristotle's definition of 'nature' in his *Physics*: some things (animals, earth) are 'natural,' according to this definition, and no thing is 'natural' if even in part it is produced by 'man.' But the reach of the convention extends beyond aesthetics into the workings of religion,

---

provinces would take over treaty-making powers with the Native peoples. Ontario shortly signed Treaty 9 with the Ojibway (a treaty that the writer D.C. Scott helped draft [see Dragland]); for several decades Quebec signed no treaty with the Cree – both actions leading to various political disputes later in the century. Did a treaty 'extinguish' Native hunting and fishing rights, for example, off reserve lands? One reading of the law said it did. (The law, until 1952, also asserted that a Native person could not leave the reserve without permission of the Indian Agent, and, until 1960, asserted that a Native person who left the reserve to attend university ceased being an Indian.) Another reading of the law said that, *in practice*, Natives during these decades frequently went hunting off the reserves, and Indian Agents were infrequently on the reserves to grant permission or to refuse permission to do so – hence the precedent of actual behaviour made it clear that rights were not extinguished, and that, in consequence, all opportunities were not limited by a particular demarcation of land.

science, law, and social custom. In English, the very word *wilderness* derives its understood meaning from an overlay between conventional usage and, loosely speaking, 'reportorial' meaning.* The *wilder*-ness was the place of the *wild deer*,† and hence, by tacit understanding, the territory beyond the reach or authority of English common law. The basis for this distinction lay in an attitude to land. Land was, or could be, property, that is, privately owned. Such ownership declared authority; it also expressed a participation in a system of civil order or organization, or a shared notion of 'cultivation.' Hence the (cultivated) *garden* was civil, but the *wilderness* was 'un*tract*able': unruled, hence unruly. European explorers consequently moved through the world with a sense of their potential authority over it. They saw themselves as separate from the world they navigated and claimed, but able to impose their will upon it, and, moreover, sanctioned to do so. 'Here' was separate from 'there'; 'cultivation' was separate from 'wilderness'; mapping the world was a way to declare the territoriality of rule.

Native North American cultures, by contrast, conventionally read nature and themselves as extensions of each other (implying, among other things, that damage to one would damage the other: the land was them, and they were the land). This sense of wholeness is illustrated in part by the overlap between human beings and environment in contemporary Eastern Woodlands art, or by one of the features of West Coast totemic design, or by dance. The prairie sundance, for example, directly invoked the forces of nature, and, like visceral movement, visual design could also perform this function. In the totems (see plate 1.1), the configurations interconnect – the head of one animal also serves as the body of another; human heads are used to design an animal's nostrils, eyes, and ears; a bird's wing is transformed into a human arm – and the interconnections encode the cultural belief in the totality of being. Totemic crests, moreover, signified a spiritual clan relationship between humans and other beings. A somewhat different technique of visually

---

* Linguists would classify this form of meaning as *constative* as opposed to *performative*. A *constative* utterance 'states' its meaning, that is, declares that something is or is not true; a *performative* utterance 'enacts' its meaning, that is, constructs meaning through a statement such as 'I promise to do X,' wherein the *act of declaring* itself signals the act to be done (whether or not it will in 'fact' be fulfilled).

† The Old English term *wilddeor* meant, more generally, 'wild beast' before *deor* came to mean 'deer.' The French word *sauvage*, which came to mean 'savage,' derives in parallel fashion from a term meaning 'woods-dweller.' The word *garden*, by contrast, derives from the Old English term for 'enclosure,' related to the modern word *yard*.

representing human beings' involvement in nature occurs among the
Anishnabec, where the characteristic 'X-ray' design – as is apparent, for
example, in the contemporary paintings of Norval Morriseau and Carl Ray
(see plate 1.2) – is equated with a shaman's accepted power of seeing past
the surfaces of things. A shaman was able, so to speak, to reduce himself to
skeleton. This process did not diminish but rather enhanced his power: for
by reducing the reliance on the physical dimensions of self, the shaman
could engage with, embrace, and become one with the forces of all nature.

The patterns or designs of dance and visual depiction could thus be
analogous in function to the verbal paradigms of oral tale-telling. Consider the Inuit tale of Sedna, which tells of what happens when Sedna's
father cuts his daughter into pieces and throws them into the sea. To a
European-trained ear, this action sounds like sheer butchery; heard as
metaphor, however, the process can be reinterpreted against different
cultural referents: the various severed body parts turn into the creatures
of the sea (fingers into seals and hands into walruses, etc.), until Sedna
is at once woman and fish, person and spirit, her own narrative epitomizing the potential for oneness in nature. Invoking the spirit of the animals
and the land was, in addition, considered to be a necessary act, a ritual
of respect, a way of replenishing the relationship with nature and thus
maintaining the stability of the culture.

Various other tales (of creation, transformation, tricksters, culture-
heroes) also gave people access to the wholeness of nature; indeed, in
these tales, '*Human* people' ('How the Human People Got the First Fire'
is a representative title) had frequently to be so designated to separate
them from *all* 'people' or 'beings' generally. As Robin Ridington observes
about the Dunne-za of the Subarctic, in *Trail to Heaven*, they

assume, I came to learn, that events can take place only after people have known
and experienced them in myths, dreams, and visions. Even their concept of
person is different from ours. In Dunne-za reality, animals, winds, rocks, and
natural forces are 'people.' Human people are continually in contact with these
nonhuman persons. All persons continually bring the world into being through
the myths, dreams, and visions they share with one another. Western culture views
'myths' and 'dreams' as false and illusory. The Dunne-za experience myths and
dreams as fundamental sources of knowledge. (xi)*

* Underlying this relationship is a 'non-Western' understanding which rejects – or does
  not even take into consideration – the border between subject and object that
  'Western' perceptions of reality accept as natural. In part using Jungian paradigms,

Differences between European mapping (which was intended to determine boundaries and fix empirical truths) and Aboriginal mapping (which was often sung, charting a person's spiritual connection with the land) further emphasize the disparity between traditional cultures.* The 'Trail to Heaven' among the Dunne-za, Ridington explains, begins at the place where a human person meets all his or her relatives (*ya dikwonchi* – 'all our relations'†), when the people from before 'come down to meet

---

David J. Tacey argues relatedly that, until non-Aboriginals can connect psychically with the landscape, they will never be able to appreciate the nature of Aboriginal myth and the ecological and religious bond it articulates between human being and land. Gerhard Hoffman further theorizes that in 'postmodern' First Nations art, paradigms of the material replace those of organic life, myth becomes the subject of play, artifice replaces nature but points still to the possibility of an ecological consciousness (272). Annie L. Booth and Harvey M. Jacobs also argue a relation between Native religion and ecology. Yet it is important to keep in mind Thomas King's emphatic distinction between (1) general North American policy makers' ability to rise to an ecological crisis, (2) ecology, and (3) a Native American 'land ethic' (a distinction that also informs the paintings of Laurence Paul): see his interview with Hartmut Lutz. See also Silko's reflections on the relation between the dance, or ritual circuit of landscape, and psychic and social balance among the Pueblo (91–2), and Martine Reid's comments on the iconography of 'tongue-exchange' in Bill Reid's bronze relief mural *Mythic Messengers*, in Burnaby, BC.

* Two essays in Fisher and Johnston touch directly on the issue of cultural representation. Glyndwr Williams contrasts George Vancouver's surveying accuracy with James Cook's 'instinctive' understanding that the European myth of a Northwest Passage needed to be dismissed, and discusses explorers' map making in the context of European expectations. Victoria Wyatt examines the impact of new experiences and materials (contact with Europeans and European trade goods, primarily, but also feathers from the Society Islands, brought to the Pacific Coast of North America by European sailors) on Tlingit and Haida art. In particular, Wyatt emphasizes that ceremonial artworks among the Tlingit and Haida traditionally permitted the people of these cultures to 'collapse the boundaries' between past and present, ancestor and descendant, human being and other creatures of the natural and spiritual world (183); referring to a Haida bowl with the head of a whale at one end and the head of an eagle at the other, she observes that the same ovoid form on the side of the bowl signifies the whale's pectoral fin and the eagle's wing – indicating that a 'system that uses the same formations of lines ... to represent the body parts of all animals is very well adapted to making statements about shared boundaries' (185). While European trade goods were adapted into traditional designs, however, representations of Europeans themselves were not, which suggests that at least one conceptual boundary line persisted: that is, that the artists did not deem it appropriate to fit non-Natives into the style that was 'designed to emphasize communal relationships' (187–8).

† Thomas King explains the phrase as one that conventionally begins or ends an oral story; it asserts a relationship with family, including an extended kinship with animals

you' and 'give you a song,' and (in the words he quotes from Old Man Aku) 'the circle of song will be completed / when you see the tracks before you / as your own' (291).[4]

Religion, Science, and Codes of Representation

Obviously, a 'reading' of this design (or dance, or story) is influenced by cultural context. Traditional aboriginal listeners heard the religious message that their culture had trained them to hear: that is, that the shamans were allowed to have access to the spirit world to the degree that they were conceived of as pure essence, whose flesh and blood were cut away. Europeans heard differently – not irreligiously, but against the codes of a different religion. For a Christian European, to hear such a story as that of Sedna was to respond only to the apparent surface violence and to recoil dismissively from what was taken to be savage pagan practice – even though that same Christian might easily accept the parallel European ritual narratives of crucifixion and transubstantiation: of 'killing God' and 'eating the body of Christ,' which would not necessarily translate out of Christian culture, at least in anyone's initial encounter with Easter festivals, as symbolic re-enactments. Not only are the structures of language a culturally-established convention, in other words, but so are the relations between language-in-action (the paradigms of *rhetoric*) and effective *meaning*.

Further confusion affects this process when observers think they understand another culture because the structures and images at first glance look the same as those they are already familiar with. Images, clearly, can translate readily from culture to culture; not so the body of understanding for which the images are signs. All 'deserts' in literature do not necessarily invoke Ishmael's wanderings; all 'doves' do not necessarily imply the Holy Ghost; all literature is not inherently 'Christian.' Hence complications arose at the time of European–Native contact when one culture interpreted the other culture's images of nature as though the observer (rather than the participant) had devised the cultural signs. Misconceptions occurred especially because, at the same time, the very

---

and environment, and therefore asserts morality and responsibility as well (those without 'relations,' by extension, are those who abjure their responsibilities to others and to the earth) ('Introduction,' ix).

fact of their being from somewhere else merely reconfirmed Europeans' sense of their own superiority and their suspicion of what they had already imagined as North American wilderness anarchy. For the idea of wilderness – and the representation of it – were, by the seventeenth century, indissolubly linked with notions of paganism and savagery.[5]

By the nineteenth century, story collectors were in search of a politically more acceptable position, but they still read others' culture through the filter of their own. Christian overtones, for example, turn up in some aboriginal creation stories, though it is hard to determine whether the parallel results from Christian influence or predates it. Certainly the 'Christianity' of the 'overtones' is made apparent in the English-language retellings. One of several Ojibway diver stories about Nanabush (and the mud at the bottom of primeval water), for example, tells of a flood that parallels the story of Noah. And a Seneca creation story tells of twin boys who resemble Cain and Abel; one tills the earth and makes it fertile, the other makes animals and land more difficult for human beings – then quarrels with his brother and kills him. (Human difficulties, moreover, stem from the fact that the violent brother is our collective ancestor.) Yet these stories have to be read cautiously; culture-crossing invites distortion. Jungian psychologists might claim the parallels as signs of a Collective Unconscious; contemporary anthropologists might find them evidence for structuralist analysis; certainly nineteenth-century missionaries, who taught Christianity to the Native peoples and listened to stories in return, used many of the Native stories they translated as evidence of an all-abiding Christian spirit. They then published the translations as modern exempla in missionary journals (such as the *Algoma Missionary Journal*), often modifying the stories in the process, sometimes removing the earthiness of the originals and ignoring the intrinsically different attitude to environment* that the stories articulated.

European religion thus served as a filter to reading the land. It became a means not only for converting the aboriginal people from one belief to another, but also for modifying the sign systems they used. To the degree

---

* Rudolf Kaiser traces four variant versions of one mid-nineteenth-century speech attributed to Chief Seattle; he shows that the text was altered (in diction, length, substance, and slant) so as to serve four separate purposes: to emphasize the archaic nobility of the Native peoples, to demonstrate simple political honesty, to provide a model for contemporary ecological politics, and to romanticize the ecological cause; such re-writings in each case served the need of the re-recorder, and in all cases leave the authorship in doubt.

that the missionaries and politicians could make the Native cultures seem
less civilized and of less consequence than others, even to Native peoples
themselves, they actually could alter behaviour and belief systems. The
missionaries, and others who governed public institutions, could (and
did) classify Native design as 'quaint' or 'primitive' (many Europeans,
missionaries among them, collected artefacts, either for themselves or for
museums, but seldom for *art* galleries); they could (and did) legally
proscribe such social exchanges as the sundance and the potlatch; they
could (and did) redefine Native religions pejoratively as *primitive* or
childish 'mythologies,' and they did so in part, well into the twentieth
century, by limiting access to languages and training people to a different
set of signs. While some Native languages – Beothuk, Nicola, Pentlatch,
among them – indeed perished, it is clear that the design techniques of
most Native cultures did not disappear; the tales (handed orally from
generation to generation) also survived, as did some substantial knowledge about shamanism and other religious customs. Yet their impact on
European-Canadian culture was predominantly more conventional than
reconstructive. 'Change' primarily worked in the opposite direction,
being the requirement that the preponderant group asked of the
marginalized.

Thus, in the culture at large, Christianity became the paramount
religion, and the verbal formulas of oral literature began for most people
to lose the religious function that for traditional Native cultures they once
had. Church and school privileged Christian iconography and the written
word over Native literary paradigms, and as far as European-language
narrative is concerned, until the later twentieth century the oral tales
belonged essentially to the past. In writings intended for adult readers,
at least, the idea of Eden, the Fall, and the faith in Resurrection displaced such references as Gitchi-manitou, Sedna, and the Trail to Heav-
en. Phrased more bluntly, the Christian garden replaced the shaman's
skeletal designs as a public sign of spiritual grace, and the untilled Canadian land outside the garden (the land with which Native cultures spiritu-
ally identified) became defined as pagan, barbaric, wild, the land of *les
sauvages* (see plate 1.3). European-language literature might sometimes
question this set of cultural values; more often it simply embodied what
writers took to be common knowledge, or common sense. In the early
European-language writings of Canada, in consequence, one notion
(territorial expansion: what the land represented) came to overlap with
another (religious right: how the land was, and was to be, seen).

The language of religion thus permeates Contact literature, and fashions one way of retrieving the past or perceiving environment. But it has not been the only system of conventionalized thought to shape perceptions and the deductions that follow from them. 'Science' offers a second approach to the reading of aboriginal–white relations and to the process of perceiving the past and the land.* Although ostensibly more empirical than religion, science, too, makes rhetorical, culturally marked choices, for it is fundamentally a manner of observation – and therefore of interpretation – and what it accepts as data, or evidence, varies with environment and time. Knut Fladmark's *British Columbia Prehistory*, a 1986 publication of the Archeological Survey of Canada, provides a contemporary example. When Fladmark cautiously attempts to reconcile the terms and impact of mythology with the systems of 'science' or technological rationalism, he demonstrates how a scientific set of assumptions determines the way evidence is measured. 'Indian folklore,' he writes,

is intricately bound with rich symbolic imagery and to minds moulded by contemporary scientific attitudes ... [it] can seem mystical and lacking in explicit historical 'facts.' As a result, archaeologists and others have sometimes dismissed Indian traditions about their past as *simply poetic* and *non-historical.* (my italics)

He then suggests that these attitudes 'complement each other,' and he recounts the religious mythology in general terms:

---

* On the relation between science and aesthetics, see Stafford, whose account of paradigmatic design is more complex than that of Porteous, and her bibliography extensive. Of particular interest is her account of the interconnections between the rise of empiricism, the 'voyage into phenomena' (i.e., 'penetration,' as opposed to the desire for an Olympian detachment, 285), the preoccupation with 'finding' both in art and in science, the travel discourse that presumed that 'new' lands were 'free of culture' (285), the obsession with particular 'charged' sites (xxi) – as, for example, hollowed rocks, natural bridges, geological eccentrics, monadnocks, basalt columns, precipices, crags, volcanoes, caves, waterfalls, glaciers, earthquakes, and ruins, all of which satisfied a fascination with 'havoc' and 'astonishment' (264) – and the discourses of natural history and 'objective' report. Pamela Regis also comments on natural history as a form of politicized discourse; and William Cronon, arguing that plants, animals, soils, and climates are 'coactors and codeterminants' (1349) in any history of *earth* as well as any history of *people*, tries to explain how events give rise to narrative – settlement stories in the American Great Plains, for example, conventionally are told in linear fashion, with the idea of progress or improvement in mind, but this plot inherently erases the history, the world of nature, and the sense of place that existed before the settlers, and suggests that the grassland 'deserved' to be transformed (1354). On the rhetoric of science, see Gross.

Native historical traditions varied considerably from group to group, but some coastal stories told of a primeval ocean that covered the earth's surface, with one or more deity figures, such as Raven, floating in space. Raven then caused an island to be formed, which grew and in various ways became populated with plants, animals and the first people, while the sun and moon were placed in the sky. For a time the world-island was in a kind of plastic state, with landforms and creatures shaped by the actions of powerful supernatural beings. Animals and humans were less differentiated than now, able to talk and freely transform their physical appearance. Through time the world and its inhabitants slowly solidified into the present condition, with animals taking their current forms and human culture evolving through a series of trials, often including actions of ancient heroes and crises brought about through individual folly. In some tales, floods caused people to be dispersed around the world, accounting for the diversity of tribes. From these apparently ancient themes, broadly shared by many New World peoples as well as others, the folklore gradually moves and blends into descriptions of events that are clearly more recent, eventually including incidents that occurred after the arrival of Europeans. To the native people, the truth of their traditions was attested to by concrete evidence, such as the widespread occurrence of 'beings-turned-to-stone' and other natural features transformed by ancient supernatural forces when the world was young. This tangible proof of the old legends also confirmed a people's belief in their eternal association with the land.

These traditions explain why some Indians object to archaeologists claiming that they have been in British Columbia only 11000 to 12000 years, when their own lore teaches that they have *always* been here, or at least since the present world was created. However, this need not represent any fundamental disagreement between contemporary archaeology and the ancient traditions, merely that in all our minds 'eternity' and 11000 years are essentially the same, and real comprehension of a time span beyond a few centuries eludes archaeologists and non-archaeologists alike.

Fladmark then recounts the story of Raven creating the world and hazards guesses about how 'science' might 'explain' it. He admits the value of 'folklore' and 'legend' (terms that he none the less implicitly equates with 'fiction,' and therefore 'untruth'), but he is also determined to find a *scientifically* acceptable explanation of 'story' in order to make narrative functional and hence give it a higher value within his own system of priorities. His own rhetoric gives precedence to empirical evidence:

Twelve thousand to eleven thousand years ago British Columbia was still emerging from the last glaciation and, as the ice melted away, seashores, lakes and valleys began to acquire their present forms. For a time, parts of the province may have supported powerful but now-extinct animals, such as large bison and perhaps mammoths and mastodons. Is it possible that such creatures or their bones gave rise to some of the supernatural beings of legend? Could fluctuating sea-levels and glacial damming and flooding of rivers at the end of the last Ice Age have contributed to the prevalence of flood stories in native folklore? We do not know for certain, but all these natural phenomena are scientifically supported. (10–11)*

Cultural values, in other words, give priority to one measure or another of 'truth.' Western culture in the twentieth century places its collective faith in science and technology, some versions of which dismiss 'poetry' – just as they seek 'rational' explanations for the supernatural beings, flood stories, and other elements of Native lore. Just as clearly, traditional Native societies heard some storytelling as cultural history, while European story-collectors in the nineteenth century were determined to explain aboriginal story-making by appeals to European religion.

Native Lands and Post-Contact Forms

It is possible to conclude from this process that history *reads* circumstances selectively, and that whatever need or notion prevails at the time of interpretation will affect the character of the interpretation itself. A 1984 book, *The Raven Steals the Light*, by the Haida artist Bill Reid in collaboration with the poet Robert Bringhurst, provides a relevant contemporary example. For while in one sense it can be read as a straightforward retelling of several Haida tales – especially Raven tales of trickery and creation – what is most straightforward about the book is its political intent. Its ironic tone does not undermine this purpose; the form is chosen deliberately – it is part of the Raven sensibility, the world of the creative trickster, hence part of the political effect. The book's preface establishes this sensibility by debunking, to begin with, the European trope of exploration (the figurative and structural motif of finding, claiming, and naming) and the European faith in documentary; and

---

* Subsequent comment on the 1990–1 Gitksan-Wet-suwet-en land-rights court case in British Columbia has stressed the spatiality and the theatricality of court procedure and the relation of both to the legal issues; it has also critiqued the judge's findings, and their basis in part on his rejection of *anthropological* and his acceptance of *historical* 'evidence,' dismissing the one as 'tale' and accepting the other as 'truth.' See, for example, Pinder, and Fisher ('Judging History').

among other things it uses the familiar 'rose' metaphor from English
literature (Shakespeare's *Romeo and Juliet*, Gertrude Stein's famous
maxim) to do so:

Haida Gwai, the Islands of the People, lie equidistant from Luxor, Machu Picchu,
Ninevah and Timbuktu. On the white man's maps, where every islet and scrap of
land, inhabited or otherwise, sits now in the shadow of somebody's national flag,
and is named for preference after a monarch or a politician, Haida Gwai are shown
as the westernmost extremity of Canada, and they are named not for the Haida, who
have always lived there, but for a woman who never saw them. Her name was Sophie
Charlotte von Mecklenburg-Strelitz, but the British called her simply Queen Charlotte, for she was the wife of the Mad King of England, George III.
So the Raven, who often likes to call a rose a skunk cabbage, just to see what
trouble he can cause, has tricked us again, Haidas and whites alike, with this one.
He has us trained now to point to Haida Gwai and say 'Queen Charlotte Islands.'
These stories were told there well before Queen Charlotte's time. (n.p.)[6]

In illustration, Reid's earthy creation story 'Raven and the First Men'
closes with a sly suggestion that – given what pollution and 'land development' have done to nature on the 'Charlottes' – it might be time to
create the world anew, to try for another beginning.

A *parodic irony*, however – which also permeates the stories of Tom
King (Cherokee) and Basil Johnston (Ojibwa), the plays of Tomson
Highway (Cree), and the paintings of Lawrence Paul Yuxweluptun (Coast
Salish/Okanagan; see plate 1.4) – is only one of several formal techniques that contemporary Native artists have used in order to readjust
conventional European post-Contact judgments of Contact, history, culture, society, and land. Some – Jeannette Armstrong (Okanagan) in *Slash*,
Beatrice Culleton (Métis) in *In Search of April Raintree* – have openly
attacked institutionalized systems of social repression, using *linear narrative*
to expose the cruelties of racial intolerance, whether examined or unexamined, intentional or fostered by accident, ephemeral or somehow
incorporated into social practice. The power of *invective* to dismiss Eurocentric views of Native cultures is also amply demonstrated in the
speeches of Lenore Keeshig-Tobias (Ojibwa), and *polemic* in the poetry of
Duke Redbird (Métis) and the visual art of Joane Cardinal-Schubert
(Piegan).

A poem such as 'i lose track of the land' by Kateri Damm (Ojibwa)
illustrates how verbal organization structures a social protest even within
what first appears to be a straightforward lyric:

at night there are no voices
singing me gently to sleep
though i know they whisper
outside these strange walls

i look to the sky
for the sweet light of stars
but night is never dark here

i long to join the dance of the earth
– i knew the movements once

i dream of the wind
the damp smell of the earth
and the footsteps of animals
dancing by moonlight

my body is tired and aching

blood rushes to my feet
drains into the pavement
is pulled through my scalp

i lose track of the land[7]

The poem uses a series of stated and implied contrasts to emphasize how
the loss of the past (of cultural traditions, epitomized in the image of
land) results in dislocation, dispossession, and deracination. Song is
reduced to whisper; 'sweet light' disappears in urban glare; movement is
stilled; dance is surrendered to unproductive dream, one that no longer
has living access to the tales of preceding generations. The ache, the
'strange walls,' the paling from loss of blood, the disappearing into the
city's waste-drains, even the symbolic scalping: all construct through
metaphor a critique of the way white society has marginalized Native
peoples – but the particular metaphors here reinforce this critique in
part by parodying the terms (*garrison, blood, scalp*) that constructed the
margins in the first place. The closing line (and title) reiterate this process of critical reconstruction. What for Europeans had been a trackless
wilderness was for the Native societies at once *a track* and *the land*. To lose
this land is both to lose one's way and to 'lose track' – that is, to lose

1.1 *Bear with Killer Whale*, a cedar pole carved by Henry Hunt (Kwagiutl), shows the bear's body becoming the whale's head, and the whale's dorsal fin as a human form (reproduced from *Looking at Indian Art* [Vancouver: Douglas & McIntyre, and Seattle: U Washington P, 1979] courtesy of the author, Hilary Stewart). The whale on the totem pole is an orca, the crest of the carver. The pole itself now stands inside the Swartz Bay ferry terminal on Vancouver Island.

1.2 (*top*) *Mother Earth and Her Children* (India ink and acrylic on brown paper, 70 × 60.1 cm, 1975, collection of Dr B. Cinader), by Carl Ray (Ojibwa), shows animals and earth to be interconnected, and designs the world as one with nature; (*bottom*) the 'X-ray technique' of *Jo-Go-Way Moose Dream* (tempera on building paper, *c.*1964, 132.1 × 81.3 cm, Glenbow Collection, Calgary, Alberta, Canada, #9509), by Norval Morriseau (Ojibwa), expresses the ability of a shaman to reduce the body to skeleton and become one with the spirit world.

1.3 *La France Apportant la Foi aux Indiens de la Nouvelle France* (France bringing the [True] Faith to the Indians of New France) (oil on canvas, *c.*1675, 227 × 227 cm), attributed to Frère Luc (1614–1685), depicts the arrival of French Roman Catholic priests among the Huron. The iconography of the painting also indicates that the 'wilderness' is being taken over by the symbolic designs of Christianity – and that, in the process, 'les sauvages' are becoming subservient to European political authority. Reproduced courtesy of Les Archives des Ursulines de Québec.

1.4 Lawrence Paul Yuxweluptun (Coast Salish/Okanagan), *Red Man Watching White Man Trying to Fix Hole in Sky* (acrylic on canvas, 1990, 142.24 × 226.06 cm), ironically depicts the distance between a First Nations landscape and the European technicians who ostensibly control it; here, technology (with all its accoutrements: the white lab coats, the automobiles, the television sets) proves an inefficient way of coping with the hole in the ozone layer. By means of its own technique, the painting also replies to the landscapes of Emily Carr and Salvador Dali, using the Salish cultural signs to undermine the presumed 'universality' of artistic insight and artistic method. Reproduced courtesy of Lawrence Paul Yuxweluptun and the Canadian Museum of Civilization.

1.5 This woodcut print (*above*) by Giacomo Gastaldi (*La Nuova Francia*, 1556), depicting Newfoundland (Terra Nuova) and the coast of Quebec, illustrates how early map-makers decorated 'known' areas with human activity, assigned devils and monsters to areas less known (here, the untested ocean deeps and the 'island of demons'), and 'named' still other areas 'unknown parts' – such maps much later became the subject of Earle Birney's poem 'Mappemounde.' Reproduced from *From Sea Unto Sea* courtesy of Joe C.W. Armstrong.

1.6 (*opposite, top*) Thomas Davies, *A View of Montreal from St. Helen's Island* (water-colour over graphite on laid paper, 1762, 35.3 × 53.5 cm; reproduced courtesy of the National Gallery of Canada, Ottawa, #6272); (*opposite, bottom*) William Ellis, *View of Ship Cove in King George's Sound, on the N.W. Coast of America* (watercolour, 1778, 32.7 × 47.5 cm; reproduced courtesy of the National Library of Australia, Canberra, ACT, Rex Nan Kivell Collection NK 53/J). Davies uses 'picturesque' techniques to frame his urban subject and to distance the observing eye; Ellis is less pictorial, imposing the familiar curved shapes of conventional tree-form rep-resentations upon what was to him the unfamiliar landscape of the 'wilderness' West Coast of Vancouver Island.

The Cataract of NIAGARA, some make
this Water-Fall to be half a League while
others reckon it no more than
a hundred Fathom.

1.7 (*opposite, top*) Richard Wilson, *View of the Cataract of Niagara, with the country adjacent* (oil on canvas, 1774, 41.5 × 52.8 cm; after a 1771 sketch by Capt. William Pierie, engraved by William Byrne; reproduced courtesy of the National Archives of Canada, C-041378), demonstrates the eighteenth-century European conventions of the 'sublime,' whereas (*opposite, bottom*) Thomas Davies, *Niagara Falls from Above* (watercolour on paper, *c.*1766, Collection of The New-York Historical Society), attempts a 'picturesque' version of the falls, enclosing them within a frame. Cf. the engraving (*above*), *The Cataract of Niagara* (reproduced courtesy of the National Archives of Canada, C-16758) – an insert (23 × 23 cm) on Hermann Moll's map of 1715, based on a 1698 map (*L'Amérique divisée selon letendue de ses principales parties*) illustrated by Nicolas de Fer and engraved by H. van Loon – which adds a beaver colony to the depiction of Niagara and fancifully categorizes the wilderness figures according to their imagined work roles (including loggers, carpenters, porters, masons, an architectural supervisor, and one individual who is 'sick from having worked too hard').

1.8 Four versions of the Montmorency ice cone (*pp. 48–51*), in four different media, indicate the continuing appeal of this phenomenon as a subject for artistic representation during the nineteenth century: (*above*) Robert Todd, *The Ice Cone, Montmorency Falls* (oil on canvas, *c.*1850, 34.5 × 45.9 cm; reproduced courtesy of the National Gallery of Canada, Ottawa, #6763); (*right*) Lt-Col. James P. Cockburn, *The Cone of Montmorency, as it Appeared in 1829* (etching and aquatint with hand-coloured watercolour on wove paper, 1833, 54.4 × 72.9 cm; reproduced courtesy of the National Archives of Canada, c-95622). (*continued on p. 50*)

1.8 (cont.) (*above*) Attrib. to Alicia Killaly, one of six Robert & Reinhold coloured chromolithographs from a series called *A Picnic to Montmorenci* (1868) – No. III: *Coming Down is Easier but More Dangerous* (960 × 276.94 cm; reproduced courtesy of the Royal Ontario Museum, Toronto, Canada); (*right*) Alexander Henderson, *Ice Cone, Montmorency Falls* (albumen photographic print, 1876; reproduced courtesy of the National Archives of Canada, PA-138521). The social function of these versions also differs. Cockburn's print, for example, is one of a set of six Quebec scenes dedicated to 'His Most Excellent Majesty William the Fourth.' The museum copy of Killaly's more comedic print (on old card) adds the following comment: 'Shows Capt. Buzbie and Miss Muffin in centre foregrd. coming downhill by sleigh. Two ladies in grey dresses in foregrd. watching.'

1.9 These illustrations – (*top*) Major Williams's *The Citadel of Quebec from Prescott Gate* (engraving from the *London Illustrated News*, 4 August 1860), and (*bottom*) F.B. Schell's *Halifax, from Citadel* (engraving from *Picturesque Canada*, vol. 2, 1862) – reveal five of the conventions by which popular designers, in their representations of landscape, reconfirmed the social status quo: they emphasize height as a vantage point, military command, the spread of a 'protected' domesticity, the aesthetics of industrial smoke, and the erasure of 'wilderness.'

one's sense of priorities. To recognize what leads to such losses, however, is perhaps already partway to re-calling – speaking again for – a coherent relation among individuals, community, and environment. Such verbal complexities readily counter any vague generalizations about the 'naïve simplicity' of the rhetoric of Native tale-telling.

Another story by Bill Reid, 'The Raven Steals the Light,' reinforces this appreciation of complexity; it opens with a series of figurative comparisons and structural and lexical repetitions that take a simple determinist rationalism and turn it around:

Before there was anything, before the great flood had covered the earth and receded, before the animals walked the earth or the trees covered the land or the birds flew between the trees, even before the fish and the whales and seals swam in the sea, an old man lived in a house on the bank of a river with his only child, a daughter. Whether she was beautiful as hemlock fronds against the spring sky at sunrise or as ugly as a sea slug doesn't really matter very much to this story, which takes place mainly in the dark.

Because at that time the whole world was dark. Inky, pitchy, all-consuming dark, blacker than a thousand stormy winter midnights, blacker than anything anywhere has been since.

The reason for all this blackness has to do with the old man in the house by the river, who had a box which contained a box which contained a box which contained an infinite number of boxes each nestled in a box slightly larger than itself until finally there was a box so small all it could contain was all the light in the universe. (12)

The effect is multifold. To single out two particular features: (1) the imagery explicitly finds beauty (*as well as* ugliness) in the kind of environment that the European imagination characteristically defined as wilderness tract; and (2) the narrative structure reclaims the power of authority from the exterior world (the world of empirical logic, which would see contradiction in the finiteness of infinity) and gives it back to the people who tell the tales. The act of telling is, in fact, key to the spiritual effectiveness of the art. In oral tales of creation, utterance is itself an act of shaping. Hence the act of making land, or light, or life – or of articulating the politics of starting again – is reiterated in the process of the telling of the tale.

European Forms and Post-Contact Lands

When Walter Ong, in *Orality and Literacy* (31 ff.), writes of the 'psychodynamics of orality,'[8] he alludes to this power of speech, and differentiates between the structures of oral and written discourse. He distinguishes, for example, between composition-in-process (whereby meaning is established in the act of communication) and composition-by-process (whereby meaning is a result of communication). He further distinguishes between the tropes and formulas used both to pattern and to 're-call' the spoken word and the tropes and formulas that in the written word are susceptible to visual re-examination and analysis. In its 1984 published form, Reid's tale 'The Raven Steals the Light' is palpably *in print* – that is, *written*; and it uses the subordinative or hypotactic techniques (the *which* and *who* clauses) characteristic of written discourse, as well as the additive or paratactic techniques (the *and* structures) characteristic of oral discourse. But the presence here of some techniques of written communication neither denies the passage its oral force nor reduces, within a marginalized culture, the political impact of reclaiming for oneself the power to name. To develop the point further, the act of *naming* constitutes yet another trope, but it functions differently in oral and written discourse. In particular, speakers in oral cultures and writers in written cultures attribute different kinds of social power to the *process* of naming, and listeners and readers attach different cultural values to whatever each process names (in this instance, the land).

Walter Ong refers, further, to the 'magic' of naming as a feature of oral cultures (e.g., 32–3, 51). A cursory glance at European exploration journals between the early sixteenth and late eighteenth centuries reveals the extent to which written cultures also invested power in names and the act of naming. Yet to label the oral system according to a belief in 'magic' and the other system according to the documentary impulses of 'exploration' reiterates the earlier distinction between 'religion' and 'science,' especially in so far as it establishes a hierarchy between two versions of transformation. The Native (oral) system is dismissed as superstition and *tale*; the European (written) one is accorded the authority of empirical *evidence.* Yet such 'evidence' is problematic, for cultural codes intervene (see plate 1.5). The European explorers' journals, for instance, are not straightforward, nor are their versions of documentary 'objective'; indeed, they rely on a spiritual code, covertly (or at least unthinkingly), to define a cultural connection with the land, and they rely on the political expectations of their time (and on editorial shaping to such political ends) for their perceived effectiveness.

The European explorers and the Native tale-tellers, that is, both drew on religious codes, and both used these codes to particular cultural ends. But the European codes exerted more cultural power in the society at large to the degree that the prevailing political system gave more credence to them than to the other. In the system that shaped how the *explorers* saw, land existed apart from the observer, as a thing seen, an object or entity susceptible to the senses – whereas *indigenous* religious tales identified the spirituality of the land as an extension of human sensibility. Both of these perceptions are political, but for European readers – that is, for those persons within the reach of European institutional power – the politics of the explorers' words is at once constituted in and defended by an appeal to the enlightening force of civilization. This idea, 'civilization,' is of course another social construction, in which journal-writers, editors and publishers, and readers (those of an earlier time as well as those of the present) all participate. It is a construction, however indirectly articulated, of a particular cultural dominance and a particular group dominance within that culture, served by a kind of covert syllogism. The explorers, naming the land in accord with the conventions of current politics, were deemed to be dealing with documentary reality and to be on the side of God. Church, state, and the publishing industry were all agents of the powers invested in *literacy*. Documentary form, in consequence, being ostensibly empirical, was approved as truth. But in this context, documentary can be seen to be one of many systems of presumptive translation, one that does not possess intrinsic value but which is given value within a particular society. Its version of land, and of 'landing ashore,' which serves as a particular version of cultural power, can consequently also be read as a site of contesting systems of authority.

Jacques Cartier's sixteenth-century journal furnishes a familiar instance of the European claim to (and by) naming – and of the cultural transformation that mapping and claiming together effect. One passage especially clearly demonstrates how speech and land interconnect. To be more precise, the excerpt that follows comes from John Florio's 1580 English translation of Giovanni Ramusio's Italian translation of a journal purported to have been written by Cartier in French – which puts a contemporary reader on thrice shaky ground. To read the 'document' in English is consequently to read a political process, a system of translating or transforming that accords in some figurative measure with what Cartier himself was doing: crossing boundaries, landing imaginatively as well as physically on unfamiliar earth that was shortly to be made more familiar by the terms used to name it.

Florio's Cartier is not much impressed by what he sees at the mouth of the *St Lawrence* River in 1534, and he writes:

If the soile were as good as the harboroughes are, it were a great commoditie: but it is not to be called the new Land, but rather Stones, and wilde Furres and a place fitte for wilde beastes [the French reads: 'pierres et rochiers effrables et mal rabottez'] for in all the Northe Ilande I didde not see a Carloade of good earth; yet went I on shoare in many places, and in the Iland of White Sandes, there is nothyng else but Mosse, and small Thornes scattered here and there, withered and drye. To be shorte, I believe that this was the lande that God allotted to Caine. (6–7)*

But he proceeds to claim by naming anyway: a 'good harbour' is named after St Anthony, another 'good harbour' after St Servan, a 'good open-ing' for a river after St James (they meet a French fishing vessel at this spot but, significantly, the fishermen 'did not know where *they were*,' to use Cartier's phrase, for in effect they were without Cartier's maps and Cartier's identifying names; identifying *Location* has come to depend on an assumption about a particular system of *Locating*). Even more instruc-tive is Cartier's comment when he gets to what he calls 'one of the beste [harbours] in all the world.' The saints get the 'good' harbours, but when he arrives at the 'best' one, he writes: '*therefore* we named it James Carthiers Sound' (6).[9] The ego of naming and claiming is transparent. But the intrusive 'therefore' in this phrase, which emphasizes Cartier's ego, is John Florio's word, not Ramusio's and not Cartier's; it appears in the translation, attributing intention and thus colouring the text. Politics thus affects document. (The French text does employ the nomenclature of the Christian saints, and the reference to Canada as Cain's land is Cartier's also. Perhaps the saintly names were intended to civilize the savage: politics affects both documents – the fact that *possession* in this case also involved an act of *dispossessing* is not faced directly, or is perhaps

---

* Cf. J.M. Scott's account of a young Englishman's travels to Lábrador in 1928, *The Land that God Gave Cain*. Al Purdy's poem 'Ave Imperator' provides an interesting gloss on Cartier's text that also relates the language of contact to the language of property and class, region, and resistance. The poem contrasts the 'tough crew of Newfoundlanders' who run a twentieth-century Atlantic motor vessel both with Car-tier ('who called [this country] "The land God gave to Cain" / expecting maybe dancing girls?') and with Lady Margaret Bowater, who in 1956 donated to the vessel a painting of an English parkland ('complete with a baronial hall / and doubtless a Lord and Lady Fitzsomething'). Purdy's vernacular language punctures the presump-tuousness of religion, wealth, and class, and questions whether the élite, in their desire to raise local taste, have ever truly looked at the realities of local lives or sym-pathized with ordinary people's sacrifices, successes, and commitments.

implicitly justified, to both Cartier's and Florio's contemporaries, by the claim of land in the name of religious enlightenment.) But despite the uncertainties regarding authorship and intention, modern readers can fairly securely deduce some social attitudes from such texts; these attitudes in turn help to explain how a conception of 'the land' subsequently affected English-language literary expression.

Jurisdiction over Taste

Quite clearly, to extrapolate from Cartier's comment, two criteria governed what European eyes considered acceptable in the new world: usefulness and beauty. Whatever was *usable* in the old world's terms was deemed to be of value – that is, whatever was open to cropping and therefore to economic advantage. Whatever accorded with the old world's measures of aesthetic order, moreover, was deemed to be *beautiful*. In practice, aesthetics and utility did not always coincide, but in the language of *polite* literature, the terms of such order operate openly, as Robert Hayman's 'Quodlibets' (1628) illustrates. In these lines Hayman was writing about the new country's landscape, but with a social purpose, addressing his poem to the former governor of Newfoundland with a complimentary (and therefore in some measure functionally political) intent. He employed what was at the time a conventional four-part *system* of praise involving the four elements of 'Nature':

> The Aire in Newfound-land is wholesome, good;
> The Fire, as sweet as any made of wood;
> The Waters, very rich, both salt and fresh;
> The Earth more rich, you know it is no lesse.
> Where all are good, *Fire, Water, Earth, and Aire,*
> What man made of these foure would not live there?
>
> ('[The Pleasant Life in Newfoundland]' 1)

Hayman's question may be more rhetorical than consequential, assuming no stated reply to be necessary because the presence of all four elements already establishes a praiseworthy harmony. The composition itself is clearly artificial, verbally shaped with the idea of (elemental) balance in mind, meaning that an expectation of strict *referential* reality should not disturb how the passage is read. When Hayman was writing, stylistic imitation (of a received version of verbal skill) did not demonstrate a lapse in aesthetics, but rather a tribute to aesthetic order; the artifice would therefore have been an intrinsic part of the poem's political compliment. Artifice also, however, intrinsically reshapes 'wilderness' here into something orderly and 'therefore' cultivated – creating an equation that excludes 'wild' form from any 'civilized' definition of art.*

This context affects the language of 'Landing,' the terms of European–Native contact[10] – and these terms in turn subsequently affected anglophone writing in Canada. They encoded the systems of value that *interpreted* wilderness; and for its part, 'interpreting wilderness' meant responding to the *images* as well as the *empirical realities* of both *Indians* and *land*, often undifferentiated.[11] The received terms by which writers perceived (and so constructed) social order affected not just the polite literature of formal occasion, but also the language of ostensible documentary, the travel commentary that was framed by politically subjective eyes. For example, adjectives such as *vast* and *strange*, describing land and travel in journals from Luke Foxe in the sixteenth century to Alexander Mackenzie in the late eighteenth, speak of space and distance in such as way as to suggest that European dimensions and appearance constitute the world's cultural norms.[12] Further, they give the tinge of romantic adventure to journeys that were undoubtedly at least as much marked by hardship and boredom. They also make *acceptable* that which was beyond reach of prevailing European systems of beauty.

When Mackenzie's journals were published in 1802, the *Edinburgh Review* praised them not for their specifics of empirical detail – indeed, the realities of mud and endurance somehow disappear from the picture – but for what, inside two centuries, had become the conventional language of wilderness observation: 'There is something in the idea of traversing a vast and unknown continent [said the reviewer], that gives an agreeable expansion to our conceptions; and the imagination is insensibly engaged and inflamed by the spirit of adventure, and the perils and the novelties that are implied in a voyage of discovery ... ' (quoted by Hopwood, 30). One measure of the pervasiveness of this conventional way of

---

* Robert J.C. Young (30–3) quotes from Raymond Williams's *Keywords*, to elucidate the root meanings of the word *culture* and its influence on definitions of 'civilized' conduct: The Latin root words *cultura* and *colere* ('inhabit, cultivate, attend, protect, honour with worship') give rise both to *cultus* (hence the English word *cult*) and to *colonus* (from which comes the English word *colony*). Young adds: 'The culture of land has always been ... the primary form of colonization; the focus on soil emphasizes the physicality of the territory that is coveted, occupied, cultivated, turned into plantations and made unsuitable for indigenous nomadic tribes' (31).

viewing the North American 'wilderness' – it becomes agreeable to the degree it can also be considered novel – is the language used a generation after Mackenzie, when Frances Trollope recorded her first glimpses of New Orleans in 1827. Once again, the other-land and the other-persons who live in it are united within a literary trope that distances and demarcates them:

On first touching the soil of a new land, of a new continent, of a new world, it is impossible not to feel considerable excitement and deep interest in almost every object that meets us. New Orleans presents very little that can gratify the eye of taste, but nevertheless there is much of novelty and interest for a newly arrived European. The large proportion of blacks seen in the streets, all labour being performed by them; the grace and beauty of the elegant Quadroons, the occasional groups of wild and savage looking Indians, the unwonted aspect of the vegetation, the huge and turbid river, with its low and slimy shore, all help to afford that species of amusement which proceeds from looking at what we never saw before. (7)[*]

Clearly, it was not the *specifics* of landscape in either Canada or Louisiana that engendered such a response; it was the perceived difference from English paradigms of aesthetic and social arrangement. Using these paradigms could, nevertheless, permit specific features of North American landscape to be read for a particular political purpose. Barbara Novak, whose *Nature and Culture* considers the representation of rocks, clouds, organic foregrounds, and other phenomena, notes, for example, how the iconography of the sublime was used to construct a particular nationalist sensibility in nineteenth-century American landscape painting; expansion to the western frontier, for example, is represented in these paintings both as a conversion of savagery and as God's demonstration, through the settlers' and explorers' perception of a 'sublime' landscape, of the future possibilities of the (American) nation-state.[13]

---

[*] Susanna Moodie, in *Roughing It in the Bush*, observes: 'I was told by a lady, the very first time I appeared in company, that "she heard that I wrote books, but she could tell me that they did not want a Mrs. Trollope in Canada." I had not then read Mrs. Trollope's work on America, or I should have comprehended at once the cause of her indignation; for she was just such a person as would have drawn forth the keen satire of that far-seeing observer of the absurdities of our nature, whose witty exposure of American affectation has done more towards producing a reform in that respect, than would have resulted from a thousand grave animadversions soberly written' (214–15).

'Taste' and social order, that is, were symbiotically related. What this chapter has referred to as 'disconnection' was, in practice, a necessary attribute for the polite classes to possess, according to the fashion of the day, for it enabled them to observe the 'ordinary' world but to preserve their learned version of superiority over it. As Mrs Trollope's 1949 editor observes, the Tory press in London, when her book was first published, praised her *lady*-like exposure of the *myths* of a western paradise, whereas the Whig press chastised her for mere scandal-mongering ('Introduction' 8). The language here is revealing. In each case a desire for the 'real' existence of a particular *social* structure (a desire based on the political utility of the image of reality) determined what would be accepted as 'truth' or dismissed as 'myth.' But *literary* practice complicated how reality could be measured. Although received taste was continuously making a distinction between chaos (immediate experience, measurable reality) and design (distanceable convention, orderable art), art and criticism were themselves blurring the line by reading reality in the terms of convention and measuring design against the forms of experience.

The impact of the distinction between the measurable and the conventionally decorative shows in late eighteenth-century paintings. Thomas Davies, for example, reproduced some details of Eastern Canadian forested landscape with draughtsmanlike care (in contrast to the work of the amateur British naval illustrator on Cook's third voyage, William Ellis, whose depiction of Canadian West Coast conifers radically distorts their shape); but Davies, through his coloration and arrangement, and his imposition of conventional human figures against the landscape, none the less redesigned the wilderness as 'scene,' making it acceptable to current English fashion (see plate 1.6). Forest turned into garden.[14] Other landscapes encouraged related responses, as when numerous illustrators tried to deal with Niagara Falls as a visual icon[15] (see plate 1.7). But *this* natural phenomenon (unlike the deforested garden) had no immediate European parallel; it consequently resisted aesthetic taming longer than the 'garden' did, apparently creating something of a challenge to taste. Breathtaking, the Falls were beyond reach of what conventionally was called 'beautiful' – they were neither a fountain nor the kind of cataract that could be contained pictorially *within* a European garden or represented as 'picturesque.' So Niagara became an example of nature's 'sublimity' instead – a redefinition of aesthetic reality which had further social consequences. Like Frances Trollope, Harriet Martineau, Frances Anne Kemble, and many another nineteenth-century traveller, Susanna Moodie attempted to capture the sensation of first seeing

Niagara Falls. Her 'Niagara,' a chapter in *Life in the Clearings versus the Bush* (1853), connects the waterfall with the sublimity of God, but also with liberty and with creation itself: the 'great cataract burst on my sight ...., producing an overwhelming sensation in my mind which amounted to pain in its intensity' (248). 'Niagara,' Moodie adds, 'belongs to no particular nation or people. It is an inheritance bequeathed by the great Author to all mankind – ... at which all true worshippers must bow the knee in solemn adoration' (258). The Niagara image might typify a *sublime*, if not *beautiful* environment; but however awe-inspiring, it remained uninhabitable – which only reinforced the idea that Canada was a 'real' wilderness.

Critics, writers, painters, and philosophers – from Burke to Gilpin and beyond* – all sought at this time to demarcate aesthetic 'laws' which might articulate (hence contain, within language) a 'lawless' land. A distinction between the habitable picturesque and the uninhabitable sublime (still changing as the nineteenth century advanced) permeated both the theory and the practice of composition, and it shows up, as Ian MacLaren has argued,[16] in the landscape depictions of Samuel Hearne's mid-eighteenth-century Arctic journeys. Here the paradigm of distinction relies on differences between 'South' and 'North.' Hearne travelled 'through' the southern landscape, but 'onto' and 'across' the treeless

---

* The English writer Edmund Burke (drawing on 'On the Sublime,' a treatise mistakenly attributed to Longinus), published in 1757 his influential commentary *A Philosophical Enquiry into the Origin of Our Ideas of the Sublime and Beautiful*; Burke associated the 'sublime' with the idea of terror (embracing such intangibles as the dark, the vast, and the isolated) and the 'beautiful' with the idea of love (embracing such intangibles as the delicate, the smooth, and the fair). In response, other writers, including William Gilpin in *Three Essays* (1792), proposed a third category, the 'picturesque,' which could cope with the attractions of 'unorganized' scenery, especially rural scenery. The 'picturesque' (an idea also influenced by the paintings of Nicolas Poussin and Claude Lorrain, and by the practice of the garden designer Capability Brown) praised such qualities as the rough, the 'ruined,' and the irregular in landscape, provided that the viewer, securely distanced from the scene, had a vantage point from which to view these qualities 'as a picture,' as a pictorial representation. In North America, the sublime and the picturesque came to be associated, respectively, with 'uninhabitable' and 'inhabitable' landscapes. On landscape conventions in literature, and their relevance to Canada, see also D.M.R. Bentley's Introduction to *Quebec Hill*. Thomas King's story 'The One About Coyote Going West' satirizes the European impulse to rearrange Canadian nature into a picturesque iconography; Coyote at one point in the story is unhappy with River and Mountain in their 'happy' state (74) – the one because it is straight and runs both ways, the other because it is round and fertile and doesn't have any crags and cliffs.

North. He was not – and never could be – *of* the North. *It* (the distancing impersonal pronoun is intentional) was *Other*, because *it* was deemed '*barren.*' It could nevertheless be made aesthetically acceptable in literature *if* it could verbally be transformed into a conventional image – of ruin or desolation or barbarity. Hence, by the eighteenth century, the Canadian landscape had become a verbal territory as well as a physical one, and the ways in which language constructed this landscape affected what people thought they saw or thought was there to be seen. If it had already ceased being a spiritual extension of humankind, in the aboriginal sense, it had not given up all connection with religion, but it had turned into a written European literary trope, one that was shaping the way people could respond to the land, whether outside Canada or within.

Sometimes a publishing house even rewrote an explorer's logbook or diary to remove the evidence and flavour of empirical observation and heighten instead the conventional contrasts and elevated diction of fashionable discourse. It was the English writer William Combe, for example – the author of *The Tour of Dr. Syntax in Search of the Picturesque* (1809) – who edited Alexander Mackenzie's journal before it saw print: he altered vocabulary, changed syntax, and even (as Florio did with Cartier) sometimes inserted presumptive statements, in this case about the character of landscape. When Combe takes Mackenzie's manuscript phrase 'The Soil is Yellow Clay mixed with Stones' and publishes it as 'The soil, where there is any, is a yellow clay mixed with stones' (cited by MacLulich, 62),* he is doing more than altering orthography. The phrase 'where there is any' reconfirms the conventional image (and expectation) of barrenness. The 'land God gave to Cain' got larger, apparently, as Canada's physical dimensions became known in Europe. And this literary convention had surprising staying power – with more effectiveness, appar-

---

* W. Kaye Lamb also notes, in the Introduction to his edition of *The Journals and Letters of Sir Alexander Mackenzie*, that 'Combe could vary his style to meet almost any occasion – a gift that caused him to become a forger as well as a ghost-writer – and his method was to revise and embellish rather than to rewrite in a style of his own' (34). In his own preface to the first edition of his *Voyages from Montreal*, Mackenzie writes: 'These voyages will not, I fear, afford the variety that may be expected from them; and that which they offered to the eye, is not of a nature to be effectually transferred to the page. Mountains and vallies, the dreary waste, and wide-spreading forests, the lakes and rivers succeed each other in general description; and, except on the coasts of the Pacific Ocean, where the villages were permanent, and the inhabitants in a great measure stationary, small bands of wandering Indians are the only people whom I shall introduce to the acquaintance of my readers' (Lamb 58)

ently, than had the subsequent images (or the immediate aesthetic appeal, except within the conventions of 'novelty') of empirical irregularity.

'Veracity,' however, *was* deemed important – a necessary answer to the hyperbolic lies of earlier travel literature perhaps – and with the advent of tools of scientific measurement, the landscape records of the travel writers became more concerned with botanical taxonomies and more connected with number. Empiricism began to confront rhetorical convention. Hence John Franklin's nineteenth-century expedition reports carry on the traditions established by the Cook–Banks observations in the 1780s, and George Vancouver, writing in 1798, is preoccupied with details of latitude and longitude – 'The observed latitude here was 49°19', longitude 237°6', making this point (which, in compliment to my friend Captain George Grey of the navy, was called POINT GREY) 7 leagues from point Roberts' (300) – at least until he leaves behind what he called the 'decorum' and 'civility' of the coast-dwellers and the land in which they dwell (the southern tip of what is now British Columbia) and moves north to observe the precipitous fjord coast. Here the novelty, the very *lack* of decorum, is what fascinates and at the same time horrifies Vancouver; and for want of an accepted vocabulary of praise or an adequate numerical vocabulary of measurement, he retreats into the 'other' adjectives of conventional distanced chaos: 'stupendous barrier,' 'abrupt [rise],' 'frigid summit,' 'foaming torrents,' 'rugged surface' – 'altogether a sublime, though gloomy spectacle, which animated nature seemed to have deserted'* (300, 303). But conventionally, when decorum goes, so goes civility. Hence 'Neighbourhood,' a term resonant with notions of civil law, was in these circumstances wholly divorced from landscape. The Canadian landscape, in consequence – which turned in time into a

---

* Vancouver's sense of the sublime coast as 'repellant' is noted in Tippett and Cole, 16–17. Vancouver's subsequent naming of 'Burke's Channel' after Edmund Burke in 1793, however, likely acknowledges Burke's recent political publications (e.g., *Reflections on the French Revolution*, 1790) and his contributions to the shaping of British colonial policy, especially *vis-à-vis* the Spanish, in the Pacific, more than his earlier work on the sublime and the beautiful. Burke's indirect influence on subsequent settlement patterns shows in the work of Edward Gibbon Wakefield, who (as an influential designer of British colonial settlement policy, and as one of the writers of the 1839 Durham Report) conceived of colonial lands as 'waste' until settled. Wakefield further proposed that acreage costs be set sufficiently high that ordinary workers would not be able to purchase them outright, necessitating their having first to labour for others; such policies set a capitalist economy in place in Canada, and indirectly also helped shape subsequent social attitudes towards immigrants and immigration.

general concept, one that was extrapolated negatively from individual reactions more than it was grounded positively in the varied images of active record – was divorced from the idea of European neighbourhood by the very language that was being imported to describe it.[17] But if a terminology comes from elsewhere, what values will it carry, and how valid will the values be in its new context, let alone the old one? What, in short, will the 'natural' terminology for land be in any country, and what will it imply?

Two sets of European visual conventions are being isolated here: those of the sublime (related to notions of the exotic) and those of the picturesque (related to a way of conceptualizing the familiar). But they were not the only arbiters of visual representation, just as 'elevated language' – the approved formal style of much eighteenth-century writing – was not the only permanently acceptable feature of European verbal practice. Changes in taste repeatedly intervene, and when a taste for 'empiricism' inevitably returned, it seemed to replace the idea of 'sublimity' in evocations of nature and land. But it is important to emphasize that empiricism was not a substitute for rhetorical artifice but simply another form of it, one that embodied a different set of values. When, towards the end of the eighteenth century, European writers mastered a less adorned art of description, for example, they did so in the belief that a so-called 'plain' speech could prove as eloquent a convention as 'elevated language' had been* – David Thompson's journal and Catharine Parr

---

* The virtues of the 'plain style' had been extolled by Thomas Sprat in his *History of the Royal Society of London* (1667). Barbara Maria Stafford (*Voyage into Substance* 36), demonstrating how Sprat's views drew on Sir Francis Bacon's theories and would influence those of John Locke, notes how Sprat assumed that 'visual and linguistic tasks are identical'; he was convinced that the abandonment of metaphor would lead to 'science' and greater objectivity, and wrote (not without metaphor): 'the Genius of *Experimenting* has endeavoured to separate the knowledge of nature from the colossus of rhetoric, the devices of fancy, and the delightful deceits of fables.' By extolling the virtues of observation, he encouraged the 'scientist' to stand apart, thus equating 'distance' with 'objectivity' – whereas twentieth-century physics argues that any observation requires photons to strike an object for 'sight' to take place, thus already modifying the object during the process of observation, making 'objective' record something of an illusion. Sprat's 'plain style' also came to be considered 'masculine,' setting up a hierarchical distinction between *parataxis* as masculine, neutral, and nonjudgmental, and a metaphoric or ornamented style as feminine, personal, and biased. This distinction seems to have been undisturbed by practice, or by the subsequent eighteenth-century fashion for 'elevated language' as a sign of august sophistication, or by the ironic paradox that oral cultures were concurrently being dismissed because, in part, their paratactic storytelling forms were considered childlike.

Traill's nineteenth-century settler's guidebooks furnish examples. But the claim to be writing 'plain' speech did not mean that those who used it (in contrast to their precedessors) were *therefore* neutral or objective. In any event, eighteenth-century landscape conventions persisted for a long time into the nineteenth century, affecting fiction and poetry in Canada as well as 'documentary' prose.

Frances Brooke's 1769 novel *The History of Emily Montague* sets out a pattern. When a central fictional character named Arabella Fermor (pronounced 'farmer') is made to visit Montmorency Falls (which was also a recurrent subject for painters [see plate 1.8]), she describes the 'real' scene not so much in empirical detail as in strategies of epithet and design: hence it is the shape of the prose that matters, not the specifics of observation. A passage describing the falls and the approach to the falls in winter will suggest the flavour of the work:

The road, about a mile before you reach this bay, is a regular glassy level, without any of those intervening hills of ice which I have mentioned; hills, which with the ideas, though false ones, of danger and difficulty, give those of beauty and magnificence too.

As you gradually approach the bay, you are struck with an awe, which increases every moment, as you come nearer, from the grandeur of a scene, which is one of the noblest works of nature: the beauty, the proportion, the solemnity, the wild magnificence of which, surpassing every possible effect of art, impress one strongly with the idea of its Divine Almighty Architect.

The rock on the east side, which is first in view as you approach, is a smooth and almost perpendicular precipice, of the same height as the fall; the top, which a little overhangs, is beautifully covered with pines, firs, and evergreens of various kinds, whose verdant lustre is rendered at this season more shining and lovely by the surrounding snow, as well as by that which is sprinkled irregularly on their branches, and glitters half melted in the sun-beams: a thousand smaller shrubs are scattered on the side of the ascent, and, having their roots in almost imperceptible clefts of the rock, seem to those below to grow in air.

The west side is equally lofty, but more sloping, which, from the circumstance, affords soil all the way, upon shelving inequalities of the rock, at little distances, for the growth of trees and shrubs, by which it is almost entirely hid. (149–50)

The heavily subordinated structure, the recurrent doubling of nouns and adjectives ('danger and difficulty,' 'shining and lovely,' 'trees and shrubs,' 'smooth and ... perpendicular'), the concern for balance ('east side/west side'), the measured arrangement of contrasts ('equally lofty, but more sloping'), the establishment of background and foreground, the emphasis on prospect, proportion, and nobility: these features organize a Royal Academy painting more than they mimetically mirror wild nature. Within a page, the deliberately coquettish Arabella does go on to praise the winter, adding:

I have not told you half the grandeur, half the beauty, half the lovely wildness of this scene: if you would know what it is, you must take no information but that of your own eyes. (151)

But what is apparent here is the disparity between the message about elegant balance (conveyed by the syntax and the formal *arrangement* of the vocabulary) and the denotative meaning conventionally lodged in the words 'lovely wildness' themselves. For in this context, even the term *lovely wildness* has to be read for its *structure* – as an oxymoron – rather than as a 'natural' description. Like Hayman, Brooke appears to be praising the Wild Canadian Landscape as the work of a Divine Almighty Architect* rather than dismissing it as the land east of Eden, but she is also ordering it in the process. Hence the syntax of praise that is here *applied to* Canada leads to a further hiatus between word and place. The question here is what constitutes 'reality' for the settler society, the physical cultural experience or the learned cultural expectation of how to read that experience; if the learned expectation takes precedence over the physical actuality, then the territoriality of the mind-set sets preconditions on interpretation.

J. Mackay's 'Quebec Hill or Canadian Scenery' (1797) extends this illustration. Mackay used verse not just to describe or evoke a particular place, but also to ask how to contain the uncontainable. To cast his literary premise in such terms is to emphasize how much he saw his landscape as a verbal (artistic) problem. These are some early lines:

---

*   Andrew Allan's 1798 poem, 'A Description of the Great Falls, of the River Saint John, in the Province of New Brunswick,' also incorporates this architectural image. In contrast with the falls in summer, where the 'abyss' produces 'scenes of horror, / Delight, and wonder, with most awful terror, / From this dread gulf of never-ending noise, / Resembling that were devils but rejoice,' the falls in winter are ordered and divine: 'Around the verge what curious objects rise / To feed the fancy, and to feast the eyes! / Pilasters, arches, pyramids, and cones, / Turrets enrich'd with porticos and domes; / In artless order, – form'd by surge and spray, / And crystalline-garnet hues their rich array; / A dazzling cascade ground throughout the whole / Strikes deep with pleasure the enraptur'd soul' (62–3).

Ye who, in stanzas, celebrate the Po,
Or teach the Tyber in your strains to flow,
How would you toil for numbers to proclaim
The liquid grandeur of St. Laurence' Stream? (47)

Mackay's answer to this question – essentially a request for a metric
design appropriate to a place – is to elevate the diction and find contrast
and degree everywhere. He interprets the question, that is, as a search
less for a particularity of language and place than for the kind of convention appropriate to the way he conceptualizes size and 'grandeur.' Ac-
cordingly, his vocabulary shapes an orderly scene that in effect grants
more authority to the designs of artifice than to the less predictable (or
at least more random) exigencies of experience. Ships become 'barks';
waves become 'impetuous billows.' 'Prowling wolves,' 'rattling snakes,' and
even 'fiery tygers' dart upon their prey in the 'lofty groves' of wilderness,
as do the wild Indians who are 'deep involv'd in woods' – *hence* (and the
belief in consequence again links landscape with theology here) 'brutal
warfare fills the chequer'd groves.' These observations prove to Mackay
two things: (1) the accuracy of the Christian ethic – the dangers demonstrate the concealed 'stings that ever lurk below' – and (2) the necessity
of an imported culture, which takes shape on the land in the form of
'cottages ... *spread*' on the river banks, a 'rip'ning *increase*' in the cleared
fields, and on 'distant hills' an 'arbor richly clad' which 'afford[s] the
wild inhabitants a shade.' There is little activity in these descriptive passages, despite the river (now called 'stream' and thereby tamed) which
'pours along' (but now with 'lazy motion') (47–52; my italics).* All instead is passive, under the control of speech and rhyme, as was the poet's
intent, even if these bear little resemblance to the vernacular speech in
use in the new communities or to the empirical disorder of community
expansion. What was deemed 'natural,' the language of *literary* practice,
did not necessarily accord directly with the 'ethical' in social behaviour,

---

* Lines 95–8 read: 'High soar Niagara's renowned Falls, / whose dreadful grandeur
passengers appalls: / With force collected, down the waters roll / Condensed, spread,
impatient of control' (49). Cf. John Hunter-Duvar's *De Roberval* (1888), which batheti-
cally perpetuates this discourse; it reads in part: 'An ocean poured into a giant chasm
/ With one majestic sweep of quiet force, / Embodiment of power ineffable, / Resist-
less beyond utmost stretch of thought, / Too grand to have its features analysed, /
Too vast to pick and speculate on parts, / But in its whole so dread it numbs the
mind / And merges all sensations into awe, / Visible image of immensity' (225–6).

the 'real' in practical experience, or the 'aesthetically pleasing' in art.[18] Mackay's practice reflected a particular aesthetic taste; he attached value to a genteel class paradigm, wrote so as to design it in speech, and ignored what other (and later) observers might regard as the 'dominant' culture's alternative preoccupations and priorities.

Nineteenth-century writers were for some time to show the continuing influence of eighteenth-century notions of appropriate *degree* in the aesthetics of landscape depiction. Oliver Goldsmith was intentionally to imitate his English namesake and forebear when he described, in 'The Rising Village' (1825), nature's 'blest ... ruggedness,' its 'bleak and desert lands,' the 'low hamlet and ... shepherd's cot,' the 'vernal bloom' that 'adorns the field' (*passim*).[*] By the literary conventions of imitation, Goldsmith hoped not only to order in verse the unordered landscape around him, but also to claim for himself a position of some eminence as a literary shaper. Such eminence was to be won, it was believed, not by appealing to local detail or to Native custom, but by adopting European convention; he sought approval elsewhere, and to win it he accepted that other world's aesthetic definitions of *wild* and *wilderness*, even though (or perhaps because) these definitions attitudinally removed him from the empirical version of 'wilderness' in which he happened to live.

When Susanna Moodie began to write the sketches that subsequently appeared in 1852 as *Roughing It in the Bush*, these conventions had been normalized. Moodie used them because she had been trained in them; they marked the way she wrote because they marked the way she saw, because they determined the limits of what she could see. She complained at one point to her publisher Richard Bentley that she was 'deficient' in her power to render detail (*Letters* 129). In a way she was; a preconception about the verbal character of 'eloquence' intervened, leading her to reach for the elevated word and the distancing phrase every time she attempted to describe with emotive effect the landscape

---

* Ann Bermingham's comments, in *Landscape and Ideology*, on the Enclosure Acts in England provide a useful background to this poem. Drawing on the work of E.P. Thompson and Louis Althusser, Bermingham argues that the notion of an enclosed landscape in economic fact led to the aesthetic precedence of the 'picturesque,' which represented scenes as enclosed gardens. Cf. Denise and J.-P. Le Dantec, who argue that the forest was conventionally associated with ignorance, and the enclosed garden with civilization (13); and David R. Coffin, who examines notions of proportion and the iconography associated with garden design, noting that the flowers of the *hortus conclusus* or enclosed garden were associated with virginity (5).

(which she saw as 'Nature' with a capital 'N'). Describing how she felt on arriving at her first bush home – a *hut* more than a 'cottage,' *pace* Mackay – she relies, for instance, on those now familiar adjectives 'wild,' 'strange,' and 'drear,' along with the eighteenth-century conventions of distant 'prospect' rather than close *setting*:

I was perfectly bewildered – I could only stare at the place, with my eyes swimming in tears; but as the horses plunged down into the broken hollow, my attention was drawn from my new residence to the perils which endangered life and limb at every step. The driver, however, was well used to such roads, and, steering dexterously between the black stumps, at length drove up, not to the door, for there was none to the house, but to the open space from which that absent but very necessary appendage had been removed. Three young steers and two heifers, which the driver proceeded to drive out, were quietly reposing upon the floor. A few strokes of his whip, and a loud burst of gratuitous curses, soon effected an ejectment; and I dismounted, and took possession of this untenable tenement. Moodie was not yet in sight with the teams. I begged the man to stay until he arrived, as I felt terrified at being left alone in this wild, strange-looking place ...

The prospect was indeed dreary. Without, pouring rain; within, a fireless hearth; a room with but one window, and that containing only one whole pane of glass; not an article of furniture to be seen, save an old painted pine-wood cradle, which had been left there by some freak of fortune. This, turned upon its side, served us for a seat, and there we impatiently awaited the arrival of Moodie, Wilson, and a man whom the former had hired that morning to assist on the farm. Where they were all to be stowed might have puzzled a more sagacious brain than mine. It is true there was a loft, but I could see no way of reaching it, for ladder there was none, so we amused ourselves, while waiting for the coming of our party, by abusing the place, the country, and our own dear selves for our folly in coming to it (*Roughing It* 83–4)[*]

Despite the suggestion of detail – the *black* stumps, the *pinewood* cradle – the greater portion of the passage appeals verbally to propriety (the cattle *reposing*, the whip *effecting* an *ejectment*). Moreover, expectation and experience are at odds, in language as well as in 'reality.' The landscape which

[*] Stafford's point (*Voyage into Substance* ch. 5) that a tension between Olympian detachment and close observation affected aesthetic and scientific representation throughout the eighteenth century, influencing discourse in the nineteenth century as well, is relevant to a reading of Moodie's style. See also Buss.

'should' accord with an idea of ordered Nature defies expectation, and the balanced clauses of Art, which 'should' accord with the rules of an ordered society, are everywhere belied by the 'gratuitous' realities of the effective but impolite vernacular. Instead of a house, she finds an absence, which is hard to occupy without altering. Though she 'takes possession' of it, re-enacting the way the explorers politically staked territory, she is afraid of it, afraid of its 'strangeness,' afraid even of being alone in the world that she has now claimed as her own.

Later, trying to record what she sees when she starts to look around her more closely, she still grasps for resonance by using elevated diction (she characterizes fish as 'finny wanderers of the wave') and generalizing, non-specific adjectives, such as 'noble.' This vocabulary involves her in one of the most pervasive of Canadian literary tropes, the equation between wild Indian and wild land:

One morning we started as usual before sunrise; a thick mist still hung like a fine veil upon the water when we pushed off, and anchored at our accustomed place. Just as the sun rose, and the haze parted and drew up like a golden sheet of transparent gauze, through which the dark woods loomed out like giants, a noble buck dashed into the water, followed by four Indian hounds.

We then discovered a canoe full of Indians, just below the rapids, and another not many yards from us, that had been concealed by the fog. It was a noble sight, that gallant deer exerting all his energy, and stemming the water with such matchless grace, his branching horns held proudly aloft, his broad nostrils distended, and his fine eye fixed intently upon the opposite shore. Several rifle-balls whizzed past him, the dogs followed hard upon his track, but my very heart leaped for joy when, in spite of all his foes, his glassy hoofs spurned the opposite bank and he plunged headlong into the forest. (170)[19]

Here, despite Moodie's apparent praise for and sympathy with some wild creatures, her underlying sympathy is for one *version* of wild behaviour over another. Her vocabulary and syntax are structurally part of a rhetoric of translation. Implicitly, her description of Indians pursuing a *wild deer* does not create reality so much as it recreates a familiar romance *narrative* – a formulaic tale of a noble hero mastering the wilderness in order to elude the enemies that the wilderness conceals. In other words, Europeans brought with them to Canada some fundamental hierarchies of value and systems of evaluation, which neither their contacts with Native cultures nor their contact with North American nature rapidly altered. Although, over the course of time, many settlers came to appreciate the 'new' land more than they did on first encountering it, this change did not necessarily mean that they outgrew the systems of assessment that derived from their early education. Like many another writer, Susanna Moodie tried often to demonstrate her engagement with the land, only to have her vocabulary and her education distance her from it. Trying to begin again, she built doors for a house in which she was never quite at home.

It is this question of distance that so marks early English-Canadian literary landscape representations. The conventional English-language vocabulary was resistant. It would not permit its users to identify with a shape of wilderness that it had predesigned as barren and uninhabitable; 'utopia,' apparently, was not credibly to be located in the Canadian wilds,* and in Canada the language would not immediately expand beyond its formulaic limits enough to permit the redefinition of wilderness as home. Hence the formulae had to change before the land could be seen in another way. Aboriginal responses to the land offered a ready paradigm of identification and conservation, for those who were willing to see it. But few were. For most European observers, indigenous mythologies represented a primitive past rather than an alternative future.† Any

---

* The use of landscape to construct utopian worlds is, however, the subject of much science fiction and fantasy, on which see David Ketterer's preliminary survey of the field, and Andrea Paradis's anthology of personal and critical essays, designed to accompany a 1995 Canadian sf exhibition at the National Library, 'Out of This World.' That utopias conventionally afford consolation and untroubled fantasy, and permit fable and discourse, is an assertion Michel Foucault makes in *The Order of Things*, an issue taken up with reference to architectural design by Georges Teyssot. Importantly, Teyssot also pursues Foucault's definition of a *heterotopia* as a disturbing disjunction between two systems of order, in which language is undermined, names become meaningless, and syntax is destroyed. It is this 'heterotopian' condition, rather than the 'utopian,' that characterizes the settler society. See also Castro.

† Writing about the contemporary Native American writer James Welch, William Bevis observes not only that American readers conventionally oppose 'natural' to 'civilized,' but also that this distinction results in a stereotypical way of reading nature as symbolic rather than real. 'The famous "sacred reciprocity" of Indians and nature certainly exists, but the quality of the Indian "sacred" within novels needs elucidation.' In relation to Welch's *Winter in the Blood* (1974), Bevis adds: 'just as there is no real category "Indian," but only various tribes, so in Welch there is no "nature," only various instances – of what?' He disputes pastoral and Freudian readings of Welch's landscape; the cows, bats, and meadowlarks in it 'are not symbols. They "function" to reveal that the narrator respects what's there' (598–9). For comparison, see also the special *Landscape* issue of *Meanjin*, which contains articles on Aboriginal land ethics in

merely sentimental identification between European and Native, more-over, would simply compound the presumptuousness of power relations that already divided these groups on largely racial grounds. The 'new way,' consequently, would distance the newcomers even more firmly from the Native peoples than it had already, for it derived from the presump-tions of authority and measurement that were inherent in the explorers' claims. 'Landing' had brought with it some versions of a new, observable landscape, which – from N.P. Willis's *Canadian Scenery* (1842) to George Monro Grant's *Picturesque Canada: The Country as it Was and Is* (1882; see plate 1.9), and on into the multitude of pictorial photograph books of the twentieth century – contrived to represent Canada as a series of quaint villages, rustic harbours, dangerous places (whirlpools, rapids, canyons), lone individuals dwarfed by giant spaces, and other *scenic views.** But for many people, writers among them, 'observing' was not enough. Subsequent definitions of land turned the 'new' landscape into something that could also be owned, and 'property' is another commodi-ty altogether.

Australia, as well as on the Australian politics of horticulture, landscape, and urban planning; McNaughton, who (in the course of an anthology) distinguishes between Maori identification with the land and European exploitation of it, both reactions becoming *systems of coding* when they take literary form; Orbell; Falkiner; and Talbot.
* Willis's two volumes were illustrated from drawings by W.H. Bartlett; Grant's were illustrated with more than 500 wood engravings, under the supervision of Lucius R. O'Brien. Willis's work includes pictures of isolated clearings in spectacular surround-ings, together with suggestions regarding immigration; the essays Grant collected range from the statistical to the impressionistic, and the illustrations include such exoticisms as 'The Douglas Pine Trees' and 'A Cañon on the Homathco.' O'Brien's most famous painting, *Sunrise on the Saguenay*, is the subject Ramsay analyzes in *A Few Acres of Snow* as an example of the picturesque convention. See also Harding and Ellen Harding, who emphasize Bartlett's conventional use of picturesque technique, his appeal to European expectations of exotic wilderness in his portraits of Indians, and his representation of technology as an icon of progress that reconstructs nature.

2

Land-Office: Literature, Property, and Power

Bias and Authority

The word *Land-Office* resonates with social implications. When people say they're doing a 'land-office business,' it means they're doing well: they're a success. And the connection between metaphor and real estate is not inconsequential. For underlying much of Western culture is an explicit connection between culture and possession: the king and his castle, 'Crown lands,' 'church lands,' the family estate. With 'landmark' decisions, the law establishes boundary lines; and privacy and status interconnect in the word 'property' itself (the word derives from the French for 'one's own'). Money and property, in turn, are linked with cultural preeminence, and the acquisition of money and property is even read, by some Christian denominations, as a sign of 'election' or moral grace. Buried in this equation is the basis for another set of Canadian literary reactions to or representations of the land. Chapter 1 outlined ways in which the European explorers' literary conventions (or those textually introduced by their editors) came to influence community attitudes. This chapter examines some of the ways in which literary images of land conventionalize – or 'map'[1] – presumptions of power. The basic metaphor in chapter 1 was *wilderness*, the difficulty of reconciling oneself with experiential reality when preconceived definitions of 'garden,' 'wild,' and 'nature' have arranged in advance the character of culture. In this chapter the recurrent metaphors are the *surveyor/map-maker* and the *clearing*. For the settler culture that developed in Canada, the explorer and the land-worker (the voyageur, the lumberjack, *les raftsmen*, the farmer) often served as model social types – of stable producers or of heroic (and therefore forgivably rowdy) adventurers. School textbooks reiterated the virtues of 'land *use*' as 'progress.' But 'heroism' and 'stability,' like 'garden' and 'wilderness,' are social determinations. The value system that these models were generally made to serve had little to do with selflessness (for all their 'nobility') and much to do with hierarchies of bias and authority. Bias and authority, in other words, are associated with land.

In part the difference between 'wilderness' and 'clearing' imagery expresses a simple historical difference between a generation concerned with travelling *through* the land to get to the other side, and a generation concerned with settling *on* the land, digging *into* the land, whether to mine, to farm, to harvest timber, or to dam and so rearrange the watercourses. For both generations, the land *as given* is a problem. For the first group it is a physical obstruction; for the second it is an impediment to commerce, valuable only when reconstructed or rearranged. And because 'commerce' is a powerful social process, an institutional mechanism in its own right, the land in northern North America soon stopped being seen as a mere impediment and became a marketable commodity. If the land-as-wilderness was somehow conceptualized as savage and evil, then it could be made acceptable if it were cleared; if it were cleared, then it could also be fenced. Either way, it could be sold, and so it became necessary within the developing society to work out how to measure plots of land: to find out precisely where they were, what they were contiguous with, and in due course what lay under them. Consequently, after the first wave of explorers had finished their reports, governments authorized a whole series of surveying expeditions[*] to chart *usable* territories and define the limits of *property*.

---

[*] For example, the Geological Survey of Canada was established in 1842; Morris Zaslow writes that it 'began the systematic mapping of the vastnesses of the Canadian Shield and the rugged Cordilleran country, made the first accurate maps of most of Canada's northern rivers, and was the first arm of the federal government to make an appearance in many districts ... The men of the Survey not only mapped the geology; they collected materials from every phase of life they encountered – samples of rocks and minerals, plants, animals, fishes, birds, Indian and Eskimo artifacts, even languages and legends (3).' Following on Clifford Sifton's plans, a federal Department of Mines was established in 1907, absorbing the Geological Survey. Under Mackenzie King's administration (with T.A. Crerar as minister), several departments merged as the Department of Mines and Resources, with separate branches concerned, respectively, with Mines and Geology; Lands, Parks, and Forests; Surveys and Engineering; Indian Affairs; and Immigration – the latter two divisions indicating an institutional relation between marginal populations and resource management. In 1947, another reorganization reduced the departmental divisions to two; it created the Lands and Development Services Branch, abolished Mines and Geology, and moved the Geological Survey to the Mines,

Such definitions often ignored whatever settlement was in place, thus giving precedence to a centralized authority over a local custom or agreement. A succession of land-dealers also arose, whose marketing strategies sometimes exceeded their scrupulous adherence to truth (see plate 2.1). 'Oh ye dealers in wild lands,' Mrs Moodie berates these men in *Roughing It in the Bush*, 'ye speculators in the folly and credulity of your fellow men – what a mass of misery, and of misrepresentation ... have ye got to answer for!' (5). This was in 1852, when she still regarded herself as their victim, and when she was still regretting having left English security for what she could perceive only as 'wilderness disorder.' By 1871, when she added an introductory essay to her book, called 'Canada: A Contrast,' she had entered the new Establishment of the increasingly urban colony. Drawing on Isaiah 40: 4 ('Every valley shall be exalted, and every mountain and hill shall be made low: and the crooked shall be made straight, and the rough places plain,' a verse reiterated in Luke 3: 5), Mrs Moodie announced of the landscape that 'the rough has become smooth, the crooked has been made straight, the forests have been converted to fruitful fields' (7).* The surface rearrangement that she espouses is clear: 'order' for Methodist Mrs Moodie is the result of surveyed edges and the cultivated replacement of the wilderness. Nature is to be controlled. The word she uses to talk about this change, moreover, is *converted*. It is an important word, for it emphasizes how strongly the Evangelical underpinnings of nineteenth-century thought influenced Anglo-Protestant

---

Forests, and Scientific Services Branch of the ministry. Several further reorganizations of responsibility (and attributions of power) have since followed. Allison Mitcham (in *Prophet of the Wilderness*) tells the story of Abraham Gesner, the geologist and inventor who founded the first Natural History museum in Canada (in Saint John, New Brunswick, in 1842). Suzanne Zeller (in 'Mapping the Canadian Mind') examines in part the relevance of the science of geology to continental expansion. John MacKenzie speaks of 'the imperialism of geology' or the process through which a conventional nineteenth-century educational system 'annexed the past' (67). The enduring precedence of geology in Victorian scientific theory (from Sir Charles Lyell, professor at King's College [London] to Sir William Dawson, principal of McGill University) is, of course, also one of the targets of Paul Hiebert's satire in *Sarah Binks*: 'Literary movements grow, fashions change, and people leave the country. But geology is founded upon a rock' (54).

* Graeme Gibson's 1982 novel, *Perpetual Motion*, provides an interesting contemporary parallel; the central character in it, Robert Fraser, tries perpetually to read Ontario forest and waterway as a 'mechanician' and to substitute clock time for Nature (see esp. 95, 109, 114–15, 145).

political expansions.* The words of the prophet Isaiah were taken literally: 'Until the spirit be poured upon us from on high, and the wilderness
be a fruitful field, and the fruitful field be counted for a forest, Then
judgment shall dwell in the wilderness, and righteousness remain in the
fruitful field' (32: 15–16). By these terms, order – the sequence of surveying, clearing, cultivation, property establishment, acquisition, ownership,
and success – is no mere accident of history but a process (and a *system*)
given sanction by God.

Even Mrs Moodie's Anglican sister, Catharine Parr Traill, invokes
God's influential blessing on land use. The more matter-of-fact of the two
settlers, Mrs Traill writes in *The Canadian Settler's Guide* (1855), a handbook about how to survive in the wilderness: how to cure the ague or
cure fish, make candles or make beer, when to sow and when to reap.
Her eye is practical; she recognizes what most people – the 'dominant
culture' of her immediate environment – will want to know. Her eye is
also always on productivity, *therefore on wealth as much as on survival.*
'Owing to the rapid progress,' she writes, 'lands have increased in value.'
Economic advantage and the idea of progress go hand in hand. This
passage continues with a catalogue of empirical demonstrations of progress:

The growth of towns and villages, the making of roads, gravel, plank and now rail-
roads; the building of bridges, the improvement of inland navigation, mills of all
sorts, cloth factories, and the opportunities of attending public worship have,
under a peaceful government, effected this change; and wise men will consider
that the increased value of lands is a convincing proof of the flourishing condition of the people and the resources of the country, and feel encouraged by the

---

*   See Berger (*Sense of Power*); McKillop; and Cook (*The Regenerators*). Cf. Fuller on
    'the geography of Mother Nature' – and the prevalence of religion as a basis for the
    nineteenth-century tropes of landscape ('Ruskin – at least, the Ruskin of the first
    volume of *Modern Painters* – believed "Nature" was little more than a synonym for the
    handiwork of God,' Fuller writes [17]. John Dixon Hunt's *Figure in the Landscape*
    shows the way enclosures and statuary were used to produce a landscape of 'sensi-
    bility' and thus construct 'suitable' (26) locations of moral habits; David Hamer's
    study of the United States, Canada, Australia, and New Zealand, by contrast, empha-
    sizes the ambiguity of 'morality' as two versions of township and town design came
    into opposition: the sense of the town as the opposite to savagery and the sense of
    the town as a structure existing within a new world garden. Further studies of urban
    landscapes include the essays collected by Anna Rutherford, on metropolises, subur-
    bia, emptiness, 'limits,' class, paradise, and public libraries.

prospect of a fair return for capital invested either in land or any other specula-
tion connected with the merchandize of the country.

Traill then affirms an authority over the wilderness, spelling this out by
appealing to a scripturally sanctioned authority of male over female:

The crown lands to the Westward, in the newly surveyed counties, are selling at
12s.6d. currency per acre. The soil is of great fertility; and to this portion of the
Province vast numbers are directing their steps; certain that in a few years the
value of these bush farms will be increased fourfold; but let none but the strong
in arm and will go upon wild land. The giants of the forest are not brought down
without much severe toil; and many hardships must be endured in a backwoods-
man's life, especially by the wife and children. If all pull together, and the women
will be content to bear their part with cheerfulness, no doubt success will follow
their honest endeavours. – But a wild farm is not to be made in one, two or even
five years. – The new soil will indeed yield her increase to a large amount, but it
takes years to clear enough to make a really good farm, to get barns and sheds
and fences and a comfortable dwelling-house; few persons accomplish all this
under ten, fifteen and sometimes even twenty years.

This passage might well be drawing allusively on familiar passages from
the Old and New Testaments: for example, Psalm 89: 10–12 ('Thou hast
scattered thy enemies with thy strong arm. The heavens are thine, the
earth also is thine: as for the world and the fullness thereof, thou hast
founded them. The north and the south thou hast created them ... Thou
hast a mighty arm'), Isaiah 52: 10 ('The Lord hath made bare his holy
arm in the eyes of all the nations; and all the ends of the earth shall see
the salvation of our God'), and Luke 1: 51–3 ('He hath shewed strength
with his arm; he hath scattered the proud in the imagination of their
hearts. He hath put down the mighty from their seats, and exalted them
of low degree. He hath filled the hungry with good things; and the rich
he hath sent empty away'). Whatever the case, Mrs Traill's rhetoric then
takes a steep turn towards the cadence and periodic structures of the
moral sermon and the sentimental romance, which it is necessary to
quote at length in order to demonstrate:

I am speaking now of the poor man, whose only capital is his labour and that of
his family; and many a farmer who now rides to market or church in his own
waggon and with his wife and children, well and even handsomely clad, by his
side, has begun the world in Canada with no other capital. It is true his head has

grown grey while these comforts were being earned, but he has no parish poor-house in the distance to look forward to as his last resource, or the bitter legacy of poverty to bequeath to his famishing children and broken-hearted widow. And with so fair a prospect for the future, wives and mothers will strive to bear with patience the trials and toils which lead to so desirable an end, but let not the men rashly and unadvisedly adopt the life of settlers in the Bush, without carefully considering the advantages and disadvantages that this mode of life offer over any other; next his own capabilities for successfully carrying it into effect, and also those of his wife and family; if he be by nature indolent, and in temper despond-ing, easily daunted by difficulties and of a weak frame of body, such a life would not suit him. If his wife be a weakly woman, destitute of mental energy, unable to bear up under the trials of life, she is not fit for a life of hardship – it will be useless cruelty to expose her to it. If the children are very young and helpless, they can only increase the settler's difficulties, and render no assistance in the work of clearing; but if on the contrary the man be of a hardy, healthy, vigorous frame of body, and of a cheerful, hopeful temper, with a kind partner, willing to aid both within doors and without, the mother of healthy children, then there is every chance that they will become prosperous settlers, an honor to the country of their adoption. The sons and daughters will be a help to them instead of a drawback, and the more there are from six years old and upwards to lend a hand in the work of clearing, the better for them: they will soon be beyond the reach of poverty. (36–7)

Words such as *only* and *own* point at property as much as they stress independence. An institutionalized sexual hierarchy also functions here; the wife is *by his side*, but without equal power, hence even 'to one side,' by implication. Alliteration accentuates the melodrama of cliché (*grown grey, parish poor-house, bitter ... bequeath ... broken-hearted*); and anaphora (through the repeated *If* structures of the last part of the passage) incre-mentally builds the rhetoric to a climax that links financial success to health, work, moral outlook, and the production of children.

A subsequent passage, on the value of saving and sharing seed, openly adapts, then quotes, from the King James Version of holy scripture, using the familiarity of *rhetorical* pattern to give moral force to a pattern of *settlement behaviour.*

It is always well to save your own seeds if you can. A few large carrots should be laid by to plant out early in Spring for seed. Onions the same, also beets, pars-nips, and some of your best cabbages. – Seeds will always fetch money at the stores, if good and fresh, and you can change with neighbours.

If you have more than a sufficiency for yourself do not begrudge a friend a share of your superfluous garden seeds. In a new country like Canada a kind and liberal spirit should be encouraged; in out-of-the-way, country places people are dependent upon each other for many acts of friendship. Freely ye will receive, freely give, and do not forget the advice given in the scriptures, 'Use hospitality one to another,' and help one another when you see any one in distress; for these are opportunities cast in your way by God himself, and He will require the use or abuse of them at your hands. (49)

The reference is to 1 Peter 4: 9, but there is a covert reference also to Romans 8: 32 ('He that spared not his own Son, but delivered him up for us all, how shall he not with him also freely give us all things?'). Clearly, ideas about land use interconnect here with the rhetoric, images, and institutions of authority, which involve gender, race, and religion as well as the politics of money. A simple syllogism is at work. Control over the land is a tacit demonstration of success; success in turn reiterates and reinforces both the value of independence within the received system and the moral superiority of those who attain and maintain such independence.

It might well be that the underlying irony goes largely unnoticed here: ownership ostensibly produces independence, yet the primary guarantee of this 'independence' is participation in the system that has justified ownership in the first place. But to whom does the society permit the privilege of ownership? For many years, the answer was simple: white men – with money. (The disputes that led to the 1837 Rebellions were preoccupied with this connection; who would own the land: the wealthy, urban, politically connected, 'landed' families of the Family Compact and the Château Clique, or the squatters/settlers/small farmers who actually worked it?) The land thus signifies more than simply nature or territory in this interlocking system of social and moral values; it signifies a version of power that was tied to economic right (spelled out in Edward Gibbon Wakefield's designs of colonial capitalism), and in turn connected with gender and race. The opportunity to use power to influence the community – through voting privileges, for example – came to be tied to land ownership; in this way the community authorized its own validity, in the process circularly reconfirming its own structural principles and the values that went with them.

Traill's reference to sharing seed perhaps suggests some higher altruism governing the settlements: one has quickly to add that there were limits to what was characteristically considered 'community.' Interdependence was necessary for survival, but a border also defined the limits of this necessity, a border that was perceived as a finite edge to civilization, not as a threshold of ongoing change. Hence when Margaret Atwood refers to the notion of 'survival' in Canadian literature (facing the 'threat' of the environment, say), and when Northrop Frye (as in *The Bush Garden*) coins his metaphor of the 'garrison mentality' – the defensive community clearing that lies at the heart of the bush – neither of these generalizations applies readily to the whole of Canadian writing; both paradigms, however, are clearly rooted in the nineteenth-century Establishment Anglo-Protestant sensibility that is epitomized by Moodie and Traill. The 'pioneer' community became a community in order to survive, but it did so by determining its edges and so declaring – and sometimes attempting to extend – the perimeter of its power (see plate 2.2). On the other side of these conceptual edges were presumed to lie the territories of anarchy – by which *in practice* were meant wilderness, forest, moral corruption, Indians, Catholics, and French. Patently, the pioneer Anglo-Protestant communities were hierarchical (as were the Catholic communities in a different way), and they collectively revealed a mixed array of biases.

In their attitude to land, moreover, they reiterated the political structures accepted as the norm of Victorian anglophone Canadian society: the 'English' *man* (the household 'head') held 'God-given' authority over both women and children, and he accepted as a matter of imperial 'right' that he should also command 'others' and control nature. The lives of thousands of individual pioneers (both women and men) of course resisted and rewrote this paradigm, but the work of William Kirby, who openly advertised his Protestant, United Empire Loyalist ancestry, clearly illustrates it. Kirby's 1877 novel *The Golden Dog* – subtitled *A Romance of Old Quebec* – explains the history of English supremacy in Canada by locating a corrupt hierarchy at the heart of *francophone* civil and religious structures; hence Kirby leads the reader inferentially to proclaim the greater virtues of the British system. This is historical fiction as propaganda. But the opening paragraphs, which set the scene, point to a further dichotomy:

A group of French and Canadian officers in the military uniforms of Louis XV, stood leaning on their swords, as they conversed gayly together on the broad gravelled walk, at the foot of the rampart. They formed the suite in attendance upon the Governor, who was out by sunrise this morning to inspect the work done during the night by the citizens of Quebec, and the *habitans* of the surrounding country, who had been hastily summoned to labor upon the defences of the city.

A few ecclesiastics, in black cassocks, dignitaries of the Church, mingled cheerfully in the conversation of the officers. They had accompanied the Governor, both to show their respect and to encourage by their presence and exhortations, the zeal of the colonists in the work of fortifying the capital.

War was then raging between old England and old France, and between New England and New France. The vast region of North America, stretching far into the interior and southwest from Canada to Louisiana, had for three years past been the scene of fierce hostilities between the rival nations, while the savage Indian tribes ranged on the one side and on the other, steeped their moccasins in the blood of French and English colonists, who, in their turn, became as fierce and carried on the war as relentlessly as the savages themselves.

Louisbourg, the bulwark of New France, projecting its mailed arm boldly into the Atlantic, had been cut off by the English who now overran Acadia, and began to threaten Quebec with invasion by sea and land. Busy rumors of approaching danger were rife in the colony, and the gallant Governor issued orders which were enthusiastically obeyed, for the people to proceed to the walls and place the city in a state of defence; to bid defiance to the enemy. (13–14)

The metaphors here are military – geography turns into a series of defences, bulwarks, mailed arms, which the man-made *walls* only reinforce. These walls sustain a particular paradigm of power, for those who do the *work* in this context are not the figures of authority but the ordinary people. This distinction is part of Kirby's political rhetoric, his aim being twofold: to discredit the authoritarian system of the *ancien régime* but at the same time to praise the *habitant*, who would be a citizen of the new Canada. And yet the rhetoric is still more involved, for it does not question British authority in Canada; on the contrary, it justifies it – or at least justifies the course of Canadian history to a readership (ten years after Confederation) eager for signs of progress and national identity. As part of this justification, Kirby's rhetoric consigns that which is considered naïve or powerless or inconsequential to the past. For example, his text contrives to praise the *habitants* in such a way that giving credit to their agricultural skills is balanced by a patent dismissal of their 'peasant' sensibilities. Kirby exploits, in other words, the conventional nineteenth-century image of land as possessable property, using it to advance an Anglo-Protestant perspective on imperial military history and also to justify the political inequities evident in the Canada of his day. The image of the French-Canadian *as a habitant* reiterated the 'normality' of a social hierarchy based on ethnic differences, and for those who enjoyed the status quo, it also reconfirmed the 'normality' of their own power. This image lasted well into the twentieth century in English-Canadian litera-

ture and in the education system. In the popular mind, 'Quebec' consequently came to equate with 'rural,' a mind-set that writers and illustrators readily and perhaps unthinkingly drew on for several decades. In the
1940s, Duncan Campbell Scott complained that Thoreau MacDonald, the
modern illustrator of his 1890s story sequence *In the Village of Viger*,
seemed to think that the village he was writing about was somewhere in
the Northern Barrens rather than on the edge of a big city.[2] In the 1950s,
schoolteachers and anthologists still praised William Henry Drummond
for his pastiche *habitant* verses; collectors and critics still praised Cornelius
Krieghoff for his romantic (but to Quebec eyes clichéd) portraits of
habitant life.[*] As late as the 1960s, literary histories were still labelling
Scott's book a collection of 'regional idylls'; and Scott himself, despite his
earlier demurral, continued in consequence to be categorized as another
perpetrator of the *habitant* stereotype rather than as a psychological
analyst of at least some of the structures of social power.

Troping Categories: Property and Propriety

More than simply recording a series of social biases, however, this chapter
is concerned with examining how and why certain paradigms of social
power (rooted in questions of received propriety and control over property) came to be associated with certain modes of aesthetic expression
(written books, heroic adventures, epic proportions).[†] Indeed, the seman-

---

* The work of Charles William Jefferys (1869–1951) illustrated textbooks and popular
  publications for many years, producing an iconography of Canadian social history for
  more than one generation of readers. M.J.H. Liversidge claims that Jefferys was one
  of the first Canadian landscape painters to express, both in subject and technique, a
  'consciously Canadian identity.'

† Susan Wood's posthumously published *The Land in Canadian Prose* presents a detailed
  thematic survey of shifting attitudes in francophone and anglophone Canadian literature; the strength of the book derives from its reference to a large body of non-fictional
  as well as fictional texts, finding contexts for literary themes in a variety of educational,
  religious, and other institutions. Its themes include the city–country contrast, 'la surviv-
  ance,' and the patriotic force of the notion of 'home and native land.' Focusing on
  Robert Stead, F.P. Grove, Ringuet, Ralph Connor, Louis Hémon, Leo-Paul Desrosiers,
  and Lionel Groulx, the book contains a number of insightful comments, as when it
  refers to the connection between landscape and commerce epitomized by the portrayal
  of scenery on Canadian banknotes; or when it observes (83) that a folk-song such as
  'Ballad of New Scotland' celebrates the freedom from *landlords* (and from duties and
  taxes) as the substantive issue underlying an idyllic dream of the new world. Commenting on John McMullen's *The History of Canada* (1855), moreover, Wood also emphasizes
  how McMullen (representative of his time) celebrates property, in that he praises mer-

tic link between the words *property* and *propriety* further elucidates the
political connection between the rights of ownership and the assumptions
about behavioural order. Clearly the systems and expectations of polite
literature did differ in some respects from the terms and definitions of
vernacular speech – though the distinction is not absolute, and though
critical generalizations sometimes make it sound as if it were. The division
between written and oral literatures, that is, sometimes unquestioningly
equates 'written' with 'respectable,' and 'oral' with 'casual.' This distinction affected conventional judgments of both Native art and 'popular'
European art. Historically, although the ritual forms of much speech can
scarcely be equated with the vernacular, the very fact that Native literatures were *spoken* was sufficient for most educated European immigrants
to consider them 'primitive.' The 'folk' arts of ordinary settlers – the
tales, songs, carvings, and dances – likewise enjoyed less stature than
books did, among those who had been educated to the dominant forms
of European taste.[*] In this hierarchy of taste, moreover, certain genres
held higher status than others. Epic and pastoral, for example, were long
regarded as more exalted forms (and therefore more important and
aesthetically significant statements about life) than such prose forms as
the novel and tale. The novel, by virtue of length (a questionable criterion at the best of times, which in this case likely reiterated the preference
for epic dimensions), was in turn deemed more significant than the short

---

chants and a land-based class as the basis for the new community emerging in Canada –
as opposed to the 'extreme' democracy of the United States (105–7). Wood goes on to
suggest the influence of this sensibility on the Protestant version of nature later
espoused by Connor. See also Bentley (*Gay/Grey Moose*, 153, 304) on Sir William Blackstone's legal commentaries on 'Property, in General,' which affected Oliver Goldsmith's *The Rising Village*, and on Blackstone's distinction between the claims of 'natural
law' (whereby Natives held 'transient' rights) and the claims of 'regular connexion and
consequence' (which stemmed from 'the art of agriculture').

[*] Yet there was another dimension to the construction of the very category 'folk.' Ian
McKay, for example, draws on the social analysis of Benedict Anderson's *Imagined
Communities* to demonstrate how the existence of the category served the interests of
the Establishment and how the category itself was concocted by Establishment desire.
By associating the unlettered poor, he argues, with (1) the simple life and values of
the past; (2) an ethnically 'pure' golden age, which produced 'true and original'
versions of songs and ballads; (3) honest labour; and (4) nature and the land; for
example, poverty could be aesthetically romanticized, a nostalgic version of ethnic
'purity' could be made to serve the political cause of nationalism, and social disparities could be made to seem 'natural,' a sign of beauty, and successfully marketed
within a tourist economy (xiv, 15, 32, 197, 248, 265, 275–6).

story and sketch. And the romance (especially the sentimental romance, to the degree that it became associated with female readers) came at the same time to be marginalized in social status. Within the European community, that is, the value attached to a given literary pattern or articulate oral expression varied in part according to custom and training. The attractiveness (and the degree of acceptance) of particular literary modes was related to *class* perceptions, and to race and ethnicity and gender, not just to language.

But (like the others) 'class' is a problematic category in Canada: it is associated with education (though not uniformly with grammatical accuracy), with money (though not uniformly with taste), and with position (though not uniformly with birth or family). Nor is it fixed in character or permanently passed from generation to generation. And yet an adopted version of a *fixed* class–taste connection can sometimes govern cultural perceptions; it can come to seem more like a determining than a negotiable criterion of cultural aspiration and evaluation, and hence to distort the social function of, say, literacy or art.[3]

The fate of the Mechanics' Institute libraries is instructive in this regard. These libraries came into existence in Canada – between 1827 (in St John's) and the 1850s – because many among the already educated classes saw literacy and literature as agents to homogenize cultural taste. Assuming their own taste to be the desirable norm for all, they set up the Institutes with an Evangelical urge to 'raise' the taste of the community by sharing their enthusiasm for book-length treatises on serious subjects. Conveniently, this plan ignored the predilection of the 'educated' to pay at least some attention to several *oral forms*: for example, rumour, gossip, innuendo, jest, conversation, discussion, and political oratory. As might have been expected, in a fluid culture, the Institutes, with their reading-rooms and lending libraries, did not produce the expected result. They reached their greatest extent in the 1890s – but more middle-class people than labourers joined them; and more of the Institutes' members sought out newspaper journalism and 'popular fiction' than indulged in scientific, religious, and aesthetic enquiry. Mrs Moodie's efforts, as co-editor (with her husband) of *The Victoria Magazine* of 1847–8, to bring 'politeness' to the 'workers' (287) shows a parallel impulse, which is symptomatic of a particular class desire.* But this desire, not without admirable

---

* Their opening editorial reads in part: 'In a *town*, the inhabitants may be said to educate each other; while in the *Country*, each individual may be said to educate himself. The Farmer, of all others, *should* be a reading man. Books should be his every-day compan-

intent, could finally control neither taste nor the future. With increased access to theatre, library, newspaper, and music-hall, many newly educated persons simply resisted the received norms; they fashioned their own instead. It is not that the new norms were intrinsically 'better' than the imported ones, just as 'plain language' is not intrinsically better than 'elevated language.' But the new norms more directly met a particular set of cultural needs, and they came with their own forms of discrimination in tow. Instead of erasing the needs of distinction, therefore, social changes appeared to multiply them. Demarcations permeated the culture, and as these grew more complex, they further marked the sliding connections among social structure, language, and land.

There were thus in place by 1900 numerous social and literary ways of encouraging settlement – and through settlement, at some levels, of encouraging a settled Establishment culture. However, not all the results were as conventional as might have been anticipated. Sir John A. Macdonald had arranged for the railway to be built to the West in the 1880s, claiming a Canada that stretched 'from sea to sea.'* (The building of the railway – together with the *railway's claim* on territory – was also a way of forestalling American expansion northward into the Prairies.) But the accompanying version of nationhood differed from Quebec and Métis versions of nationhood to begin with, and the granting of lands to the Canadian Pacific Railway Company as part of the railway-building agree-

---

ions. It must be admitted that a little reading with much reflection, is better than much reading with little reflection. If the intelligent farmer will employ a portion of his leisure hours in reading, he has always plenty of time during his daily labors, which become mechanical from habit, to arrange and digest in his mind the knowledge he has previously acquired. Without any wish to depreciate the intelligence of the Towns'-people, it is difficult to conceive any occupation better calculated to form a great, virtuous and intelligent reflective character, than that of the farmer, when properly unfolded by education' (2).

* The national motto, *A mari usque ad mare*, first used about 1906, was drawn from the same biblical verse that produced the word *Dominion* in the phrase 'Dominion of Canada' – Psalm 72: 8 ('He shall have dominion also from sea to sea, and from the river unto the ends of the earth'); Macdonald accepted the term *Dominion* as a sobriquet for the new nation in 1867 (his own preference had been for the term *Kingdom of Canada*) apparently at the suggestion of his fellow politician Samuel Tilley. July First, the national holiday, was officially changed from 'Dominion Day' to 'Canada Day' in 1983, apparently because the word *dominion* had come in some people's minds to be associated only with imperial subservience (and also because there was no precise equivalent in French to the King James Bible's sense of the word).

ment extended the connection between power and land ownership west across the continent and on into the next century.

Moreover, at the turn of the century, Clifford Sifton – Prime Minister Wilfrid Laurier's Minister of the Interior – invited East European *peasants* west to fill and till the prairie lands. Advertising posters, distributed abroad, encouraged immigration through the promise of ownership, implicitly suggesting that the new world would be the same as the old, except better. The peasants could now be landlords, for example. The foreign and the familiar would combine. Canadian government posters, using the image of birds in flight, seeking a nest, encouraged prairie settlement with the promise of home (see plate 2.3). A subsequent Canadian National Railways poster advertised Canada as 'The Right Land for the Right Man' (the man in the poster wears a broad-brimmed hat and open-necked shirt, and holds in his hands a framed image of a productive farm with a train running past cultivated fields); a White Star Line poster (emblazoned with the slogan 'Canada's Call to Women') portrayed a blonde woman standing before an open kitchen window, making apple pies, while, outside, men in a prairie field are stooking wheat; a 1919 Hudson's Bay Company 'land department' advertisement in *The Country Gentleman* invited would-be immigrants to buy some of its 3 million acres in the 'Success Belt' of the prairies, where they are told they will find not only 'Independence and Prosperity' but also 'the Right Kind of Neighbours'; and CPR travel advertisements distributed in Europe insisted on Canada's domesticity and safety, saying that travel through the Rocky Mountains would not only be 'Fifty Switzerlands in One,' but that 'Swiss guides [were] to be found at all the mountain hotels.'[4] Such promises once more shaped the image of the West in European terms, with the added comfort of an image of European dependability. When Sifton invited Eastern Europeans west, however, he apparently gave little thought to the likelihood that the cultural differences they brought with them would have any subsequent impact on mainstream Canadian culture. If anything, he seems to have anticipated – as people such as D.C. Scott concurrently assumed about the Native peoples – that a straightforward form of cultural absorption would take place.[5] Both Scott and Sifton spoke an Establishment language; in both cases, too, their language derived from, depended upon, and reconfirmed some unstated presumptions about authority in place. The perspectives of the new immigrants – Germanic, Slavic, Roman Catholic, Jewish, Mennonite, Hutterite, Eastern Orthodox, and more – would over time substantially question these presumptions and open the society to further change.

Troping Empire and Manliness

To reiterate: the image of settling the land – measuring, marking, and clearing it – was political not just in so far as it claimed property, but also in the way it implicitly asserted several hierarchies of power. Europeans were deemed to be in authority over 'Indians,' 'Negroes,' and 'Asians.' Men to be in authority over women and beasts. The Protestant English to be in authority over the Catholic French. The East to be authority over the West, the South over the North. And so on. None of these distinctions was absolute, but all were presumed by a substantial portion of the society to be true. Hence they became functioning truths (or functioning untruths): that is, they had the power of any set of unquestioned 'standards' to affect daily lives. Biases were everywhere. Anti-Semitism was rife both in Catholic and in Protestant communities. Women, Native people, and Asian immigrants were denied the vote; women were denied the opportunity to hold separate bank accounts from their husbands or to own land in their own name.[6] And people with non–Anglo-Saxon names frequently anglicized them for the sake of social acceptance. Such biases ran through literature as well. Much of the reason for the popularity of Mazo de la Roche's 1927 novel *Jalna*, for example (and its multiple 'Whiteoaks' sequels), derived precisely from its romantic appeal to these values. The saga of the Whiteoaks family portrayed the landed gentry of Ontario, such as they were: a family with a name, an estate, and an estate name. Whatever soap-opera scandals the Whiteoaks novels relied on for their rudimentary plot lines, the novels also appealed to the persistence of Empire, to a sense of place and power under continuing control. Stability implied property; property meant stability. In assuming the linearity of his own version of Progress – the continuity of the social model to which he belonged by birth and training – Clifford Sifton somehow epitomized his time without containing it. Duncan Campbell Scott, in 'Poetry and Progress,' a presidential address to the Royal Society of Canada (17 May 1922), at least acknowledged that literature and life were both changing in directions he had not anticipated – he noted approvingly the 'wilderness of natural accent' (16, 23) in the blank verse poetry of younger writers, but his reaction to what he saw as a 'violence' of modern thought was to seek refuge in elegy, not to alter his own political stance. The society of the people, meanwhile, was moving on.

Yet the revelation of Imperial and Establishment attitudes is not always so clear-cut. In the work of the 'Confederation Poets' (D.C. Scott, Bliss Carman, C.G.D. Roberts, Archibald Lampman, and others), from the

2.1 (*opposite, top*) A cartoon from the popular press, *The Emigrant's Welcome to Canada* (hand-coloured lithograph, *c*.1820, 19.4 × 29.3 cm; reproduced courtesy of the National Archives of Canada, C-041067), caricatures mercantile ambition, unprepared genteel colonists, and colonial conditions; (*opposite, bottom*) *The first iron mine in Canada West, Marmora, Hastings County* (24.2 × 37.1 cm; reproduced courtesy of the National Archives of Canada, C-000172), a watercolour by one such genteel colonist, Susanna Moodie – who went on to write pointed observations about the colony – illustrates her interest in land use and productivity: she considered such modifications to the wilderness to be civilized, progressive, and necessary.

2.2 (*above*) Henry Francis Ainslie, *Entrance to the Rideau Canal at Bytown, Upper Canada, 1839* (watercolour, pen, and black ink over pencil on wove paper, 1839, 23.0 × 32.0 cm; reproduced courtesy of the National Archives of Canada, C-000518), represents the 'garrison' landscape through the garrison wall itself, the cleared hillside outside it, the mechanical regimentation of the movement of the log rafts, and the reconfiguration of the landscape into a draughtsmanlike system of steps and locks.

2.3 (*above*) A Canadian Pacific Railway travel poster (from *The Canadian Alpine Journal*, vol. 3 [1911], reproduced courtesy of The Alpine Club of Canada) configures the Rockies according to European models; and (*right*) a Canadian Government settlement poster, 'Build Your Nest in Western Canada' (undated; held by the Government Archives Division, reproduced courtesy of the National Archives of Canada), offers would-be immigrants an image of wilderness in tamed, domestic terms.

2.4 Nineteenth-century painters conventionally represented land as property, in turn emphasizing the power of wealth, separated spaces, and gender roles. (*above*) William Berczy's *The Woolsey Family* (oil on canvas, 1808–9, 59.9 × 86.5 cm; reproduced courtesy of the National Gallery of Canada, Ottawa, #5875) glimpses property as an adjunct to virility and material comfort; (*right*) Frances Jones Bannerman's *The Conservatory* (oil on canvas, 1883, 63.3 × 79.8 cm; reproduced courtesy of the Public Archives of Nova Scotia, N-7619) brings the garden indoors as woman's domain. The reverse of Bannerman's canvas shows an earlier title, in the artist's handwriting: 'The favourite corner,' signed 'F.M. Jones.'

2.5 Len Norris, editorial cartoon for the Vancouver *Sun* (4 January 1976; reproduced courtesy of Len Norris).

2.6 While nineteenth-century lithographers delighted in the aesthetics of urban smoke and busy streets, and later painters (e.g., L.L. Fitzgerald) visualized suburban homes in terms reminiscent of pastoral security, the more characteristic attitude of twentieth-century artists has been to represent cities as soulless or sterile: as the site of pollution, economic divisiveness, and working-class protest. The subject of Eleanor Bond's *II. Departure of the Industrial Workers* (from the WORK STATION series) (oil on canvas, 1985, 239.5 × 327.5 cm, Winnipeg Art Gallery #G-86-140, reproduced courtesy of Eleanor Bond) is the dehumanizing of the urban streetscape.

latter years of the nineteenth century well into the 1920s, representations of the land cease to be 'sublime' – as they had been in the usage of the eighteenth- and early nineteenth-century poets. But rejecting the notion of a wonderful, terrifying, and abstractly conceived sublimity leads the Confederation Poets at once to embrace an empirical and particular notion of place and to use this sense of place – now defined both as *locale* in general and as *their* locale in particular – as a literary setting and as an aesthetic or ethical metaphor. Still connecting *place* with *value*, they did not give up their appeal to lines of demarcation. Hence even local poetry embodied hierarchical principles. By focusing on the *identity* of locale, the Confederation Poets were tacitly asserting that the self was rooted in Canada rather than elsewhere, and attempting (by using their poetry to celebrate the details of local landscapes) to justify the validity of their own newly national 'Canadian' perspectives.

When the wilderness then came in some measure to be perceived as *home*, the trope of the evil, godless, savage, grotesque, barren land – even in its Romantic Gothic variant of 'horrid beauty' – began to alter.* Yet alteration brought with it some new problems for those who would seek consistency. For the change in attitude seemed to deny that a person acquired prosperity by putting *wilderness* under control. This paradox takes one shape in the disparity between D.C. Scott's two attitudes to the past: Scott argues, first, that the past is a form of cultural order, to be celebrated as beauty, and, second, that the past is a form of cultural danger, which he represented in his literary texts as Indian ritual and Quebec manipulation. Scott configures the beautiful past as European – especially Italian – whereas he associates Native and Quebec images with false emotionalism and bloodless ambition. (Both tropes, instructively, Scott repeatedly associates with women.) If 'home' is a site of *change*, consequently the role of a man in it is also changing – and for Scott the new male role appears to be passive and elegiac: not to readily relinquish power but to remember order while recording decay.

The writings of Sir Charles G.D. Roberts at the turn of the century propose a different but related resolution to the dilemmas shaped by change. Although they contain a set of seeming contradictions, they also

---

* William Kirby's *The Golden Dog* provides one example of the Canadian Gothic, a form that Margaret Atwood later used parodically (in the so-called costume Gothic, perhaps most obviously in *Lady Oracle*, 1976). Conventionally, the Gothic emphasizes the two faces of the Sublime: *terror* and *horror*; while terror inspires awe, horror results from recognitions of evil. See also Northey.

demonstrate how the trope of wilderness came to be rewritten as a natural setting for the evolution of virtue and as a test of the civilized intellect. Roberts acquired notoriety as the author of 'nature stories' – stories primarily of wild animal behaviour, but also of the 'naturalness' of 'natural law' and wilderness landscape. Anthropomorphic, they also depict animals and land in order to construct versions of human relationship. Coming close to nature meant perceiving the connection between human behaviour and behaviour in nature. But behaviour in nature does not initially seem comprehensible (or compatible with human moral standards); hence such identification involves fear, especially of the unknown. The opening of the story 'The Haunter of the Pine Gloom' thus reads initially as though the wilderness were hostile. But this impression is almost at once countered by vocabulary, structure, and tone:

For a moment the Boy felt afraid – afraid in his own woods. He felt that he was being followed, that there were hostile eyes burning into the back of his jacket. The sensation was novel to him, as well as unpleasant, and he resented it. He knew it was all nonsense. There was nothing in these woods bigger than a weasel, he was sure of that. Angry at himself, he would not look round, but swung along carelessly through the thicket, being in haste because it was already late and the cows should have been home and milked before sundown. Suddenly, however, he remembered that it was going flat against all woodcraft to disregard a warning. And was he not, indeed, deliberately seeking to cultivate and sharpen his instincts, in the effort to get closer to the wild woods folk and know them in their furtive lives? Moreover, he was certainly getting more and more afraid! He stopped, and peered into the pine gloom which surrounded him.

Standing motionless as a stump and breathing with perfect soundlessness, he strained his ears to help his eyes in their questioning of this obscure menace. He could see nothing. He could hear nothing. Yet he knew his eyes and ears were cunning to pierce all the wilderness disguises. (*Last Barrier* 7)

As the narrator observes – didactically – a few paragraphs later: 'The Boy's confidence in his woodcraft was well founded. His natural aptitude for the study of the wild kindred had been cultivated to the utmost of his opportunity' and 'he had trained himself to the patience of an Indian in regard to all matters appertaining to the wood folk' (8).* These passages

---

* On nature writing, see Polk, Lebowitz, and Wadland; Wadland connects the 'animal story' with Ernest Thompson Seton's 'Woodcraft Indians' and the Boy Scout move-

resonate with contrarieties which derive from the way the familiar tropes of wilderness are presented. The wild animals are 'kindred,' and are even verbally domesticated through the narrator's use of the word *folk*, in the phrases 'wood folk' and 'wild woods folk.'* But 'the Indian' is left unparticularized, made into a stereotypical, undifferentiated group. And while 'aptitude for the study of the wild kindred' is said to be 'natural' and the Boy said to respond with 'instincts,' the aptitude must be 'cultivated' and his instincts sharpened and trained. Knowledge about nature, that is, is not natural in itself. On this distinction hangs much of Roberts's argument, for if it is through knowledge (training, cultivation) that the Boy acquires control over nature, then the hierarchy of rule is not after all undermined.

This paradigm does not appear to be consistent in Roberts's work, yet the variations from it illuminate the extent to which Roberts championed authority as much as he did the 'natural' freedom to be oneself. In a poem such as 'Tantramar Revisited' (1883), which describes the Maritime landscape (and a Bay of Fundy vista) as a *prospect* – emphasizing the distancing eighteenth-century landscape word here – the speaker resists identifying with nature close at hand in order to identify with memory instead. 'Rule' is achieved only by resisting time. These lines contrive to portray a particular locale (using descriptive adjectives, active verbs, exact nouns); they also clearly delineate a conventionally pictorial background and foreground, as seen (or constructed) from a secure position:

> Here, from my vantage-ground, I can see the scattering houses,
> Stained with time, set warm in orchards, meadows, and wheat,
> Dotting the broad bright slopes outspread to southward and eastward,
> Wind-swept all day long, blown by the south-east wind.

---

ment, both of which idealized the bush as a male domain while espousing certain forms of political conservatism.

* The language can also be construed as misleading and nostalgic. Homi Bhabha's comments on 'unhomely lives' or 'the literature of recognition' are relevant here. Discussing the work of Frantz Fanon, Bhabha observes that 'colonial' cultures are 'calcified,' and hence 'subordinated' peoples would be unwise to strike roots 'in the celebratory romance of the past' or to 'homogeniz[e] the history of the present.' He goes on to champion 'unhomeliness' – 'the condition of extra-territorial and cross-cultural initiations' instead; 'To be unhomed is not to be homeless,' but rather a step towards converting 'domestic' or 'personal' space into the effectively 'political' (9–11).

Skirting the sunbright uplands stretches a riband of meadow,
Shorn of the labouring grass, bulwarked well from the sea,
Fenced on its seaward border with long clay dykes from the turbid
Surge and flow of the tides vexing the Westmoreland shores.
Yonder, toward the left, lie broad the Westmoreland marshes, –
Miles on miles they extend, level, and grassy, and dim,
Clear from the long red sweep of flats to the sky in the distance,
Save for the outlying heights, green-rampired Cumberland Point;
Miles on miles outrolled, and the river-channels divide them, –
Miles on miles of green, barred by the hurtling gusts.

Miles on miles beyond the tawny bay is Minudie,
There are the low blue hills; villages gleam at their feet,
Nearer a white sail shines across the water, and nearer
Still are the slim, grey masts of fishing boats dry on the flats.
Ah, how well I remember those wide red flats, above tide-mark
Pale with scurf of the salt, seamed and baked in the sun!

(*Collected Poems* 79)[7]

The character of the portrayal is as important here as are the details of
the portrait. These lines *recall* in order to *describe*; they turn reality into
illusion in order to maintain for the observer some control over the *shape*
of the knowledge he possesses. The military metaphors in the poem –
rampired, bulwarked – reinforce the paradigm of measured authority that
is established through the surveyor metaphors, the property/border
metaphors, of *fence* and *dyke*. And the domestic, clothing metaphors
(*riband, skirtings*) rapidly become part of the same sequence of images
involving containment or enclosure. Celebrating control, the poet ultimately seeks a control of his own devising, not that of 'natural' time or
others' communities; hence he asserts a personal authority ('I will') in
order to maintain his distance from others and to defy the possible
efficacy of randomness. The poem closes with these four lines:

Yet will I stay my steps and not go down to the marshland, –
Muse and recall far off, rather remember than see, –
Lest on too close sight I miss the darling illusion,
Spy at their task even here the hands of chance and change. (79)

Consequently, while Roberts claims the power of the wilderness, he also
paints the present as a convention of the past. In these terms the wilder-

ness is acceptable only as an acquired understanding, however; and – extending the property metaphor – the cultivation of the land is acceptable only if it does not alter the customary structures of authority that ostensibly give him control over reality.

Roberts's technique here to some degree adopts the nineteenth-century traditions of the picturesque (as in G.M. Grant's *Picturesque Canada*). 'Picturesque' gardens were designed with the wilderness in mind (under control, in its *place*), and ruins were sometimes imported or artificially constructed – as, even later, in the Gatineau hills, neo-Gothic ruins were arranged on Prime Minister William Lyon Mackenzie King's Kingsmere estate to provide a fillip of romance to the landscape and make it serve as an escape from empirical fact. With Roberts, neither the wilderness nor the contemporary landscape is congenial on its own terms: both chaos and change seem resistant to easy control. Therefore he transforms the physical landscape, using metaphors of attitude. Paradoxically, these metaphors (particularly as they function in the animal stories) were then accepted as *empirical* truths about nature by a couple of generations of Canadian readers and critics who were less eager for 'facts' than they were for a reputation as both a cultured and a distinctive people. Roberts's wilderness provided the image: it was *Canadian*, and yet it was also *cultivated knowledge*; it was *natural*, but at least by implication it was also *safely* in the controllable *past*.

Troping Hierarchies

Later writings – Ralph Connor's turn-of-the-century Presbyterian romances (*Black Rock*, for example), E.J. Pratt's verses with their poetic fascination with giantism* – fed the same set of social desires: for naturalness and cultural distinctiveness together, for safety through authority and in propriety. The effect of the disparity between the items in this set of desires is particularly apparent in Frederick Philip Grove's 1927 novel *A Search for America*. Here the narrator openly disputes the validity of land ownership and expresses an ideal of freedom; he admires 'the lower valley of the Missouri' for its 'suggestion of width, of large spaces, of an infinite beyond which has always thrilled me' (381). But the effect is ambivalent, for Grove's protest against ownership ultimately suggests a

---

* Pratt's notes about his own poems (collected in *E.J. Pratt on His Life and Poetry*) are punctuated with such words as *dramatic intensity, colossal, tyrannical power,* and *magnitude*.

profound attraction to it.* Declaratively in love with width and space, that is, Grove's narrator, Phil Branden, is nevertheless determined to criticize expanse when he construes it as an attribute of ownership and a consequence of patriarchal inheritance. Hence, when contemplating a farm in the American Midwest, shortly after his paean to the Missouri Valley, he uses a distance metaphor to circumvent any identification between himself and the farmer. This farmer/*owner* is named Mackenzie, and Branden is at pains to ensure that a metaphor of closure contains this character whom he professes to dislike:

A farm, many square miles in extent, owned by a single man! Nothing was further from my thoughts than envy; had somebody offered me the place as a present, I should not have accepted it. But it struck me as incongruous. I was awed and felt as if I had run up against some barrier in a valley along which I had been travelling – a barrier of forbidding aspect, unsurmountable. (404)

The residential buildings, the 'small park,' the *encircling* 'well-kept lawns' (405): these subsequent details reconfirm the image of the farm as a *hortus inclusus*, a walled garden – created, in this case, by the wealth and industry of a now-absent father. Grove then goes on to portray the character named Mackenzie himself:

This pleasant-faced boy was the owner of all these square miles! And he lived with his mother! That seemed to imply that he was unmarried. The fact that his mother kept house for him made the whole thing somehow seem still more preposterous; it made the young man seem still younger; it made it a certainty that this farm was not earned. I felt as if some uncomfortable facts, some disquieting realities were obtruded upon me. (405)

Here the unstated message reveals itself to be as significant as the surface declarations. For it seems that Mackenzie's *youth* and Mackenzie's *mother* disturb the narrator as much as ownership (or patriarchy) does. Though not directly argued, a notion of 'manhood' is at issue. In the now-conventional tropes of nature, an *earned* 'manhood' is repeatedly

---

* In 1936, Grove responded to William Arthur Deacon's request for information for *A Literary Map of Canada* by sending him two sketch maps, one of which draws Phil Branden's travels in *A Search for America*, giving the novel the authority of 'truth' by using the medium of the map, which asserts authority over territory. See Thomas and Lennox.

equated with the unbounded, uncontrolled, and de-femaled wilderness. The 'boy' is deemed not to be a 'man' because (unlike the narrator, inferentially, though again the protest leads the reader to equate the narrator *with* boy-manhood rather than to accept the implied differentiation from it) he has neither left home nor embraced 'wilderness.' Reversing this paradigm emphasizes the presumption that informs it: if this person has neither left the domestic home nor embraced wilderness, then he cannot be a man and must therefore be 'womanish'; and 'woman' is seemingly defined as a person without social consequence.

However psychologically symbolic these tropes of manhood and wilderness might be, they obviously do not exactly describe everyone's daily experience.* But they provide some insight into the attractions of social power. Because they derive from and perpetuate the prevailing conventions of authority, they not only contrive a literary design but also encode an influential social paradigm, one that was to affect people's conventional judgments of the authority of measurement and the authority of gender. Even in the hypothetically socialist designs of Grove himself, for example, the literary images established wilderness as an adjunct to property – that is, *property* remained the norm by which to identify, appreciate, and judge *wilderness*. While Grove, by means of this imagery, thus claimed for himself the manhood of wilderness, he at the same time – ironically? or cautiously? – kept property under man's authority (see plate 2.4).

The force of convention and the disparity between declaration and practice become even more apparent when *A Search for America* is placed beside *Over Prairie Trails* (1922). In the autobiographical earlier book, Grove shows himself to be altogether willing to accept the benefits of measurement: he leads his horse along established trails, knows his way by fence lines and surveyors' markers, accepts *correction lines* in the roads he travels (thus acknowledging the prairie surveyors' compromise between the vast size of farms and the curvature of the earth's surface). Not, however, openly acknowledging the effects of his own self-centredness, Grove then criticizes *others* for their obvious aspirations, as when he writes:

* The American poet Robert Bly, in his influential and commercially successful *Iron John*, which became a kind of bible for the consciousness-raising, resensitizing 'men's movements' of the late twentieth century, reiterates this connection between manhood and wilderness, and argues that psychological relations with garden and wilderness do indeed characterize men's daily lives.

The road was a trail again for a mile or two. It led once more through the underbrush – wilderness interspersed with poplar *bluffs*. *Then it became by degrees a real* 'high-class' Southern Prairie grade. I wondered, but not for long. Tall cottonwood *bluffs*, unmistakably planted trees, betrayed more farms. There were three of them, and ... here on the very *fringe of civilization* I found that 'moneyed' type – a house, so new and up-to-date, that it verily seemed to turn up its nose to the traveller. I am sure it had a bathroom without a bathtub and various similar modern inconveniences. The barn was of the Agricultural-College type – it may be good, scientific, and all that, but it seems to crush everything else around out of existence; and *it surely is not picturesque* ...

It is unfortunate that our farmers, when they plant at all, will nearly always plant in straight lines. *The straight line is a flaw where we try to blend the work of our hands with Nature.* They also as a rule *neglect shrubs that would help to furnish a foreground* for their trees; and, worst of all, they are given to importing, instead of *utilizing our native forest growth.* Not often have I seen, for instance, our high-bush cranberry planted, although it certainly is one of *the most beautiful* shrubs to grow in *copses.* (22–3; my italics)

As the italicized phrases here cumulatively indicate, Grove produces an aesthetics of degree out of local nature as though by doing so he were himself leaving the wilderness ungardened. Clearly, in his prose, he does 'garden' – not just by representing landscape as a painting but also by accepting the aesthetic priorities of a particular painting school: one that champions the necessity of foreground, the picturesque validity of the curved line, and the convention of perspective. Moreover, he uses the local word *bluff* (for a *grove* of trees) only to criticize the particular trees as imports, and then he praises the local cranberry bush only to connect it with the 'imported' word *copse*, possibly making some circuitous auto-biographical claim for his own superiority.* In rebelling against (and

---

* The etymology of the word *copse* (or *coppice*), interestingly, suggests that the term refers to a stand of *cuttable wood*; hence Grove is perhaps unconsciously reasserting here the precedence of use over conservation, or property over 'nature.' Grove's masks – as the immigrant writer who claimed an aristocratic Swedish ancestry but who turns out to have been Felix Paul Greve, a writer with a working-class German background, who was once jailed for fraud – were revealed by Douglas Spettigue in *FPG* and elsewhere; in the current context, with reference to landscape terminology, disguise, and Grove's 1925 novel *Settlers of the Marsh*, see also Stich. Given Grove's comments here about the 'flaw' of straight lines in picturesque designs of nature, moreover, it might be possible also to read Thomas King's 'The One About Coyote Going West' as a parody of *Over Prairie Trails*.

criticizing) the uniformity of 'moneyed' (and in his declared terms *therefore* 'tasteless') local practice, he nevertheless covertly appeals to a different received authority to reinforce his own positon. In his life – ironically, though not unexpectedly, given what he writes in *A Search for America* – Grove also claimed an estate for himself when he subsequently moved from rural Manitoba to Simcoe in Ontario and tried to live out his life as a landed gentleman. In this context, the phrase that comments on the 'earned right' to land no longer reads like a fixed moral principle; Grove seems, rather, to use the phrase relatively, to condemn others' behaviour while justifying his own.

Intrinsically, Grove's version of land represents the image and exercise of power, subjects that relate to the gendering of space. These subjects also feature clearly in the poetry of E.J. Pratt. While money underlies Grove's depiction of a primarily rural world (through its account of the systems of production and the system of ownership), for urban Pratt (Newfoundland-born but a Torontonian by election), the landscape was a manifestation of *size* in North America. Size – or distance – was, moreover, a sign of power. For once it had stopped being perceived simply as hardship or grand vista, size repeatedly connects in Canadian writing with the prospect of ownership and mastery. Pratt also turned size into a metaphor of challenge, and linked authority and hierarchy with notions of 'manhood.' As with Connor directly (and Grove at least by declaration), the land for Pratt represented a test of heroism, faith, will, individuality, and endurance – the very qualities that Canadian criticism prized from 1900 to the 1950s. Hence when Pratt coupled these attributes with the transcontinental tale of the building of the Canadian Pacific Railway, in 'Towards the Last Spike' (1952), the Anglo-Protestant national myth (of ethics and power) coalesced with the now-conventional wilderness image of Canada – and was granted *aesthetic* precedence. Subject and method alike served a particular cultural desire.

Pratt's poem tells of the forging of links between East and West in Canada and the conquering of distance; at the same time, it reveals how language has the power to fire the imagination into practical support for such developments. The railway and the metaphors of language both, however, in Pratt's terms, impose the control of the *status quo* political and commercial Establishment upon the character of the newly joined territories. The poem does not anticipate that change will derive *from* the margins, and consequently it re-enacts in many ways the kinds of *presumptive* discovery that were apparent in the explorers' journals. It casts British Columbia, the farthest margin, as a lady and a Pacific lass; it minimizes the role of the Asian coolies who made up many of the railway gangs; and it portrays the Canadian Shield, the rugged country north of Lake Superior, as a prehistoric reptile destined to be mastered by man. These structures of relationship all articulate a conventional hierarchy.

Two passages will illustrate. The first depicts Sir John A. Macdonald taming both the Western wilderness and his own sleepless turmoil by rehearsing names, using them to read the unfamiliar through convention and cliché:

> 'Twas chilly at the window. He returned
> To bed and savoured soporific terms:
> *Superior*, the *Red River, Selkirk, Prairie,*
> *Port Moody* and *Pacific.* Chewing them,
> He spat out *Rocky* grit before he swallowed.
> *Selkirk!* This had the sweetest taste. Ten years
> Before, the highland crofters had subscribed
> Their names in a memorial for the Rails.
> Sir John reviewed the story of the struggle....
> He could make use of that – just what he needed,
> A Western version of the Arctic daring,
> Romance and realism, double dose.   (*Complete Poems* 206)

The second passage establishes the Canadian Shield north of Lake Superior as an antediluvian, serpentine object and a jealous female:

> On the North Shore a reptile lay asleep –
> A hybrid that the myths might have conceived,
> But not delivered, as progenitor
> Of crawling, gliding things upon the earth.
> She lay snug in the folds of a huge boa
> Whose tail had covered Labrador and swished
> Atlantic tides, whose body coiled itself
> Around the Hudson Bay, then curled up north
> Through Manitoba and Saskatchewan
> To Great Slave Lake ...
> So motionless, she seemed stone dead – just seemed:
> She was too old for death, too old for life,
> For as if jealous of all living forms
> She had lain there before bivalves began
> To catacomb their shells on western mountains.

> Somewhere within this life-death zone she sprawled,
> Torpid upon a rock-and-mineral mattress.   (*Complete Poems* 227–8)

Sprawled on a mattress, hybrid and reptilian, a jealous female who is snug with a snake and who will sooner or later be ruled by man: the iconography here is that of Eve in a frontier bawdy-house. The tacit dismissal of women's power is clear.

While the lady of British Columbia may be wily, and to that degree more dynamic than the geologic temptress, she is never *in Pratt's portrait* a real threat to the Men (with a capital 'M') who build the railway and the nation. And while the image of the reptile landscape suggests the difficulty of expansion, it never really suggests opposition, nor does it even hint at an alternative culture in place. The romantically animated giantism of the landscape merely stimulates the nascent heroism of the extraordinary (because ordinary) Canadian Male: to dream, survey, measure, build, and so to rule. Culturally, the poem appealed to androcentric as well as anglocentric biases, and hence typified its time. The *form* of Pratt's poem simply confirmed this sociocultural message. Adopting the techniques of the romantic epic – the extended metaphor, the catalogue of heroes, the journey motif, the appeal to immemorial history – the poem coupled the distinctiveness of distanced wilderness with a literary model borrowed from a more long-standing civilization. In this combination, the culture had found its paradigm. And in this paradigm, the image of the measurable wilderness became a sign at once of social purpose and social progress, and of the received social order through which purpose would be declared and progress achieved.

Edward William Thomson's story 'The Privilege of the Limits,' published in *Old Man Savarin and Other Stories* (1895), suggests that an ironic redefinition of property values might be possible within this ordered environment. Thomson's narrator is female, and as with Pratt this perspective initially hints at the existence of a political alternative, but as with Pratt the irony here does not really question the status quo. The narrator tells of her grandfather, one Mr McTavish, who is jailed in another town on a trumped-up debt charge, but at the jail is given the 'privilege of the limits': that is, free movement over the sixteen acres around the jailhouse, the limits marked by white cedar corner-posts planted in the ground. When McTavish learns that his child is ill, he resolves to revisit his home. Being an honest man he cannot go past the limits; being a resourceful man too, however, he moves the limits – by pulling up one of the corner-posts and taking it with him, being meticulously careful to keep it always on the far side, with himself between it and the jail. Bending the rules of property, he maintains control over his own decisions, and manages to resist the imposition of others' control over him. In so far as cleverness wins out over arbitrary rules, the rebel would seem to be the hero here. The story is anecdotal; the 'oral' and dialectal method it uses is also itself resistant, in some measure, to conventional codes of value. Except that the story is not intrinsically revolutionary; it insists less upon a change of values than upon the separate implementation of them. Which means, of course, that the story appeals to the very codes of individual power which it appears at first to be undermining. More effective forms of resistance would have to take the politics of alternative perspectives more fundamentally into account, and irony – or 'realism' – work to undercut the pervasive assumptions of 'natural' language and law.

Troping Women and the Limits of Stasis

For although Pratt's version of British Columbia explicitly connects gender with politics, and Thomson's version of manliness embraces fatherly concern, neither narrative espouses social change: just as the lady of British Columbia was a distant colony on the continent's margin, there to be acquired by the new nation, so 'she' was also characterized *diminutively* as a 'Pacific lass,' there to be wooed and won by the right nation-state suitor. The expansion of the nation-state into distant territory, that is, is configured as a gendered romance, one in which person as well as territory constitutes property. But the literary forms that oppositional writers employed began actively to resist this paradigm and oppose the limits of social convention. Irony could be made political; the romance could become a force for social education; speech-making and letter-writing could be crafted as effective modes of literary and political exchange. Although, in the early twentieth century, women still could not readily fit into the property-*owner* mould in Canada[*] – despite Mazo de la Roche's *Jalna* – many women had long been articulately campaigning

---

[*]   The implications go further than economics. Historically, property ownership in Canada has often been a requisite for the right to vote. In 1887, the British Columbia MLA and 'coal magnate' Robert Dunsmuir celebrated this connection when he observed that 'property [was] the standard of intelligence' (quoted by Patricia Roy 42); the exclusion of women from the one category implied, conventionally, assumptions about the other. For parallels and differences involving American literary representations of and by women, especially with relation to the land, see Kolodny, and Fairbanks.

for social reform, and occupying influential positions in society. (A list would include, among others, Cora Hind, Emily Howard Stowe, Anna Leonowens, and Nellie McClung.) Sara Jeannette Duncan's insightful analyses for the Toronto *Globe* in the 1880s and 1890s have to be read against this whole context. Perhaps the ironies she used might to some readers of the *Globe* at the time have seemed mere entertainments, but others would surely have recognized the newspaper articles' literary force and their social intent. They do more than simply observe society; they also probe the language of convention and expose how social conventions (including language) linked women with property, and with marriage.

In the deliberately amused stance of 'The Veritable West,' for example, Duncan cuts through the expectations of Winnipeg society to reveal the presumptuousness that feeds them. As in Pratt's 'Towards the Last Spike,' the geographical margin is represented as both capacious and female; a kind of social allegory underlies the politics of gender relationships. But Duncan's essay is neither epic in form nor heroic in intent:

One's feeling about Winnipeg, just rolling over its splendid streets in a cab and before speaking to a soul in it, is a vague perception of breadth and calm and promise. The city seems lying in a dream, content for the moment with having shown her magnificent possibilities ... There is no compromise with the East, no imitations, no mixing of meretricious old things and crude new ones. Winnipeg is honestly and openly new, in people, in brick and mortar, in ways and manners. It is very tonic.

Another thing that one does not expect in Winnipeg, for some inexplicable reason, is the artistic modern wooden house. Why ... the reign of Queen Anne should be shut out of one's western conceptions does not readily appear, perhaps because the shanty of the pioneer is so intimately associated with prairie architecture ... Yet the 'Fort Rouge district' is full of such houses, each with its gables, its square windows, its modern dress of neutral paint, each set in a wilderness of oak and poplar, and each with its pleasant glimpse of the brown Assiniboine rolling past. Tennis lawns there are and boat houses on the rear grounds that slope down to the water's edge. Past them six canoes abreast, full of young men and maidens, singing as they float down the river in the clear moonlight of the prairies, often make an idyllic picture on a summer evening ...

As Government House is undergoing repairs and has been almost ever since Lieut.-Governor and Mrs. Schultz entered it, it is impossible to get a very definite idea of the character of the new *regime*. By opening the Legislature in citizen's dress His Honor has given one indication that it is to be marked by a disregard

for the forms and ceremonies of the past, a departure which is variously com-
mented upon ...

Society in Winnipeg is noticeably young, with the highspiritedness of youth and
something of its impatience of control ... There appears to be a great abundance
of young men in the place, young Englishmen, and English-Canadians. The
number to be met at a five o'clock tea, usually contemned of masculinity, is
surprising. Femininity is chiefly youthful, pretty and married. Something in the
air of the country makes everybody vivacious – whether the extraordinary attractiveness of the young married ladies is to be accounted for on general grounds
by the climate or not, is difficult to say ... (79–81)

But it is not difficult to interpret. Duncan is not so enamoured of the
new that she does not also see the degree to which it is being settled by
(*old*) young Easterners – and that this new West in turn aspires to Ontario status. All the signs of propriety and possession are there, imposed
upon the land, once again remodelling wilderness into property in a way
that 'society' is unable to resist. (That such aspirations to property persist
in Canada, even to a late-twentieth-century push to have property rights
guaranteed in the constitution, and that, in turn, these aspirations continue to be ironically undercut, is apparent from the editorial cartoons of
Len Norris, among others [see plate 2.5]; the ongoing gendering of
political discourse, moreover, is apparent in the journalistic metaphor
recurrently used in the 1990s to describe Quebec separatist sentiment:
that of a 'divorce.') In the 'new' Winnipeg of the 1890s, Duncan sees that
an artificial 'oak wilderness' surrounds the wooden *Queen Anne* houses;
that the lieutenant-governor who rebelliously wears 'citizen's clothes' is
none the less having his house *remodelled*; that the 'idyllic picture' on the
brown river reinscribes as many values as it questions. Only Duncan
herself stands apart, weighing the Establishment values by tone if not by
direct critique. What is 'veritable' about this 'West' is its pretence; the
irony undercuts the illusion of documentary and it exposes the illusion
of sophistication. Duncan, demonstrating the limits of 'form,' thus opens
up for discussion the values that such forms – of manners, of address –
embody.

This metaphor – of the *body* – is one to which commentaries on the
relation among women, the land, and the state repeatedly return, often
in order to demonstrate the kinds of slippage that make a pervasive 'land
language' so unreliable. The 'body' is at once a physical body, sexually
marked and either empowered or vulnerable, and a metaphoric construct, still marked by the gender/power association, which can apply to

architecture, the state, language, or any other structure – including land. Rosalyn Diprose and Robyn Ferrell argue in *Cartographies*, for example, that 'map making' – any system of representation and codification, in other words – is bound up with the production of what it represents. A line produces space and demarcates territory, and the territory so produced is contingent upon the nature of that line. To extend the analogy as metaphor, then, is to see that the design of the 'body politic' is contingent upon the criteria that grant political authority. To the degree that political authority is conceptualized in androcentric terms, the body politic will be a male body. But if this design at once encodes males as property-owners and the land as female, the sexualized female body is tacitly turned into the territorial prerogative of the hero/owner/explorer/ adventurer, a condition of existence that is both presumptuous and unacceptable.*

Hélène Cixous articulates the feminist theory that informs this body–land–language association, and as 'Sorties,' a section of *La Jeune Née* (1975)† reveals, she derives this theory from her own life. Female, Algerian-born, French-speaking, part-Jew, Cixous declares that she quickly

---

* 'Introduction' to *Cartographies*, viii–xi. Beatriz Colomina articulates a similar position in the 'Introduction' to her *Sexuality & Space*: 'the body has to be understood as a political construct, a product of ... systems of representation rather than the means by which we encounter them' (n.p.). See also Massey, 'Woman's Place,' which analyzes the relation between capitalist industrial development and the design of 'women's occupations' in nineteenth-century England; and Pollock, who examines the construction of Interior and Exterior in women's painting, rejecting the idea that the paradigms of representation simply document women's condition (sexuality and class) and instead emphasizing 'the practice of painting' as 'itself *a site for the inscription of sexual difference.*' Gillian Rose argues that the 'geography of the female subject' (354) is not a question of naming a 'specific kind of spatiality' but rather one of being vigilant about the consequences of different kinds of spatiality.' David Bell and Gill Valentine assemble a series of essays on the geography of (primarily gay and lesbian) sexuality – that is, on the spatialization of such subjects as 'gay neighbourhoods,' sites of resistance, and intimacy itself. Of relevance, too, are Teresa de Lauretis's comments (esp. 55–8, 118–19) on the rhetoric of 'mapping' gender difference, and conventional associations of boundary-crossing with (heroic) males and closed spaces with females, constructing the male as an active agent in culture and the female as simply a *topos*, a resistant matrix.

† Translated by Betsy Wing as *The Newly Born Woman*, 63–131. Verena Andermatt Conly suggests that the French title can also be read (emphasizing ambiguities of gender and the resistance of which language is capable) as *la Genet* and as *là-je-une-nais* ('there I am being born as one') (37). Cixous's theory is not, of course, uniformly received. The writings of Nicole Brossard reveal its influence. But Toril Moi, for one, critiques the water-troping of female writing (117–19) as another kind of convention.

learned that her experience and her language were in conflict with each other, the marginality of the one (her experience as a woman, as a colonial) being not just dismissed but even crafted by the authority attributed to the other. In the face of authority, represented here by the French language, the gendered body and the colonized space become one, and her childhood taught her, Cixous writes, to want to flee colonial space – a desire that led her to identify with the oppressed. Arguing that the language of Empire is an agent of oppression, she goes on to argue that 'phallogocentrism' (maleness, phallic rule, and the use of language as phallic rule: over body, over land) always serves a hierarchy, a system of patriarchy or imperial power – and yet that the alternative is not to place 'femaleness' in power but to resist the concept of 'mastery' altogether. She consequently construes an alternative language as an 'ocean' – an element that permits a merging with the Other rather than a violation ('mastery') of it. Simple binaries of sexuality and rhetoric institutionalize gender roles, in other words, a codification which this theory would resist.

While, that is, designing a 'woman's sphere' apart from that of men might be argued as a way of preserving women's liberty from intrusion, this social custom has proved in practice to enact other kinds of restriction or confinement, to be in effect an intrusion of a different kind, in that it simply reconfirmed the hierarchies of power. The problem lay not just in the specific demarcation of sphere, but more fundamentally in the power-based and gender-related terms that were used to conceptualize 'sphere' in the first place.* This sense of 'sphere' governed more than gendered opportunities; it also shaped, for example, the categories determined by ethnicity and wealth, especially in so far as these came to be associated with specific neighbourhoods or occupations, but it related gender to them.[8] Opportunities for social 'mobility' worked against these categories; and social legislation was one of the agencies of change. But what would be the conditions that would permit improvement, and how

* For a critique of the 'rigid gender-defined notions of separate spheres for male and female activity' that 'the ruling elite' imported into Upper Canada in the late eighteenth century, see Katherine McKenna's biography of Anne Murray Powell and her family. Anne Powell's three daughters, McKenna writes, reveal the 'limited range of options open to women of the upper classes in early Ontario': one is deemed a 'success' for marrying in her own class and becoming a mother; one commits herself to domestically serving the needs of other women; the third rejects these roles and becomes a social outcast (239).

might they come about? More often than not, the city was the social and symbolic site.[9]

An effective challenge to the norms of ownership in Canada – though not of territory – was thus to come when urban settings began to appear more customarily in Canadian fiction, in the 1920s and 1930s. But they did not directly bring about change so much as they redefined the terms of social interpretation. In the works set in the rugged wilderness, it was possible to hypothesize romantic heroism as the 'natural' consequence of environment and training – and the acquisition of status and property as the 'natural' consequence of 'noble' behaviour. In the urban works, the land became a metaphor of economic disparity; land ownership (and land *loss*) emphasized the deprivations which inevitably attended any unchecked system of acquisition and property measurement.[10] The short stories of Morley Callaghan provide numerous examples. More devastating, however, is the opening paragraph of Irene Baird's 1939 critique of the Depression, *Waste Heritage*:

The freight steamed clanging into the yards. The engine bell swung backwards and forwards, the heavy tolling kept up even after the long line of cars had clashed to a shuddering standstill. The sun glared down onto the burnished maze of storage tracks, and off in the distance the grain elevators and the awkward span of the old bridge stood out against a hard blue sky. Closer in, on the far side of the tracks, the pier roofs, splashed white with dried gull droppings, cut between the smokestacks and masts of the waterfront. From uptown came the screeching of a fire truck. It sounded hysterical, as though it had picked up the feel of what was going on around it. (3)

Here the only 'natural' things are the seagull droppings and the sky, and they are 'dried' and 'hard'; all else – even the railway 'street' – is mechanical. The landscape, no longer serving development, is now shaped by development; it has become an industrial by-product, a sign of ownership by system rather than by person, hence a sign of surrender to anonymity, because the source of power can no longer be identified and therefore individually claimed, or blamed (see plate 2.6).

One social position thus celebrates land as the site of order, and one critiques it as the symbol of stasis. One stresses the advantages of productivity, and one focuses on the disadvantages that derive from the means of production. One equates property with individuality and privacy, and one links it with invasive presumptuousness. Well into the twentieth century, these perspectives continue in opposition and, sometimes, they constitute a dialogue. Henry Kreisel's short story 'The Broken Globe' demonstrates how each of these discourses works, and reflects on how each becomes less communicative to the degree that it stops being an argued position and turns into an article of unshakeable belief.

'The Broken Globe' tells of a bright young man, now a 'success' as a geophysicist in the world at large, who despite his nostalgia for 'distance' and 'space,' which he misses in the crowded city, *will* not return to revisit his father or his father's farm in northern Alberta. A friend of the son's, knowing something of the generational estrangement, does visit the farm, however, partly out of courtesy, partly out of curiosity. What he finds is a stubborn Ukrainian immigrant farmer – one of Clifford Sifton's 'peasant types,' perhaps – who parentally enquires after his son, with some pride, but who has plainly given him up for lost: both physically and morally. The point of contention dates from the young man's adolescence. The boy had returned from school one day with news of the earth's spherical shape and active rotation; the father, who still 'lived in the universe of the medieval church,' not only resists the information but also forbids the expression of any scientific explanations, for he considers such explanations to be the devil's words. For the father '"The earth ... was the centre of the universe, and the centre was still. It didn't move. The sun rose in the East and it set in the West, and it moved perpetually around a still earth. God had made this earth especially for man, and man's function was to perpetuate himself and to worship God."' When the boy subsequently brings home a small globe to prove his teacher right and his father wrong, the father strikes him; the boy retaliates by *throwing the globe at his father*; the father *breaks the globe* (but keeps it); and the two resolve angrily to go their separate ways. The land intervenes. And then, in order to make his visit many years later, the friend must cross a prairie that seems endless, the paved highway disintegrating to gravel until at last a 'grain elevator hove *like a signpost* into view ... [T]here were neither bears nor hills here, but only prairie, and suddenly the beginnings of an embryonic street with a few buildings on either side like a small island in a vast sea, and then all was prairie again.' In this evolutionary sea of land, he, too, is quizzed as to his beliefs. On saying he believes the world is round, and moves, the father muses resignedly that Satan has taken over the world, and regrets that his son has left to 'tamper with God's *earth*' rather than stayed 'to look after the *land*.' But he remains consistent, declaiming with dignity his defence of his individual soul: 'His eyes surveyed the vast expanse of sky and land, stretching far into the distance ... "Look," he said, very slowly and very quietly. "She is flat, and *she stands still*"' (135–47).[11]

This story balances a reader's sympathy between the stubborn father and the equally stubborn son, each committed to a cause and to a process of interpretation that itself becomes a cause, each reading the land (and the earth) for its *signs*, each articulating a received truth about nature based on 'evidence': one metaphysical (though affirmed by the senses), the other lodged in the apparent laws of technical cartography and measurable physical motion. Precisely what 'evidence' is, and how it functions, constitutes the crux of the disagreement. This distinction, moreover, relates directly to the notion that *property* is *power.*

This chapter has been tracing several motifs that demonstrate this relationship: (1) the shift from idealistic to empirical philosophies, (2) the way that centres of empire construct dismissible margins, (3) the distinction between 'earth' (as something apart from blessing) and 'land' (as something invested with God's blessing and transferred in proprietorship to man), [12] (4) the equation between land and woman, (5) the power conventionally attributed to man to survey and demarcate, (6) the force of hierarchy that ostensibly gives ruling rights to man over woman, and (7) the 'stillness of centre,' or of a faith in centre, that (as with Roberts looking at the Tantramar marshes) uses measurement to confirm stasis and resists all forms of measure that invite or embody change.

But change was, of course, to come. Feminist criticism recurrently resists the map-making metaphor – the collocation of images that connects explorer with map-maker with claimer and namer: rejects, in short, the *maleness,* the implication of sexual conquest, claim, proprietorship, that is implicit in the explorer image of empire and *penetration* (of continent, of body). [13] In the novels of Aritha van Herk and Paulette Jiles, for example – *No Fixed Address* (1986) and *Sitting in the Club Car Drinking Rum and Karma-Kola* (1986), respectively – women take over the roles of explorer/traveller/adventurer and reconstruct them. An image of landscape-in-motion replaces the image of land-as-a-static-territory-to-be-named-into-compliance, and so confined. The alternative image challenges the validity of ownership itself, and the 'clearing' – the still centre at the heart of the woods – comes to seem a dubious image of order because it is a dubious claim to authority. The politics of rejecting the still centredness of Empire is disclosed in other ways as well: in, for example, the ways ethnicity and place have also reshaped attitudes to power in Canada. (It is not irrelevant that it is Henry Kreisel, of Austrian Jewish background, who writes, in Alberta, a story about competing versions of reality and truth.) But to point to these issues is to anticipate ways in which land also functions in anglophone Canadian literature to convey the attitudes of *region*. Clearly 'region' is not unrelated to 'locale' or to 'documentary setting,' and it certainly extends the meaning of 'marginalized property.' It also leads to a third set of verbal techniques for dealing with space, presence, and power.

3

Landed: Literature and Region

Centre and Margin

This chapter tries, broadly speaking, to differentiate between the metaphors *insider* and *outsider*, or between two kinds of relationship with centralized authority. 'Region' is a shorthand way of conceptualizing this distinction, for it raises questions about the political effects of centrality and marginalization; at the same time, it provides a way of discussing people's primary commitment to a local environment they call 'home,' a place where they 'belong.'* Sometimes this 'locale' functions to differentiate a range of specific political attitudes from those espoused or expressed by the nation-state as a whole, or at least from the attitudes associated with the state's most populous centres and 'power points' – Toronto and Montreal, say, in Canada (though a different approach would constitute Toronto and Montreal simply as alternative 'locales'). At other times, the 'regional locale' is more loosely conceptual in nature – a function of distance or time rather than of fixed political boundary.†

---

* Anne Buttimer argues that space is subjective, that the human experience of a sense of home and the 'horizons of reach' (the processes whereby other places are brought into a person's ken) shape spatial identity. See Massey ('Locality Studies') for an analysis of the trend towards locale-based theory in social geography; and Geertz, who argues that, however universalist a theory, judgments are always intrinsically relativist and local.

† That space is inherently temporal is the recurrent argument of Allan Pred, who speaks of 'time–space specific practices' ('Structuration and Place,' 'Contingent Process'). Quoting from these articles, Agnew adds: 'place is not just locale, as setting for activity and social interaction, but also location,' a *locus* for the 'reproduction and transformation of social relations' (262).

But in both instances, 'locale' is identified with a version of place (pictorially specific), with a distinguishing activity (a sport, an industry, a cuisine), and with an idiom or 'accent' of perspective. To phrase this premise differently, chapter 1 spoke of land as *there*; chapter 2 spoke of land as *mine*; chapter 3 considers land as *home*. This chapter proceeds initially with a series of references to different physical settings from across Canada; it considers how these depictions determine the character of 'home' in temporally marked ways; and it concludes by trying to see how setting – the desire to fix narrative *in place* – relates to the politics involved in the possession of the language *of* place.

Dictionary definitions of such terms as *land, place, region,* and *home* are clearly insufficient here. The *word* 'region' (defined as 'an indefinite portion of territory' or as 'a particular area or realm') is not the same thing as the *concept* 'region' (as identified by the people who live within a region, and who associate their place with a cause or culture or political leaning). The word 'home,' relatedly, obviously also means different things not only to different people, but also to different generations.[1] It can refer to *back there* (expressing a concern about origins), or it can refer to *right here* (a concern about present conditions). *Being in place,* moreover, is not the same thing as *belonging to place.* The first term suggests an awareness of existing in a physical environment, an awareness of one's external spatial surroundings and of finding them, in whatever measure is being used, 'appropriate'; the other suggests an attitudinal identification with a particular locale, a determination of self through a relationship with site, and potentially with land. *Locale,* further, is a term charged with political and aesthetic implications; it is variously the scene of action, the site of expression, a microcosm of whatever political 'whole' is relevant, and the limit of neighbourhood.

Such abstraction seems straightforward; it is complicated, however, by the question of authority. Those whose sense of land (and self, and the language of expressing this connection) reinforces and is reinforced by their dominant position within the culture at large will differ from those whose sense of land, self, and language (however acute and locally fulfilling) still divides them from the dominant forms of social power. The 'landed gentry' – I use the term metaphorically here, not to suggest that Canada *replicates* English class categories – do not see 'land' in the same way that 'landed immigrants' do. Put another way: those who identify with a body of attitudes might find some satisfaction in the place where the attitudes are dominant, and identify with the place, might even think that the place and the attitudes are one; while those who are consigned to the peripheries of power because of their attitudes – whether individually or as a group – might find themselves increasingly dissatisfied with place because they are dissatisfied with the social structures that apparently exclude them – and with the discourse that these structures have made to seem fixed. Women responding to men, Natives and immigrants responding to the dominant culture, persons on a perceived margin responding to those in the perceived centre: in all cases, the marginalizing can surface in the use of the word *region* and in its attendant images. Paradoxically, the attitude to land or place within regions is also a force that can voice local authority and claim the kinship that distinguishes mere place from a declared home. The term *region* can thus sometimes be used (by the place that believes itself to be the 'centre') as a way of declaring its current power and defining its periphery, and of consigning others – the excluded – to the margins. Yet it can sometimes also function (within the areas consigned to the edge of conventional power) as a synonym for 'leading edge'; it then becomes a watchword of unity and of alternative power, a sign of an active process of aesthetic and political resistance. If 'region' is redefined as a process, moreover, it argues against linguistic fixity and social inertia, for it takes its meaning only in and over time.

The title of this chapter, 'Landed,' refers first of all to the generations of settlers and writers who did not just observe the new land or measure it, but who identified with it, using the shapes of the land as metaphors of mood and thereby defining for themselves some settled system of custom and value. As the Trinidad-born writer V.S. Naipaul observes in his novel about emigration and resettlement, *The Enigma of Arrival* (1987), 'land is not land alone ... not something that simply is itself. Land partakes of what we breathe into it, is touched by our moods and memories' (301). This recognition happened in Canada as Canadian culture developed over several centuries of history – as is apparent, for example, in francophone Acadian and Quebec writing,* with its history of family

---

* As, for example, in the long-lived traditions of *terrien* romance in fiction and a *poésie de la terre*. While the 1920s and 1930s saw a substantial resistance to romantic conceptions of the relation between people and land in Quebec – a novel such as Ringuet's *Trente Arpents* (1938) clearly articulates ways in which the aspirations to measurement and possession were able to manipulate emotional attachments to and identifications with place – such romantic conceptions continued to persist. An image of the *pays d'en haut* (see Warwick, *The Long Journey*) was as politically useful as it was pervasive, for it intensified the sense of isolation that some Quebeckers felt. Functionally, it also hindered ready interchange with the rest of Canada and so (like the commitment to the family

inheritance and local habitation, and in writing in both official languages about the two separate conventions of 'the Arctic' and 'the North.' This chapter, however, focuses on modern *anglophone* realizations of region, and begins with two poems by F.R. Scott.

The first is 'Mackenzie River,' which opens:

This river belongs
  wholly to itself
    obeying its own laws

Its wide brown eye
  softens what it reflects
    from sky and shore

---

farm, the inhabited place with a multigeneration history) it remained even after the 1930s a cultural and rhetorical image with a certain iconic power – either to celebrate difference *or* to appeal to a sense of historical injustice, depending on the user.

As with political rhetoric elsewhere (it is the subject of Abraham Klein's poems in *The Rocking Chair*, 1948), the one argument (i.e., about political injustice or cultural difference) could be made emotionally more effective by using the rural terms of the romantic claim upon a distinctive land. Cf. Smart's comments on Ringuet, 62–102. It is politically instructive, too, to recognize the changes in rhetoric that have been used by separatist politicians in Quebec; the arguments that insisted in the 1970s and 1980s on a 'distinctive culture and language' gave way, by the 1990s, to an appeal to a distinctive 'territoriality.' (The reasons for this change are not explicit; they perhaps indicate that the narrow appeals to a '*québécité pure laine*' – referring to the families who could claim descent from the *ancien régime* settlers – were ineffective, in that they rhetorically excluded, and thus politically alienated, the citizens whose ancestors immigrated after 1759, as well as the growing number of twentieth-century 'allophone' or 'multicultural' communities in the province.) For related comments, on the use of landscape reference to solidify a political relation between landscape and identity in Australia, see Bourke.

Warwick extends his summary of Quebec writers' relation with the land in 'Continuity.' See also Kertzer, who reviews *The New Land*; Kattan, who uses the term 'espace' to refer to earth (*la terre*), country (*le pays*), the idea (*les notions*) of earth and country, and interior as well as external representations of these subjects; Stratford, who examines Quebec poetry; and Motut, who examines the francophone Prairie, and the world of the Métis, as the setting for an idea of 'masculinity.' Importantly, Motut quotes Frederick Philip Grove (*In Search of Myself* 55) to the effect that any writer who would render the 'peculiar quality' of a region such as the prairies should be a 'pictorial artist,' a 'poet' who can 're-create' the sense of the place, and a 'psychologist' who can comprehend the impact of a region on the people who live 'within its confines' (69). For a review of contemporary critical writing on Canadian regionalism, see Dionne.

The top water calm
   moves purposefully
      to a cold sea

The poem closes this way:

A river so Canadian
   it turns its back
      on America

The Arctic shore
   receives the vast flow
      a maze of ponds and dikes

In land so bleak and bare
   a single plume of smoke
      is a scroll of history.   (*Selected Poems* 32–3)

It is not hard to see the politics here as well as the description. The nationalism of the Arctic metaphor, the resistance to American intervention in Canadian affairs, the indeterminate certainties of the northern landscape: these are familiar political and literary paradigms.

These tropes also permeate a second poem, 'Old Song,' though less clearly. 'Old Song' – set in Algonquin Ontario – is the more familiar, more frequently anthologized Scott poem, perhaps because of its shorter length, perhaps because it seems less strident or at least less openly political, or perhaps because its political implications have been so widely accepted as the norm by twentieth-century readers that they no longer seem political at all. But the land – in this instance, the familiar, recognizable 'Algonquin Ontario' – is a political phenomenon, and observations of the land are inevitably also political. Hence Scott's use of a land image helps explain how the *Ontario* wilderness comes to be identified as 'home,' or as the dominant image of home, in a Canada marked by geographic diversity and a high concentration of urban dwellings. It also helps explain why the foreignness or fearsomeness of nature is built into the land/home trope. 'Old Song' reads, in its entirety:

far voices
and fretting leaves

this music the
hillside gives
but in the deep
Laurentian river
an elemental song
for ever
a quiet calling
of no mind
out of long aeons
when dust was blind
and ice hid sound

only a moving
with no note
granite lips
a stone throat   (*Selected Poems* 15)

While the politics of this poem might not at first be obvious, what *is*
apparent is the effect of the sound system and the pacing. The poem
deliberately evokes the quietness of the northern woods, the muted
echoes of stone and water. It achieves this effect, technically, by the way
it handles syllables. The liquid and labial consonants (*l, m*) – as in
'leaves ... music ... hillside ... Laurentian ... elemental' – connect with a
series of trochaic disyllables ('voices ... fretting ... music ... hillside ...
river ... ever ... calling') to suggest the river's movement. But the
precambrian stone through which the river moves asserts its own
strength, a counterforce of voicelessness, conveyed by the dental consonants (*d, t*) and the slow, stressed monosyllables ('ice hid sound,' 'no
note,' 'stone throat'). The aural effect is one of muffled sound, or
muffled message; and the full rhyme at the end ('note, throat'), after
the earlier half-rhymes ('leaves, gives,' 'river, ever,' 'blind, sound'),
invokes a kind of closure on expression.

To explain how this poetic structure is at the same time a political
declaration, it is necessary to approach it obliquely, pointing first to a
number of other apprehensions of landscape in modern Canadian writing. The landscapes that are portrayed elsewhere in the country will, in
due course, illustrate what it is that Scott has done. For the next few
pages, therefore, this chapter will appear to be a kind of aural anthology:
it asks to be listened to as well as read, for a series of varying *terms* of
recognition and identification.

Locale 1: Rural Southern Ontario

Manitoba-born Margaret Laurence describes, in *The Diviners* (1974), the landscape near Peterborough, Ontario, the country once lived *on* by Mrs Moodie and Mrs Traill:

> The river flowed both ways. The current moved from north to south, but the wind usually came from the south, rippling the bronze-green water in the opposite direction. This apparently impossible contradiction, made apparent and possible, still fascinated Morag, even after the years of river-watching.
>
> The dawn mist had lifted, and the morning air was filled with swallows, darting so low over the river that their wings sometimes brushed the water, then spiralling and pirouetting upward again. Morag watched, trying to avoid thought, but this ploy was not successful. (3)

Laurence's focus is first of all on language and memory as well as on landscape, but more, the focus on *landscape* is primarily on *movement*, therefore upon water and wind more than upon stone.* One question to ask: why is the water so important to Canadian writers – does it just reflect how much water there is in the physical environment? does it have something to do with idealism or naïvety – a thirst for new possibilities in an unspoiled land? does it derive somehow from the old voyageur experience, or the presumptive expectation of a 'Northwest Passage/Strait of Anian' water route to the Other Side? does it have more to do with the gender of the writers? does it convey more of a covert sense of loss than a myth of possibility? And in what way or ways is Laurence's description any different from Scott's *and also political?* Naïvety is not the issue,† as a

---

* 'Wood,' 'water,' and 'rock' are the three main subjects of Simon Schama's *Landscape and Memory*; Schama uses the river image to cite the power of mythological allusion in designs of the shape of history. The river that flows both ways links Laurence's narrative with Thomas King's 'The One About Coyote Going West,' where River (prior to the trickster's arrival, with 'picturesque' conventions in tow) does the same thing.

† Naïvety is, of course, a relative judgment. Pauline Greenhill's *True Poetry* investigates this issue, examining the values recorded in 'popular' verse. The book opens by quoting from Elsie Moore's 1984 stanzas in praise of Haliburton, Ontario: 'O' Haliburton / With your setting so rare / Not many villages / With you can compare / ... / The surrounding lakes / And beautiful hills / Are the finest scenery / And provide many thrills' (3–4). Greenhill finds that newspaper verses (such as these by Moore) characteristically celebrate community, community heroes, and local accomplishments, often co-opting the form of familiar songs in order to do so; characteristically also, these works

second example – Alice Munro's 'Thanks for the Ride' – suggests. Further, the two examples, side by side, also hint at distinctions between insiders and outsiders, between those who know and those who aspire to know – their sense of experience and understanding realized in an image of space.

Locale 2: Lake Huron Country

Ontario-born Alice Munro portrays, in 'Thanks for the Ride,' a western Ontario landscape not too far from the eastern Ontario site that Laurence depicts, but it is neither uninhabited nor uninformed. Munro's story concerns power, basically. In it, the naïve young male narrator is initially manipulated by his more experienced city cousin into an evening's entertainment (by which the cousin means booze, sex, and a car); they pick up a couple of girls, who are not only available but realize they are making themselves available. The narrator, with very little eloquence, loses his virginity. And this is the way Munro succinctly words the moment: 'After a while I whispered: "Isn't there some place we can go?" And she answered: "There's a barn in the next field." She knew the countryside; she had been there before' (56).*

The countryside is not unspoiled, not free from exploitation, not empty, not unused (the negative positive: *litotes* is the paradigmatic form); paradoxically, it is for these imperfect and human attributes that it starts to become evocative not just as place but as home. But what kind of home? Perhaps one that depends on (because it is shaped by) the 'landscape' – or 'countryside' – that has been already established as custom, by 'history' or previous experience; perhaps one in which the biases have been normalized, whatever damage they continue to perpetrate (this story probes the conflict, clearly, between ritualized conquests and gendered victims); perhaps one that is enclosed by proximity, power, and familiarity more than it is compelled by the need to pursue distance and alternatives.

---

are rhymed, bathetic, metrically uneven (often distorting syntax or shifting pronoun placement for the sake of rhymes). While these features generally seem unplanned, the writers of local verse occasionally use this metrical irregularity deliberately (and contribute to a sense of local pride by doing so) in order to parody or ridicule the speech or actions of a higher government, whether federal, provincial, or metropolitan.

* A later story, 'Five Points,' in *Friend of My Youth*, 1990, echoes this scene, when the character Brenda thinks she wants *commands*, not *requests*, from her lover Neil and wants to be his 'territory' (41).

These examples have, deliberately, been concerned with Ontario so far,[2] a point to be returned to shortly. But first: elsewhere.

Locale 3: Labrador

Other parts of the country produced other forms of descriptive rhetoric. Here is the Newfoundlander Harold Horwood, epitomizing the Subarctic[3] through an indirect mimicry of the palatal sounds of Inuktituk, in 'Men Like Summer Snow':

The sun glitter came pounding across the icefield. Akta squinted into it, searching the floe edge. The first rain of spring had been followed by hard frost, and the snow-covered pans were covered in turn with a hard glaze. He and his friend Innuk were surefooted in their sealskin kamiks. They could feel every undulation of the slippery surface through the thick but supple soles of ugruk – leather from the bearded seal – and they walked like dancing foxes, as they had been doing as long as they could remember.

'This might be a good morning to go look for seals, if anyone wished to do so,' Innuk had suggested to his friend.

'On such a day as this,' Akta had agreed, 'many seals will by swimming northward, far beyond the ice, and there will be seals in the leads, I expect, and many a lazy one dozing in the sun perhaps.'

They spoke to each other in English, as they did with all the young people of the village, though they had spoken since infancy the Language of Men, and used it still when talking with their elders. Their English was fluent and easy though salted with turns of phrase from the older tongue, and they wore it like a badge – there were not many ways in which a man of sixteen summers could excel: use of the new language was one of them. The girls expected it, too, as they had begun to expect fast outboard boats and rides on snowmobiles. (230–1)[*]

---

*   Discussing Rudy Wiebe's version of Arctic landscapes, in *Playing Dead* (1989), and Aritha van Herk's, in *Places Far from Ellesmere: A Geografictione. Explorations on Site* (1990), Martin Leer argues against what he calls the psychological reductiveness of Atwood's *Survival* in favour of an 'enabling' reconceptualization of psychology as 'geography' – such as is apparent, for example, in Wiebe's 'comprehension of the essential two-dimensionality of space in Inuktituk ... , where the grammar distinguishes between visible phenomena that appear to be of equal dimensions (the *areal* dimension) and phenomena that appear to be longer than they are wide (the *linear* dimension). The first are also conceived of as motionless, the second as moving, so when a man on the ice starts moving he changes from one grammatical category to another. Moreover, an expanse of ice or land is always considered as belonging to the latter category. Arctic space is never inert, impenetrable, but always moving, penetrable. If you move with it, you will

Again, the image of landscape dissolves into a discourse on the character of speech and change; the landscape is sibilant. Yet the narrative focuses on the imperfect present more than on a possibly idealized perfect past, and it does so by emphasizing how the vocabulary and cadences are altered by translation, how the absolute certainties of nature translate (laconically) into 'if' and 'perhaps' and modern expectations.

Locale 4: Annapolis Valley

Ernest Buckler, whether evoking a Nova Scotia farmland in *The Mountain and the Valley* (1952), or his own past in *Ox Bells and Fireflies* (1968), conjures up the local landscape in a prose ripe with adjectival and adverbial modification, dependent on contrived compounded words. Through this technique, familiar, observed things acquire the presumed sophistication of a latinate gloss:

Once: You were cutting hoop poles alone in the pasture, your consciousness spreading a little as always to fill the quiet. All around you was the living greenery in its infinite shapes. The saw-toothed edges of the sweet fern. The dancing-white stars of the blackberry blossoms. The pink pleating of the toadstool's lining. The purple loops of the sheepkill. The miniature chalices of the ground moss. The green-needled hackmatack with the bright-red cones that were like solid flowers cross-petaled as intricately as a rose. The daisy with its tens of white tongues encircling the thousand grains of gold mounded at its center. Each speckling, or roundness, or pointedness, or wallpaper scrolling, or shading of color into color was as perfectly in pattern as if a draftsman's lifetime had gone into the making of it. There was not a pinpoint of earth where this infinite variety did not spring up side by side, yet not the smallest member of it without a purity of diagram to dumfound gods or worlds.

But this wasteful squandering of perfection on things so slight did not mock or stagger you then. You sat down for a few wide moments in the shade of the

---

arrive' (82). Relatedly, Rob Shields argues that *space*, as distinct from *plane*, carries ideological import: 'The Canadian North ... forms the mythic "heartland" of Canada but remains a zone of Otherness in the spatial system of Canadian culture. The North is the complete antithesis of the urban civilization of the Southern metropolises. Thus it is, that places on the margins expose the central role of "spatialization" to cultures and nation-states' (4). Karen Mulhallen's analysis of R. Murray Schafer's music, especially *North/White*, adds another dimension to the study of aesthetic region in Canada.

great landmark maple where the cows sometimes stood so still the clapper of
their bells never touched against the sides. (106–7)[4]

Landscape here is an image as well as a place, an attitude as well as a
setting.* Hence the techniques for 'speaking place' (not, that is, for
simply 'describing' it) establish the perspectives of a region, a gender, a
generation-in-place, at home or not at home with the values of a time or
the values of the authorities in charge. Buckler's catalogues recall the
confidences of a male youth, confidences about sexual power as well as
about the possessibility of knowledge – *then*. But adolescent exaggerations
subsist essentially in expectation. The cast of the memoir, by contrast, like
that of the novel *The Mountain and the Valley*, is retrospective, constructed
after the boy-become-man has realized the effects of time and change.
The landscape, here, evokes *time-past* again, home (or 'home pasture')
defined in terms of its flaws and fractured promises as well as in those of
memory's rose-coloured resonances.

Locale 5: Prairie

In the Canadian prairies, an area glimpsed as space and place by numerous literary works (Sharon Butala's autobiographical meditation *The
Perfection of the Morning: An Apprenticeship in Nature*, 1994, provides a recent
example, especially for its chapter called 'The Subtlety of Land'), *distance*
is one of the chief attributes of description. Once more distance is an
image affiliated with time as much as with space, and with pressure as
much as with comfort. The opening of W.O. Mitchell's 1947 novel *Who
Has Seen the Wind* (and it is worth emphasizing that a landscape/water-
scape setting contributes the opening trope of a high proportion of

*   Raymond Williams distinguishes, in *The Country and the City*, between pastoral and
    anti-pastoral, and between landscape and working country, in terms of wealth, class,
    and production. The leisure to design landscape or pastoral was seldom granted to
    those persons charged with actually working the land; hence the very idea of 'land-
    scape' (as distinct from 'land') can be seen as one form of class marker, with ramifi-
    cations *vis-à-vis* the class bases of aesthetics and theology (what is beautiful? what is
    good?). For further analyses of the theological basis for many attitudes to nature,
    including the privileging of species, pastoralism, cultivation, conservation, and some
    forms of English regionalism, see Keith Thomas. On the 'region' or 'district' poem in
    England, see Aubin. See also W.J. Keith's two books on rural perspectives in (respec-
    tively) English poetry and English fiction, *The Poetry of Nature* and *Regions of the Imagi-
    nation*; and the works of Yi-Fu Tuan and John Barrell.

Canadian narratives)[5] spells out this connection, one that will have an impact upon the intellectual, emotional, and technological tensions in the subsequent story:

Here was the least common denominator of nature, the skeleton requirements simply, of land and sky – Saskatchewan prairie. It lay wide around the town, stretching tan to the far line of the sky, shimmering under the June sun and waiting for the unfailing visitation of wind, gentle at first, barely stroking the long grasses and giving them life; later, a long hot gusting that would lift the black topsoil and pile it in barrow pits along the roads, or in deep banks against the fences.

Over the prairie, cattle stood listless beside the dried-up slough beds which held no water for them. Where the snow-white of alkali edged the course of the river, a thin trickle of water made its way toward the town low upon the horizon. Silver willow, heavy with dust, grew along the riverbanks, perfuming the air with its honey smell. (3)

Beside this landscape – or perhaps against it – people have built frame houses, constructed sidewalks, sown lawns, given the place names. Mitchell's focus, however, apparent in these paragraphs, falls initially on the grassy prairie itself, the sense of *surround*. But surrounding what? Surrounding 'the town' – the human habitation (the fences, the roads), which is almost overlooked because the 'prairie' so forcefully impresses itself on the imagination. Mitchell's setting thus sets up a *contrast* – between the reality (both literal and metaphoric) of the conventional constructed *houses*[6] in which the townspeople live and the competing reality of the 'natural' environment that influences how they see, how they construct an image of *self* and *home*. Mitchell might be underscoring a simple disparity here – between the empirical experience of modern Canada (most people live in towns and cities, and their true 'regions' are urban) and the rural, wilderness image which these same people continue to use to distinguish their lifestyles. It is not irrelevant that it is the writers focusing on *minority* status – writers concerned with particular examples of class and gender discrimination, and of ethnic immigration, adaptation, or resistance to adaptation – who have recurrently used urban settings.[*] But Mitchell's point is also partly ecological: he is saying that

---

[*] Sherrill Grace ('Quest') argues that urban environments are characteristic settings for female literary protest.

people affect the wilderness as much as it affects them.* Introduce people into the equation based on the 'common denominators of nature ... land and sky,' and you no longer have a neutral natural seasonal cycle; the sequence that lists wind, grass, topsoil, alkali, the 'thin trickle of water,' and dust on the silver willows implies drought, failed crops, failed cropping techniques, and a poverty of spirit. These people will ignore ecological interdependence only if they are stupid, if they pretend that their knowledge of nature is already complete, and if they believe that technology (because it has wind and land under measurement) therefore has the forces of nature under control. In the world Mitchell chooses to depict, people are, finally, not stupid. And nature is not intrinsically averse to help.

Locale 6: West Coast

The mountainous British Columbia landscapes of Earle Birney's narrative poem 'David' furnish still more examples of place perceived as strange but familiar. The coastal rainforest sketches of Emily Carr's *Klee Wyck* (1941), or her seemingly mobile expressionist paintings (see plate 3.4), or the verbal landscapes of Ethel Wilson also emphasize the human connection with place. With Jack Hodgins's 1977 novel *The Invention of the*

---

* Of relevance here is C.J. Taylor's 'Legislating Nature: The National Parks Act of 1930,' which traces the changes in public and governmental attitude that led to this particular act. (It replaced legislation passed in 1911 that used the idea of 'parkland' to preserve some areas as exploitable forest reserves.) Both acts nevertheless permitted natural-resource exploration in national parks. Although public rhetoric often equates national parks with conservationist causes – and while a substantial body of general commentary (including that by Jonathan Bate and Judith Wright) also links perceptions of the land with conservation – it is therefore important to recall that expediency has also governed much actual park designation and construction. Bill Waiser documents the fact that the Canadian government used relief workers and alien prisoners-of-war (during the First World War) as labourers to construct and develop the Rocky Mountain park system, for instance. The idea of making the 'wilderness' *accessible* through the designation of parkland is, of course, also implicitly paradoxical. Cf. Tom Wayman's 1973 poem 'The Ecology of Place,' which reads in part: 'The place begins with water. / Lake, inlet or river / eddies into a clearing, turns / to planks and houses, businesses. / The forests go elsewhere. / ... / Distant law begins to stop / the geography. A mountain is cut / by a noun. / ... / There is a startup of railroad, and thruway. / The air fills; the harbour is / crushed rock ... / ... / Then the City alone / without the forest / ... / wants to create again / wilderness, but the trails are marked / *for power toboggans* ... / ... / Fish offshore / begin to cough' (709–10).

World, this cross-Canada sampling of landscape images reaches its western extent. Hodgins's work isolates the apparent exaggerations that separate Vancouver Island from the several Mainland cultures – and yet here, too, landscape not only evokes place but also attempts to grasp in words the extraordinary features of a culture in time. Hodgins's character Strabo Becker, for example – named for the classical Greek map-maker – hopes to know all, by gathering data, as though the catalogue* were itself sufficient to understand the character of a cumulative culture; and his text (as the text of this chapter has just been doing) proceeds in catalogues to emphasize both the effect and the limitations of this process of understanding:

Strabo Becker, ... this bushy raccoon of a man, with his long narrow red-rimmed eyes calmly filming the world, and his large bent-forward ears recording all that the world might say, this man has pretensions. He has chosen to nest on a certain piece of this world and to make a few years of its history his own...

Sometimes this god-man almost believes that he owns this island, that he has perhaps invented it. He expects that he should be able to conjure it up for you out of the thick air above his kitchen table: twelve thousand square miles of rugged stone mountains and timber stands and logged-off slopes and deep green valleys, sprinkled with fishing villages around rotting wharves, with logging camps of tarpaper huts on skids, with towns and resorts and hobby farms, with snag-spiked lakes and long crooked green rivers. In words, if you let him, he will decorate the tree-furry coastline with used-car lots, rotting hay barns, smoke-blooming pulp mills, weedy estuaries, log-booming grounds, and brand new subdivisions, with old beached freighters painted up for restaurants and rusted wartime destroyers sunk for breakwaters, with mountains of gleaming white shells growing right up out of bays and topped with tiny shacks selling oysters ... And he will act as if he himself had set all this down in the ocean, amidst foamy rocks and other smaller islands where sea lions sunbathe and cormorants nest and stunted trees are bent horizontal from the steady force of the Pacific wind. (8–9)[7]

---

* The *catalogue* is formally related, that is, not just to *epic* structure, but also to the *encyclopedias* and the Linnaean *taxonomies* of the eighteenth century. As Barbara Stafford (esp. chs 1 and 6) points out, such catalogues came to be associated with an empiricist model of the mind, with an assumption that the senses could record 'reality' directly and accurately, and that sensory data (particularly if recorded 'on the spot' and/or if recorded through the 'international Latin' – that is, the non-*national* language – of 'scientific' classification) was intrinsically 'objective.'

Like Buckler's character, or Munro's, or Birney's narrator in 'David,' Becker acts *as though* he had power – in place, time, and language – while the narrative (through its conditional semantic restrictions: *sometimes, almost, perhaps, should be able, if you let him, as if*) indirectly shapes a counter-message, about those who are self-deluded about their relation with the landscape, about those who remain disenfranchised, and about the margins of understanding.

Region, Nation, Heartland

What inferences can be drawn from such a selective sampling? As plate 3.1 makes visually clear, the first point to emphasize is that the concrete *terms* of landscape description differ from area to area in the country.* A second point is that, in all cases, the appeal to the character of home comes equipped with a narrative subtext, a set of markers that delineates the degree to which appearances lie. The narratives imply more than they tell, requiring the reader to assemble (rather than receive) one of the ranges of literary communication that is taking place in the text. Landscape is a place, but it is also a body of attitudes in time,[8] couched in the manner of speech and asking to be read in its own terms.

In Sinclair Ross's 1941 novel *As For Me and My House*, one central subplot makes the point about marginalization directly. The narrator, Mrs Bentley, watches her husband, Philip (a minister without faith), give counsel to one of his prairie congregation during the 1930s Depression, and at the same time she listens (as does the reader) to the ironic, self-defensive, contrapuntal conversation of Paul Kirby, the local schoolteacher:

Philip preached well this morning ... They were a sober, work-roughened congregation. There was strength in their voices when they sang, like the strength and darkness of the soil ... Five years in succession now they've been blown out, dried out, hailed out; and it was as if in the face of so blind and uncaring a universe they were trying to assert themselves, to insist upon their own meaning and importance.

---

*   I am speaking here of geographic terms; it is possible that a more detailed sampling would demonstrate regional ties with particular generic choices: allegory in the Maritimes, for example, fable in Quebec, romantic mystery in Ontario, anecdote (as Robert Kroetsch's writing suggests) in the prairies, tall tale in British Columbia and Newfoundland.

'Which is the source of all religion,' Paul discussed it with me afterwards. 'Man can't bear to admit his insignificance. If you've ever seen a hailstorm, or watched a crop dry up – his helplessness, the way he's ignored – well, it was just such helplessness in the beginning that set him discovering gods – on his side ... That was what you heard this morning – pagans singing Christian hymns ... *pagan*, you know, originally that's exactly what it meant, *country dweller*.' (26–7)[9]

The sequence in the subtext shows how the image shapes the reader's response. Through comments on the local landscape, that is, the text once again reveals its more fundamental concern with language, and through language the reader is asked to appreciate the way people attach multiple resonances of meaning to place when they claim 'place' for an identity. Ross is specific that the identification with land is a claim upon significance.* He also makes clear that the claim to be noticed, the desire for some measure of influence, is a direct function of a felt *lack* of power.

At this point it is possible to return to F.R. Scott's poems about Canada's empirical/political distinctiveness and about the character of the Laurentian 'uplands,' so instructively known in Canada as the '*Canadian Shield*.' First of all, the shield image, visually descriptive, is also romantic and defensive. Second, the 'Laurentian' river evokes a 'northern' wilderness primarily from a southern – and specifically Southern Ontario and Quebec – perspective. Its quiet wilderness separateness is, in other words, a metropolitan, urban construction.

Like his colleague A.J.M. Smith, who wrote of 'The Lonely Land' that it had a 'beauty / of strength / broken by strength' that was 'still strong' (31),† Scott was influenced by the Group of Seven painters in the

---

* Cf. the comment in Mordecai Richler's tonally more sardonic novel, *The Apprenticeship of Duddy Kravitz*: 'A man without land is nobody' (48). Duddy Kravitz's grandfather, for whom this statement is almost a mantra, uses it to epitomize his aspiration to independence; when the acquisitive Duddy misinterprets the advice as a blanket recommendation to own property at any expense, the novel takes one its many satiric swats at modern Canadian urban 'culture.'

† The association between strength, the Shield, and the waterway/river image also reinvokes the masculine image of the explorer/voyageur. John Warkentin's edition of excerpts from the journals of the explorers and surveyors who 'mapped' the West, *The Western Interior of Canada*, provides ample evidence for the prevalence of this group of connected images; the verification of knowledge and of an idea of what it was necessary to know came together in the scientific mapping of waterways and geology, actions which were configured as heroic or manly enterprises and which practically served the political and commercial interests of 'centres' elsewhere.

3.1 (*pp. 132–4*) 'Regional' landscapes became the subject both of academically approved painters (such as Carl Schaefer) and 'folk' painters (such as Joseph Norris); these four examples illustrate some of the conventions brought to the depiction of different 'regions' of Canada: (*above*) the settled coast of village Nova Scotia, busy with separately observed and separately delineated community activities (Joseph Norris, *A Fine Day at Long Point*, oil on plywood, 1988, 24 × 48 in.; reproduced courtesy of Houston North Gallery, Lunenburg, NS); (*right*) rural Ontario, at one time perceived as pastoral, but represented symbolically here as hinged on the edge of change (Carl Schaefer, *Fields with Stubble*, watercolour over graphite on wove paper, 1937, 39.0 × 57.5 cm; reproduced courtesy of Mark Schaefer, Collection of the National Gallery of Canada, #5793). (*continued on p. 134*)

3.1 (cont.) (*above*) The rural prairies, where the sense of distance is demarcated by means of a vanishing-point perspective (Robert Hurley, *Untitled (red sunset)*, watercolour on paper, *c.*1947, 16.2 × 24.5 cm.; courtesy of the Mendel Gallery, Saskatoon, MAG 81.32.6; reprinted with the permission of Douglas & McIntyre); and (*right*) the marginal West Coast, where foreshore dwellings are depicted on temporary wooden pilings and against a mountainous backdrop (Walter J. Phillips, *Jim King's Wharf,* colour woodcut, 1927, 27.6 × 20.5 cm, Collection of Robert and Mary Adamson). Two earlier (and perhaps less romantic) versions of Phillips's woodcut (a pencil drawing from 1926 and a watercolour from 1927) depict a fishboat in the place where the later version substitutes a Native canoe; the pencil drawing also portrays the figure on the left in Western clothes rather than wearing a Native blanket.

3.2 Two examples of Group of Seven technique – (*above*) F.H. Varley's *Stormy Weather, Georgian Bay* (oil on canvas, 1920, 132.6 × 162.8 cm; reproduced courtesy of the National Gallery of Canada, Ottawa, #1814), and (*right*) J.E.H. MacDonald's *The Solemn Land* (oil on canvas, 1921, 122.5 × 153.5 cm; reproduced courtesy of the National Gallery of Canada, Ottawa, #1785) – emphasize the character of brushstroke and the representation of sea and sky. The prominence of a single tree in Varley's work, and of a particular rockface in MacDonald's, suggests the continuation, among some of the Group's members, of the conceptual ways of representing landscape that Barbara Stafford discusses in *Voyage into Substance*.

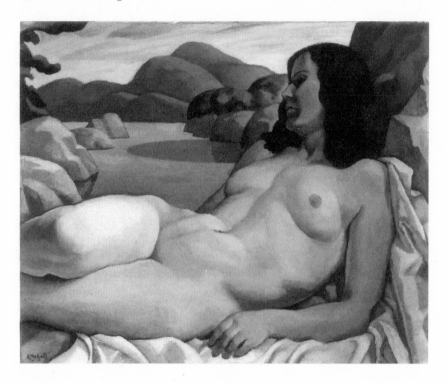

3.3 One of the political differences between (*right*) Kathleen Munn's *Composition* (oil on canvas, *c.*1926–8, 45.5 × 53.3 cm, from the collection of Ken & Lynn Martens) and (*above*) Edwin Holgate's *Nude in a Landscape* (oil on canvas, *c.*1930, 73.1 × 2.3 cm; reproduced courtesy of David Rittenhouse, Collection of the National Gallery of Canada, Ottawa, #3702) is suggested by the titles; Holgate (a member of the Group of Seven) portrays woman *in* (or perhaps *against*) a landscape, whereas Munn represents woman *as* the landscape. Holgate's painting designs parallels between the female form and the forms of the landscape. Munn's painting can be read both for its identification of woman with the rhythms of nature and (perhaps implicitly) for its 'composed' protest against male conventions regarding the 'femaleness' of 'virgin land' as 'conquerable territory.'

3.4 (*right*) Emily Carr's *Reforestation* (oil on canvas, 1936, 110.0 × 67.2 cm, the McMichael Canadian Art Collection, #3702) represents landscape as movement; (*above*) Christiane Pflug's *Kitchen Door with Ursula* (oil on canvas, 1966, 164.8 × 193.2 cm, Winnipeg Art Gallery, #G-66-89) represents a young girl only in a reflection, from the vantage point of a kitchen interior. Feminist readings of these works foreground the way the artistic techniques conceptualize gender as a *social condition.*

1920s – whose vision of the Laurentian wilderness came widely to be accepted as the distinctive visual paradigm of modern Canada (see plate 3.2). In retrospect it is possible to see how much more closely this view of Canada was to the wilderness sensibilities of Sir Charles G.D. Roberts than was thought at the time, how closely tied it was to the new CPR posters of travel and tourism, how dependent on Scandinavian models of northness, and how Ontario-based.* This is the view of Canada that underlies Northrop Frye's 'garrison mentality' paradigm of Canadian literature. In other words, Scott's 'elemental' Laurentian river, while evoking a *regional* Ontario/Quebec landscape, was articulated as though it were the semiotic equivalent of *nationhood*.[10] 'Old Song' is both under-pinned and on closer analysis undermined by a politics of extrapolation (from local scene to national character). By reinscribing the wilderness as it does, with reference to its temporal distance from (urban, and perhaps urbane) civilization, it also reinscribes the value system of the society that would claim the power to rule. This political perspective would also claim, by extension, its own centrality, and in so doing it would assume its authority over the 'regions' that it has designed as its own periphery. Along with this claim goes the presumed authority to 'read' the regions (the margins, the 'other,' the excluded-from-power) without reference to their own (alternative) points of view. The effective silencing of landscape (the 'other' with its 'stone throat') reasserts the rule of hierarchical power; it is a way of constructing nationalism in the name of nationality.

This view – of a wilderness 'heartland'[11] painted in Canadian Shield colours – underlies the standard anglophone literary, geographical, and historical designs of Canada that appeared during the 1940s and 1950s: the railway sensibility of Pratt, the 'Laurentian thesis' of the conservative historian Donald Creighton, the essays of the newspaper journalist Bruce Hutchison (especially those published as *The Unknown Country*), the national allegories of Hugh MacLennan, and a 1948 poem by Douglas LePan called 'A Country Without a Mythology.' LePan portrays an image of a place where 'No monuments or landmarks guide the stranger / ... among' a 'savage people' with 'an alien jargon' under 'barbaric skies.' He

---

* The Scandinavian connection is made clear in J.E.H. MacDonald's 'Scandinavian Art' and in Robert Stacey's 'A Contact in Context.' Related comments, on ways in which popular pastoral landscape painting in Australia served to romanticize the Aboriginal relation with the land and to help construct an Australian national identity in the early twentieth century, appear in Ian Burn and in Graeme Turner.

makes claim for heroic individuality, using a now familiar nineteenth-century paradigm:

> Lightnings in August
> Stagger, rocks split, tongues in the forest hiss,
> As fire drinks up the lovely sea-dream coolness.
> This is the land the passionate man must travel.
>
> Sometimes – perhaps at the tentative fall of twilight –
> A belief will settle that waiting around the bend
> Are sanctuaries of childhood, that melting birds
> Will sing him into a limpid gracious Presence.
>
> The hills will fall in folds, the wilderness
> Will be a garment innocent and lustrous
> To wear upon a birthday, under a light
> That curls and smiles, a golden-haired Archangel.

The poem then closes reiterating its fear of the unknown:

> nothing alters.
> Mile after mile of tangled struggling roots,
> Wild-rice, stumps, weeds, that clutch at the canoe,
> Wild birds hysterical in tangled trees.
>
> And not a sign, no emblem in the sky
> Or boughs to friend him as he goes; for who
> Will stop where, clumsily constructed, daubed
> With war-paint, teeters some lust-red manitou? (11–12)

This is landscape as allegory; the images (in speech) are of Speechlessness, Indians, and Nature – and all are distanced from the poet/observer because (however 'Canadian' they are, or are taken to be) they remain still beyond the limits of European standards both of propriety and of design.

LePan himself argues, in a 1979 address to the Royal Society of Canada, that critics who equate the 'country' of the title with the more politically limited idea of 'nation' do disservice to the integrity of the poem; by omitting any reference to the line 'This is the land the passionate man must travel,' they fail to see that the entire poetic landscape is an 'objective correlative' for the experience that a 'passionate man ... must suffer.' LePan specifically rejects the idea that the poem is 'exclusively about Canada,' and observes in an aside that he 'had in mind an implied contrast between Ireland, with its rich mythic overlay and its legend-laden skies, and Canada, where stark rock is often so very close to the surface and where the skies are so often sharp with actinic clarity.' Yet he then goes on to characterize the 'Laurentian Shield' (on which the 'landscape of the poem' draws) as 'the one uniquely Canadian physical feature' and 'the most characteristically Canadian landscape' (94–6). Clearly the central subject of the poem does concern the passionate man's state of mind; the poetic images of the Laurentian Shield have a metaphysical intent. Nevertheless, these images work in addition in a way similar to the images designed by the Group of Seven paintings: they carry *cultural* resonances or assumptions, and they generalize from particular details to a panoramic truth about a *characteristic* – even if metaphoric – 'Canadian' landscape. This particular Laurentian regional perspective had a national impact, for it suggested to many writers (whatever the realities of their own local place) that the 'savage' Laurentian wilderness (*tangled, hysterical, friendless*, without a set of received '*emblems*') is the norm to which they should write – perhaps to be 'Canadian.' The Laurentian images came, that is, to embody a centralist political attitude: one that effectively dominated a generation's thought, yet that remains a regional, not a national, version of place and myth.

Bruce Hutchison's claims follow a related line. In *The Unknown Country*, Hutchison characterizes Montreal as the only place in Canada with 'city manners, an acceptance of the city as a natural home and way of life, where most other cities are only villages trying to ape New York' (56). In addition, Quebec is European; Toronto is 'great and gracious' (115); Fredericton is the whole nation's 'home town,' lying on a 'gentle flat by the stream which bore the first settlers up ... from the sea' (192); Vancouver is a 'spectacle,' a 'combination of shadow, bulk, and light' (273).*

---

* Cf. the language of the poet and geographer Wreford Watson's 'Canadian Regionalism in Life and Letters,' which reiterates conventional images of place and power. Watson writes that Maritime culture is characterized by ship and wave, while Quebec's is characterized by plough and soil; that Ontario is characterized by cities, and the Prairies by 'vastness ... deceptive openness ... surprising secrecies ... huge enigmatic skies' (28); about British Columbia he writes that 'the strength and grandeur, the toughness and turbulence of mountain and river have entered into the people and made them exceptionally venturesome and determined' (31); and of the North

The terminology is fascinating. Implicitly it consigns the Maritimes to a warm but irrelevant *past*, reads the West as a sparkling but still-*frontier* sensibility that one day will learn to earn respect; and it locates *settlement* and *power* as 'Eastern' (shortly to be renamed 'Central') Canada. Power rests not with history or the future, in other words, but in numbers, and therefore in the Laurentian Lowlands triangle that embraces Windsor, London, Hamilton, Kitchener (formerly Berlin), Toronto (formerly York), Kingston, Cornwall, Ottawa (formerly Bytown), and Montreal (an instructive set of primarily English place-*names*), whose collective fascination with self and Shield is taken to be the iconography of the whole. In *The Empire of the St. Lawrence*, the historian Donald Creighton turns this geographical territoriality into an explanation of economic power, then in turn *designs* an image of the nation – 'the Laurentian Thesis' – on the basis of the economic centralization he has seemed merely to have *observed*. And Hugh MacLennan takes this image of centrality, in his 1945 novel *Two Solitudes*, combines with it the image of the military/fortress landscape and the rudimentary truths of wilderness rock and wilderness water, and fashions a fictional Laurentian version of nationhood.[12] However fictional, it, too, was to influence the way writers and readers imagined Canada. The notion of two competitive (and loving) 'solitudes' filled many subsequent years of critical and political rhetoric – as though this conceptual biculturalism expressed a fixed and 'natural' truth.

MacLennan's novel opens with a now-conventional passage of symbolic landscape description:

Northwest of Montreal, through a valley always in sight of the low mountains of the Laurentian Shield, the Ottawa River flows out of Protestant Ontario into Catholic Quebec. It comes down broad and ale-coloured and joins the Saint Lawrence, the two streams embrace the pan of Montreal Island, the Ottawa merges and loses itself, and the mainstream moves northeastward a thousand miles to the sea.

Nowhere has nature wasted herself as she has here. There is enough water in the Saint Lawrence alone to irrigate half of Europe, but the river pours right out of the continent into the sea. No amount of water can irrigate stones, and most of Quebec is solid rock. It is as though millions of years back in geologic time a

---

(referring to the Canadian Shield, the paintings of Tom Thomson, and the poetry of A.J.M. Smith) he writes that it is 'distinctively Canadian' (31). Edward Gibson, however, singles out Watson's article for special praise.

sword had been plunged through the rock from the Atlantic to the Great Lakes and savagely wrenched out again, and the pure water of the continental reservoir, unmuddied and almost useless to farmers, drains untouchably away. In summer the cloud packs pass over it in soft, cumulus, pacific towers, endlessly forming and dissolving to make a welter of movement about the sun. In winter when there is no storm the sky is generally empty, blue and glittering over the ice and snow, and the sun stares out of it like a cyclops' eye. (1)

Setting aside the classical simile, the implicit Biblical allusion,* the notion of savagery, the question of utilitarian function ('waste,' 'useless'), and the ecological inexactness of the St Lawrence being a reservoir of 'pure' water, the passage relies fundamentally on the allegorical notion of 'mainstream.'[13] In this image lodges a basic social premise of the Laurentian mythology, one involving centrality and the absorption of any 'tributaries.' Curiously, the notion of centrality is a regional presumption – for 'centrality' is the consequence of asserting power (often through the control over a communications system): the consequence of declaring that one region's own form of economic or social behaviour has political precedence. This power manifests itself in a particular definition of the word *region* itself. For a 'centre,' the rest of the country constitutes a set of regions grouped around it, there to serve its needs and listen to its standards; for the rest of the country, this ostensible 'centre' simply constitutes yet another 'region' or portion of the whole. Real differences in social power nevertheless make the former definition more economically effective, which in practice tends to turn 'regions' into marginal entities and which makes the very definition of *region* a political act.

The Language of Definition

This process of defining 'region'[14] is affected by the distinction between

---

* Cf., for example, Numbers 20: 7–8 ('And the Lord spake unto Moses, saying, Take the rod, ... and speak ye unto the rock ... ; and thou shalt bring forth ... water out of the rock'); Deuteronomy 8: 15 ('Who led thee through that great and terrible wilderness, ... who brought thee forth water out of the rock of flint'); Psalm 114: 7–8 ('Tremble, thou earth, at the presence of the Lord ... Which turneth the rock into a standing water'); Isaiah 48: 21 ('he caused the waters to flow out of the rock for them: he clave the rock also, and the waters gushed out'). This part of MacLennan's text, by asserting a *sword* in *geologic time* as the effective metaphor of origin, has thus to be read in part for its silence about conventional religion.

nationality and *nationalism*.* National*ity* is a matter of citizenship, and is
taken in many places to confer degrees of freedom; national*ism* can imply
something rather different, can even suggest a sense of enclosure and
exclusion that might not free people at all. If, indeed, nationalism
becomes a political imposition upon art, then it becomes a kind of imperialism in small, which, deriving from a nineteenth-century notion of national 'identity,' cultivates a notion of cultural uniformity (i.e., singleness,
cultural or tribal 'purity,' not to be confused with social 'unity'). Such
uniformity differs markedly from most people's social experience, whether
in a mixed, ancient society such as India's or in a mixed, twentieth-century
society such as Canada's.[15] In any society there are social variations affected
by economics, gender, race, creed, region, mobility, and so on; these in
turn affect language, and hence the voice and structure of literature.

But for politics to affect language and literary form is a social process,
not a fixed phenomenon. One way to examine how politics and literature
interconnect in Canada is to consider the notion of *region* as a way of
discussing the aesthetics of region*alism*. At first glance this would seem to
be a fairly conventional enquiry. But because region*alism* (and certainly
regionalism in Canada) is a term that carries a variety of resonances,
these differences inevitably influence any consideration of regionalism as
a Canadian *literary* phenomenon (as distinct from, though related to,
social alliances and geographic territory). To look at the way the term is
used is not to find a uniform definition, but rather to encounter some
two-pronged implications that involve the rhetoric of definition and the
politics of this rhetoric.

---

* Another view of the political consequences of regional labels is provided by James R.
Shortridge, who traces the American term *Middle West* as far back as the 1880s, observing how it came first to be associated with place, then linked with traits that
matched Americans' self-image (e.g., youthful vigour and pastoral idealism), then
identified as the cultural heartland of the United States. Michael Kowaleski surveys
recent commentary on American regional writing, focusing in large part on 'bio-
regionalism' (an effort to separate regionality from the artifice of political borders,
localism, and provincial boosterism). Resisting simple urban/rural stereotypes,
Kowaleski argues that 'region' is too often constituted in opposition to something
else (a nation, a city), that regionalism represents more a desired condition than a
lived reality, and that (for the insider) a notion about place derives from the specifics
that come to be accepted as the distinguishing properties of *a* place. Kowaleski also
sums up four dangers associated with regionalism and writing about region: 'redemp-
tive pseudotheology,' 'appeals to emotional determinism,' 'geographical ignorance,'
and 'representational melodrama' (182–83).

Eli Mandel articulates the essential difficulty of definition when, in his critical collection *Another Time*, he writes: 'The theoretical basis of literary regionalism is rather less firm than the historical or geographical but a sense persists that writers work out of locale or area, boundaries of some sort of defining sensibility' ('Writing West' 68). The notions of locale and boundary are of course themselves problematic. How and where, for example, can one put a boundary around sensibility? Yet many writers suggest that such a practice is both possible and actual. For example, Rudy Wiebe's narrator, in his 1983 novel *My Lovely Enemy*, at one point observes: 'On the prairie the only graspable image for time is the movement of a body in space; consequently the only image for a person's outlook on humanity is direction' (156). In this literary world, that is, forms of expression are rooted in the need to make meaning from experience. But to place Wiebe and Mandel beside two comments that emerged from a symposium on regionalism conducted in 1983 by *Waves* magazine, the term *regionalism* extends its meaning. Place remains a basic element, but the idea of sensibility narrows. Barry Callaghan, for example, observes: 'There will always be defenders of those local lusts, regionalism and provincialism, because people act in their own narrow interests unless enlarged by tolerance and laughter.' And Elizabeth Brewster, asked if she is a regional writer, says, 'I'd like to feel I was a human first' (Billings 38). The structure of their language raises an interesting point. Brewster's mode of argument is arithmetic and sequential; Callaghan's is algebraic, appearing to claim that limitation by space (regional) is equivalent to limitation of mind (provincial). Both are implicitly hierarchical answers, which therefore move away from commenting on 'simple' space to seeing space as a political dimension. Indeed, to invert the question, and ask if authors can ever *not* be in space, yields either absurd answers or openly political ones – political statements that constitute new definitions of the relation between spaces within a society. The results affect language. Defining the significance that particular spaces have, people parenthetically define or at least hint at their preconceptions about the significance of statements that will emerge from those given spaces, locales, regions. The notion of region, that is, contains within it a hidden notion of total structure, and it is often the artifice and the emotional reality of this implied total structure that literature encodes.

In an effort to clarify one of many connections between language and ideas, the poet George Bowering once observed that the word *region* derives from the Latin *regio*, the area ruled or directed from a central

authority ('Reaney's Region' 38).* But does this definition adequately
describe Canada? (Political cartoonists repeatedly return to this theme,
using vernacular idiom to characterize Canada's 'regional' attitudes. A
Gable cartoon in the Toronto *Globe and Mail* (11 December 1995), for
example, depicts a map of Canada in which seven 'regions' – roughly
corresponding to BC, Alberta, the rest of the prairies, the North, Ontario,
Quebec, and the Atlantic – are respectively labelled 'Outraged,' '<u>MORE</u>
Outraged,' 'Downright Gnarly,' 'Seriously Ticked,' 'So's Yer Old Lady,'
'Don't Even <u>ASK</u>!!,' and 'Step Outside And Say That!' A Jenkins cartoon
in the same paper (30 March 1996) runs a variation on the same motif,
in which a map of the provinces, overprinted with such substitute names
as 'No Salmon,' 'No NHL Team Soon,' 'No Jobs,' and 'No One Cares,'
carries the general caption 'Canada: Just say NO!' In both these
examples, the drawings mock the pettiness of certain kinds of competitive
territoriality, but in so far as they largely equate region with existing
provincial and territorial boundaries, they perhaps reinforce at the same
time a set of conventional assumptions about political consequentiality
and a set of conventional counter-claims upon distinctiveness.) Where in
Canada, one might ask, is an *agreed-upon* centre, whether political or
literary? Finding no answer (except another version of the Laurentian
Thesis), one might conclude that etymology, while it explains certain
presumptions in the language, does not necessarily define the realities of
current usage. But will another definition of region provide an acceptable
alternative? To presume that regions are not the outflung territories of
a central empire but are, instead, all contributing portions of a unified
whole, provides another model by which to understand Canada and
Canadian *land*. One recurrent, if misleading, image depicts the nation as
'mosaic' (misleading in that it suggests the necessity of *fixed units* for the
whole design to be visible). Such fixity would not guarantee equality any
more than a fixed hierarchy does. The notion of equal regional parts,
moreover, is also questionable, perhaps as naïve as the easy acceptance
of single-centredness. For if the imperial structure can be reduced once
– turning 'nation as empire' into 'nation as a set of regions' – then it can
be reduced more than once, and perhaps in an infinite number of ways.

---

* Bowering's point is primarily one about literary practice; he goes on to differentiate
'region' (which he associates with James Reaney, the idea of community, modernist
referentiality, and some form of nation-centred political discourse) from 'place'
(which he associates with himself, individuality, postmodern self-reflexivity, and
decentred or 'ex-centric' discourse).

Such a paradigm might just be designing the region as a new centre, each with its own territorial imperative, with smaller and still smaller units in the offing, subregions and sub-subregions, in a great long line. 'Regionalism' would thus become a form of 'nationalism,' or of 'imperialism,' written in an increasingly diminutive hand.

Here the social scientists' approach to Canadian regionalism helps clarify the political implications of the term. The Manitoba historian Lovell Clark, for example, simply dismissed regionalism as 'irrationalism':

The Fathers of Confederation challenged Canadians to the bold enterprise of a nation from sea to sea and the result has more than justified their great vision. Contrary to delusions currently held in some quarters, they provided us with a very good Constitution, one which in spite of mangling by the Privy Council has served us well and still does. Any proposed change should have to meet the test of good old fashioned pragmatic grounds, not the aspirations of the provincial potentates who have stalked the western and eastern landscapes of recent years, or the airy theories of a handful of professors. (124)

The implications of rhetorical structure here are as important as the overt message is. In this respect, Clark's historical comment links with the words of a political economist and a geographer. The political economist, David G. Alexander, writes as follows:

In countries where discontented regions are politically impotent and the possibility of separation is poor, grievances have a habit of becoming ancient artifacts. They begin with the people of the region identifying some grievance, assigning it an exogenous origin, and demanding a solution from outsiders. Externally the grievance is regarded as insignificant, lacking a solution, or having its cause somewhere else – mainly in the region itself. The aggrieved then become embittered, turn in upon themselves, and manifest hostility towards the exogenous enemy in usually futile ways. The region's enemy regards this behaviour as distasteful, revealing both a shocking nativism and a peculiar inability to see the grievance within the context of national interest. (44)

For his part, the geographer Cole Harris writes of pre-Confederation settlement patterns that (in contrast to the American experience to the south)

There was no continuous, expansive Canadian experience with the land. What was common was the lack of continuity imparted by the close limits of confined lands.

Settlement proceeded in patches, island by island ... But ... What was empire to some was colonialism to others. Islands that would rather have danced to different tunes were on strings held by the same puppeteer.

And ... there were people on all the islands ... who would not believe that the surrounding rock and climate were real ...

[Despite the people's plans for unity, the] geography of Canadian settlement remained disjointed and discontinuous. This is the underlying structure of Canada on which ... economic circumstances and political events would work their more ephemeral passage. ('Emotional Structure' 12, 15)[16]

By such routes, a reader is led back to those notions of topography, climate, and distance with which 'regional' writing has so often been identified. But wariness is still in order. Topography and climate constitute the simple descriptive elements that critics and sociologists alike have declared to be much more than superficial markers of regional difference. And geographical determinism is too simplistic to be an adequate explanation of behaviour.

Quite clearly, moreover, in the passages just quoted, the metaphors the writers have used derive less from bounded spaces – from a sensibility limited by space – than from the words of their profession: the geographer talks in terms of islands, the political economist in terms of enemies, the historian in terms of empire. But there are further implications still to their alliterative metaphors, for when they are applied to region they articulate a structure of relational thought. Whether, that is, one considers Clark's language of old empire ('provincial potentates') or Alexander's of military confrontation ('exogenous enemy') or Callaghan's of sexuality ('local lusts'), one sees that each writer is concerned not so much with place as with power, with perceived effectiveness, with lines of connection and authority – and not so much with the nature of power as with the possession or placement of power. So place remains important, but it comes to operate as a metaphor of structure.

When the poet/critic Eli Mandel observes that 'the writer's subject *is* his own dilemma, writing west' ('Writing West' 74) or in another essay in *Another Time* declares that 'my own sense is that the literature of Western Canada has its own coherence, not in relation to place, society, or history, but to its own developing forms' ('Romance and Realism' 66), he is in parallel fashion using the vocabulary of his trade to elucidate the possession of power. And in his verbal terms, the possession of words, of forms, of literary power, is not simply an indication of local authenticity or familiarity with local history and local allusion; it is tantamount to possessing a political voice, one that is fluid, that 'develops' over time. Any time a society begins artificially to declare a uniformity of character, that is, or to institutionalize an artificial norm of culture, the 'regions' – that is to say, the social variations within the society (the 'margin' as 'leading edge' perhaps) – will emerge to declare otherwise. In this sense the truly regional voice is one that declares an internal political alternative: in possession of the immediate and local, representing the voice of the *polis*, the people, it makes of the vernacular, the local attitude and the spatial allusion, not simply a descriptive posture but a political gesture. But to what effect? As Alexander observed, it is one of the companion ironies of regional utterance that, outside its own context, its voice may be dismissed (even ridiculed) and its political implications may often go unrecognized. Yet inside its context, such utterance can engender a quite remarkable political force, which any 'dominant culture' would be foolish to ignore.

Marginality and Minority

What this chapter has been saying is that criticism can look too shallowly at 'regionalism' and expect too little of it. A sensitivity to region might at one level make critics aware of place and landscape, but a sensitivity to regional nuance – that is, to the literary structures and metaphors of region – will make them aware of the link between language and political attitude. At its most sensitive, regional criticism can also usefully indicate that literary texts have social value. They are not to be dismissed as ornamental foibles or as artificial aberrations from some authoritative documentary norm. They emerge from specific social contexts. They are charged with particular social meaning. Hence they are contributing actively to an attitudinal dialectic in a society still very much concerned with change.[17]

Given *this* context, it is perhaps not surprising that it should be Coast-dwellers, Westerners, Quebeckers, Maritimers, Northerners, Newfound-landers, Women, Native writers, and Ethnic Minorities – writers on the political margins of so-called 'Central' Canada (the industrialized St Lawrence basin) – who should be among the most forceful challengers to the normative presumptions of anglophone Ontario male history. Admittedly, some writers write of marginality and regionalism from *within* the cultural or institutional 'centre': Laurence, Birney, Mitchell, and Mandel, to name four who have been referred to in this chapter, have all for substantial periods in their life made 'Central Canada' their home.

Yet this experience seems in some measure to have intensified their sense of political and cultural disparities, of differences in political and cultural perspective. Admittedly, too, not all writers on the margins are innovative, and some writers (on the surface at least) appear to use the vocabulary of existing power and so to espouse the normative structures of the national culture.

In Ethel Wilson's 1954 novel *Swamp Angel*, for instance, the central character does respond imaginatively – one might even say psychological-ly – to the *systems in place*, and she does so through the familiar image of cartographic 'discovery':

Maggie opened a map upon her knee. What will it mean, all this country? Flow-ing, melting, rising, obliterating – will it always be the same ... rocks always bare, slopes always bare except for these monumental trees, sage-brush country poten-tial but almost empty, here, except for the sage and the wind flowing through the sage? The very strange beauty of this country through which she passed disturbed Maggie, and projected her vision where her feet could not follow northwards – never southwards – but north beyond the Bonaparte, and beyond the Nechako and the Fraser, on and on until she should reach the Nation River and the Parsnip River and the Peace River, the Turnagain and the Liard, and north again to the endless space west of the Mackenzie River, to the Arctic Ocean. What a land! What power these rivers were already yielding, far beyond her sight! Even a map of this country – lines arranged in an arbitrary way on a long rectangular piece of paper – stirs the imagination beyond imagination she thought, looking at the map, as other lines differently arranged in relation to each other have not the power to stir. Each name on the map says 'We reached this point, by broken trail and mountains and water; and when we reached it, thus and thus we named it.' (73–4)

This passage is not unmarked by the political rhetoric of Hugh MacLen-nan or Bruce Hutchison; the catalogues of naming, the enchantment with imperial expansion, the faith in utilitarian potential: all speak a socially conventional language. Also important here, however, is the factor of illusion. The landscape description that begins the novel seems at first to adopt the familiar fortress image, but the reader soon finds out that the fortress is an imposition, a convention, not permanent, and only solidly real to those who cannot countenance change:

The mountains seemed, in this light, to rear themselves straight up from the shores of Burrard Inlet until they formed an escarpment along the whole length of northern sky. The escarpment looked solid at times, but certain lights disclosed slope behind slope, hill beyond hill, giving an impression of the mountains which was fluid, not solid.

Indeed, movement is the only thing that ultimately makes sense to Maggie Vardoe, the only thing that releases her from the stupid man who appears to control her life simply because she is married to him. Only change, paradoxically, constitutes order for *her*, and the passage goes on:

Mrs. Vardoe had become attached to, even absorbed into the sight from the front-room window of inlet and forest and mountains. She had come to love it, to dislike it, to hate it, and at seven-fifteen this evening she proposed to leave it and not to return. Everything was, she thought, in order. (7–8)

Even moving inland, noticing dwelling-places, she resists the impulse to locate order by identifying it with apparent settlement:

There is a second way that lies between Vancouver and New Westminster. It is called the river road. The river is the Fraser River, never far distant from the road. On the high north side of the road there is still some forest or large bush, and there is the agreeable illusion that the few pleasant and rustic small houses that stand alone amongst the trees above the road are really permanent in their aloneness, so that the road will keep its intrinsic quality of appearing to be far removed from a city. But over the ridge that descends to the road the city of Vancouver is crawling on. Bulldozers are levelling the small trees and laying bare a pale and stony soil. The landscape is being despoiled, as it must, on behalf of groups of small houses, a golf course, schools, a cemetery, all the amenities of living, learning, playing, and dying. The north side of the river road has no intrinsic quality of permanence after all, we see, and will soon be just another road, but the river flows below the south side and commands the scene. (17–18)

Implicitly, this fiction argues for the recognition of an Other-world; it also defines this 'Other-world' in terms of self as well as in terms of land: that which appears 'without' has the function of shaping – or paralleling, or corresponding with – whatever pertains 'within.' Or whatever pertains 'within' might shape whatever appears 'without.' Hence the novel argues not for resistance to the natural wilderness, but for a sympathy between wilderness and the innermost self. 'Innermost,' however, creates a problem, for it suggests an absolute condition, whereas Maggie's narrative rejects absolutes as being contrary to the process of living. Yet the novel

permits an *absolute* 'innermost' to at least be conceptualized if never quite
defined. The 'passing scene' – landscape rendered as observed time –
reminds Maggie that fixity is an 'agreeable illusion.' For her, as individual
person and as representative woman, change is the only form of permanence (see plates 3.3 and 3.4).

Thus her narrative begins and ends in disruption. In Wilson's British
Columbia, the city encroaches both upon untravelled nature and upon
the idea of 'rustic' that city-dwellers have constructed to lend charm to
a rural social reality they do not identify with and regard as unsophisti-
cated.[*] Maggie Vardoe, leaving the city for a fishing camp, does not
thereby escape from her social training into 'natural' absolutes; indeed,
she embraces neither city nor wilderness unambiguously – and Wilson's
rhetoric engages with this uncertainty,[†] depicting 'the land' as at least
three kinds of phenomenon: an empirical context for human action, a
social construction, and a condition of perception or of understanding
that is equivalent in some intangible way to the process called 'life.'[‡] This

---

[*] Michael Bunce discusses such related topics as the urban fascination with the rural,
    the cottage–townhouse dichotomy, playgrounds and city parks, and the degree to
    which countryside nostalgia perpetuates the economic and social disparities that di-
    vide those who dwell in central city core communities from those with access to sub-
    urban, exurban, and recreational landscapes.
[†] On Wilson's rhetoric, see Murray, who writes: 'Maggie's journey will be a movement
    from the city grid to unbounded space, which Wilson expresses as a movement from
    time to Time' (243); Murray argues that this progress is rendered stylistically, by a shift
    from 'the predominantly predicative structure of narrative to the structure of descrip-
    tion ... , from the complete past of the narrated ... to the literary present of the narra-
    tion ... , and from the language of action to the metalanguage of assessment and
    interpretation' (243); further, 'for Maggie, nature cannot constantly and reliably pro-
    vide direction. Its effect is inspirational but intermittent, silent and therefore in need of
    interpretation' (245) – the self requires community as well as nature, in other words,
    and cannot be fulfilled by a death-wish *identification* with a 'selfless' nature – a distinc-
    tion that Wilson communicates in part by her indeterminate handling of metaphor and
    metonymy (249–51).
[‡] Ronald Bordessa uses related terms (landscape as *design, context,* and *condition*) in order
    to distinguish three 'moral' categories of literary treatments of landscape: respectively
    (1) representation (citing MacLennan as an example: the working terms of categoriza-
    tion being *religious, anthrocentric, conformist,* and *realist*), (2) reportage (citing Ross,
    Mitchell, and Buckler: *scientific, biocentric, connective,* and *realist/symbolic*), and (3) experi-
    ence (citing Kroetsch, Lowry, and van Herk: *existential, ecocentric, contingent,* and *sym-
    bolic*). Bordessa cites both Atwood's *Survival* and Malcolm Ross's *The Impossible Sum of
    Our Traditions* as a basis for this paradigm, though both Atwood and Ross stress a great-
    er fluidity of perceptual and interpretive process than does Bordessa.
      Of relevance here also is the binary distinction between 'arborescent' and

flux also suggests that the various versions of 'land' and 'landscape' that have been considered so far – versions that might be called spatial, hierarchical, and ecotopian – are themselves neither absolute nor mutually exclusive.

Country, City, Home

But how can this conclusion be a reasonable one when, within Canadian culture generally, a city/non-city binary tends to operate more restrictively – and perhaps in fact more clearly epitomizes the national political dynamic than does any division between Ottawa and the provinces, English and French, South and North, East and West. Recurrently, 'City' represents (across a range of perspectives) a mix of wealth, power, noise, violence, sleaze, crowding, corruption, potential anonymity, multicultural proximities, aesthetic ferment, the loss of old values, the acquisition of new values, and sophistication. In parallel fashion, 'Non-city' (a term that embraces farms, rural communities, and small towns, and includes but sometimes extends only gesturally into 'wilderness') represents old values, family, purity, peace, stability, reliability, and space, but also ethical and aesthetic stasis, an uninformed literalism, and a naive willingness to accept facile political truisms as though they might actually apply to political relations. Both terms – 'City' and 'Non-city' – are paradoxically associated with 'real life' (consistency is not a strong argument here); and of course neither set of associations makes any sense. Violence occurs

---

'rhizome' models of thought that Gilles Deleuze and Félix Guattari advanced in *A Thousand Plateaus*. The 'arborescent' or tree model, to use the authors' own terms, is *phallogocentric, individual- or state-centred, unitary* (one image being the edifice-with-subordinate-branches), *hierarchical, defensive* (one image being the fort), *grid-designed*, and *definitive* (defining 'other' as 'not-self'). By contrast, the 'rhizome' or network model privileges *multiplicity, heterogeneity, action, affirmation, parataxis*, and *open horizontal space*. The same authors, in *What Is Philosophy?*, discuss what they call 'geophilosophy' (85–113). They use this term to describe what they see as a constant process of 'deterritorialization' and 'reterritorialization' in people's behaviour – a moving between 'territory' and 'earth' – by which they mean a moving between competing codes of understanding: codes of desire (the 'territorial' and hierarchical claims that they say capitalism encourages) and the codes of what might be called appreciation (a 'deterritorialized' opening up to the possibilities of a world without hierarchy). This process, they argue, is sequential, not dialectic; they theorize no ultimate synthesis between the two attitudes. Marlene Goldman applies the theories of Deleuze and Guattari to a reading of Aritha van Herk's *No Fixed Address* and *Places Far from Ellesmere*.

statistically as often in city and in small town; sophistication and naïvety are possible anywhere; and 'real life' eludes identification with any one setting only. Indeed, the mix of ideas that is associated with these two lists of 'representative' characteristics indicates nothing so much as a mutual aspiration for and dismissal of the condition of the other.

The portraits of (invented) small towns in Canadian writing – D.C. Scott's Viger, Sinclair Ross's Horizon, Alice Munro's Jubilee, Stephen Leacock's Mariposa, Margaret Laurence's Manawaka – focus on hypocrisy as much as community, making it appear that duplicity is one of the most highly celebrated of those rural 'community values.' And for their part, city portraits in Canadian writing – Montreal in Gabrielle Roy's *Bonheur d'occasion* and Mordecai Richler's *The Apprenticeship of Duddy Kravitz*; Toronto in Margaret Atwood's *Life Before Man* and *The Robber Bride*, Michael Ondaatje's *In the Skin of a Lion*, Morley Callaghan's *Such Is My Beloved* (though Timothy Findley's *Headhunter* likely constitutes an exception) – all construct visions of rural/garden/wilderness alternatives to the city (all of them ironic and perhaps equally duplicitous) as prototypes of hope and possibility. *Headhunter*, for all its structural desire for resolution, constructs a Toronto of unremitting corruption and unrelieved gloom.

But what precisely constitutes a 'city' in Canadian literature? Winnipeg in Adele Wiseman's *The Sacrifice* suggests the limits of ghetto more than the freedom of urbanity. Halifax in Hugh MacLennan's *Barometer Rising* suggests city size but not metropolitan consciousness. Ethel Wilson's Vancouver is more an aberration in landscape than a working community. The metropolitan areas of Toronto and Montreal suggest that size and economic advantage are the only working criteria of definition (though each city also has its own internal centres and boundaries – Rosedale, Westmount – complete with 'leading civic figures,' who are, for the most part, those whom the media find most narratable). But *relative size*, along with location and local influence and reputation, also determines the image that any urban area projects. Vancouver, Calgary, Winnipeg, Halifax: each represents city-ness to and exerts limits upon the neighbouring communities it serves. Each, moreover, claims size, substance, significance: *as* an urban centre and, sometimes, *in contradistinction to* the idea of 'metropolis,' which it places at a distance, elsewhere. Each is torn, that is, between the desire to grow and be 'recognized' and the desire to stay neighbourly and small, and the perennial desire among some civic enthusiasts to claim their place in 'world-*class* cities' betrays a curious skewing of a global perspective. What, then, of 'small cities': Kelowna, Regina, Saint John, Trois-Rivières? As far as power is concerned – at least, *felt* power, whatever the unequal biases of a rural-based distribution of electoral constituencies – Sudbury and Kapuskasing might be as distant from 'Toronto' (i.e., declared, perceived centrality) as Kelowna and Corner Brook are. ('Ontario' does not equate with 'Toronto,' nor the province of 'Quebec' with the city of 'Montreal,' whatever precedence the media and popular rhetoric might give to cultural generalities about 'Central' Canada and the 'Regions.') A sense of political injustice follows upon such a perception. But so does the claim on the purity of rural idyll or wilderness, for it is in large part dependent on an illusory distance from the city – 'illusory' because farms rely on urban markets, 'wilderness parks' are praised for their accessibility, small towns turn into bedroom suburbs, and so on. The land that gives substance to this sense of distance is itself, that is, a kind of rhetoric, one that demarcates difference, and hence gives rise to regional claims.

Thus the political base to the floating relation between 'land' and 'region' becomes clear. It is not, strictly speaking, *areal* (that is, based on the statistical evidence of measurement and dimensions) so much as it is *conceptual.* And a working plurality of vision disrupts the city/non-city binary even as it appears to confirm it. Any absolute distinction between the sophisticated metropolis and the backward hinterland simply reinscribes the familiar dichotomy between civilization and savagery, or that between *avant-garde* and 'folk,' or that between centre and region. But in practice, this binary breaks down; the categories move, being constantly in negotiation with each other, as the *conceptual distance* 'from' the metropolis (which metropolis? London/Paris/Boston/New York/Toronto/Montreal?) alters.

Margaret Laurence's work illustrates this negotiation, whether in the early narratives (which construe Africa both as its own centre and as the conceptual margin of Europe);[18] or in the urban setting of *The Fire-Dwellers* (1969), where Stacey MacAindra discovers that the problems and the strengths of the city of Vancouver derive from the (often originally rural) people who live there, at once in the neighbourhood and in flight from recognition; or in the north–south division that lies at the heart of 'Horses of the Night,' one of the stories in the linked series called *A Bird in the House* (1974). At one point in this short story, the young narrator, Vanessa MacLeod, listens to her older cousin Chris tell of his home in northern Manitoba. Sensitive, imaginative, *able to read the landscape,* he speaks selectively about the two versions of empirical reality that immediately affect him, one (domestic fact) that he doesn't want to remember and one (intellectual knowledge) that he wants desperately to fathom.

But he is deprived by circumstance; the terms he uses to convey this tension show him to be fascinated by science but rooted in the Eden story of Genesis.* His past so shapes him that he is not free to embrace a different future. Meanwhile the child Vanessa, the listener, is busy transforming what Chris tells her from a 'photographic' image into 'some beckoning country beyond all ordinary consideration,' into an ideal world of her own creation, full of mystery and romance. He says that his house is 'made out of trees grown right there beside the lake,' and Vanessa later has to try to free herself from the burden of Chris's dreams:

I could see it. The trees were still growing, and the leaves were firmly and greenly on them. The branches had been coaxed into formations of towers and high-up nests where you could look out and see for a hundred miles or more.

'That lake, you know,' Chris said. 'It's more like an inland sea. It goes on for ever and ever amen, that's how it looks. And you know what? Millions of years ago, before there were any human beings at all, that lake was full of water monsters. All different kinds of dinosaurs. Then they all died off. Nobody knows for sure why. Imagine them – all those huge creatures, with necks like snakes, and some of them had hackles on their heads, like a rooster's comb only very tough, like hard leather. Some guys from Winnipeg came up a few years back, there, and dug up dinosaur bones, and they found footprints in the rocks.' (134–5)

Elsewhere in *A Bird in the House*, Laurence shows how the Canadian West (as an Alternative Region) has historically disputed several of the hierarchies of settled power in Canada – hierarchies of race, religion, gender, language, class, and ethnicity. Here the narrative is not just reiterating the misplaced faith of one character in the power of knowing, and conveying the naïve misapprehensions of another character still too young to know the limits of the adult world; it is also demonstrating the danger of trying to live inside other people's dreams.

Yet one has to live somewhere, and Canadian writing recurrently takes characters on journeys home; far from the standard American model of eternal progress – 'you can't go home again' – Canadian writing advises

---

* In some sense, therefore, the story reiterates the dilemma that Barbara Stafford (*Voyage into Substance* xxi) sees as the challenge faced by writers and artists in the later seventeenth and early eighteenth centuries: how to be involved in the 'secular emancipation of the earth,' how to read the land as a set of 'signs that require the lexical gaze of the natural historian rather than the transformational vision of the theologian.'

that you must return, in order to place the past apart, to read its other-centred rules in a fresh way, and to make the present and future home, whatever its relationship with a distant childhood, your own. Margaret Atwood's narrator in her early novel *Surfacing* (1972) declares sardonically and self-deprecatingly, on entering Quebec at one point, that she's now 'on home ground, foreign territory' (11). In some ways this phrase at once characterizes the adult Vanessa's preoccupation with her cousin's story and epitomizes what 'region' is all about: it's about people recognizing the degree to which they are shaped by others' maps of territory and possession – the degree to which they are all immigrants in the lands of the gentry – and about people like Vanessa MacLeod learning, however slowly, to dispute the gentry (however defined) and to read the landscape, in their own way, for themselves.

4

Landscape: Literature, Language, Space, and Site

The Artifice of Landscape

In many respects the foregoing chapters, on literature in Canada, have only on the surface been about land. More fundamentally, they have been concerned with language. It is to this connection that chapter 4 now turns directly, acknowledging a paradox, a chaotic loop of cause and effect. Does language come before society, or society before language? And what effect does one's answer to this question have on literary intent and literary form, cultural production and cultural consumption, social organization and social desire? Speech clearly shapes social perception and understanding, as do other codes of communication (visual, aural, and numerical signs, for example – or, in economic terms, 'the language of money'). Yet language codes are also themselves social constructions, conventionalized exchanges – often of such long standing that their access to 'meaning' no longer seems crafted or 'unnatural.'

By the 1980s, many writers were impatient with what they interpreted as the false 'transparency' of any assumed direct relation between word and referent. Critics accepted, then modified, the distinction the French literary theorist Ferdinand Saussure proposed, between *signifier* and *signified*, that is, between the word or sign and the set of associations that are taken as the sign's 'meaning' – the 'gap' between these two categories then becomes a third category in its own right, one open to free play.¹ Importantly, while 'play' suggests freedom of action or movement, amusement, diversion, perhaps performance, in practice it likely never implies inconsequentiality, and for this reason is likely never altogether 'free.' One familiar 'land' image of the late twentieth century, for instance, is 'the level playing field,' which has been used widely to justify conservative economic and political theory. In these circumstances it is a 'signifier' drawn from sport, but used less to suggest frolic than to associate an ideal of egalitarian opportunity with a particular commercial freedom from governmental restriction or other forms of social restraint. But what is being championed here: 'team spirit' or 'individual achievement'? egalitarianism or precedence? As with many other representations of the sports ground, the term *level playing field* indirectly invokes certain kinds of privilege at the same time as it is being used ostensibly to espouse parity and fair practice (see plate 4.1). Given such a division between signifier and signified, late-twentieth-century critics began to reject the notion that language is an act of *representing* reality at all. They redirected their attention instead to the *artifice* of verbal arrangements – and to the artifice of conventional genres, and the artifice of the medium of expression.

Clearly, technology can alter the mode and site of production, and it can reconfigure the artifice of 'landscape.' The choice of a given medium of communication – sales catalogue, paperback novel, radio program, B-movie, TV sitcom, documentary, mall display, Internet code – affects the character of the message being delivered. But technology only trains the imagination; it does not curtail it. And writers and critics during the last decades of the twentieth century found that technology did not constrain them to accept the printed word as the limit of their subject. Critics were often as willing to interpret advertising copy and pop-music lyrics *as literature* as they were to read novels and poems for their socially redeeming virtues; conventional literature came to be seen simply as one of the many 'sign-systems' of a given culture, along with freeway designs and electronic games, opera and elevator music. Those writers who did continue to use *the printed word* often crossed genres as they did so, combining the techniques of one medium (filmscript, say, or comic art) with the format of another (the satiric or romantic novel). Some writers combined a written work with a sound diskette. Some 'journals' began to be available only electronically – most notably *Swift Current*, with its punning allusion both to electricity and Saskatchewan geography.* A few writers

---

* Changes in technology made possible the mobility of the publishing industry as well as changes in medium; from the 1960s on, as technological change led from mimeograph machine to photo-offset production to desk-top publishing, small presses opened outside Toronto and Montreal and other publishing 'centres,' often in very tiny communities. The involvement of Victoria residents Dave Godfrey (who teaches Creative Writing at the university there) and Ellen Godfrey (who writes mystery novels) in running both the publishing company Press Porcépic (later Beach Holme)

even resisted binding the pages of their writing into linear sequence, asking for the 'reader' also to be an 'arranger' (and rearranger) not of 'narrative' so much as of image and impression. Often writers undertook these experiments, moreover – whatever they might say about the non-referentiality of art – in the name of social reform. Though they were by no means the first to emphasize the *constructedness* of language, the writers of the 1980s were repeatedly concerned with politics.* In the process of writing, they designated language not just as a medium, but also as a *site* – of power, resistance, and revelation.

One critic, Gaile McGregor (in *The Wacousta Syndrome*), goes so far as to talk of 'langscape,' which punningly – verbally – codes landscape *as* language, as a set of associated ideas constructed in and by language,† and simultaneously to code language as a 'landscape' of another kind (see also plate 4.2). The title of another book will extend a sense of how this process of verbal reconstruction works. In 1986, Mark Abley published a personal travel book, a venture into both 'past' and 'prairie,'

---

and the computer-software company Softwords, represents yet another interconnection between literature and technological change. Dave Godfrey was also a featured speaker at the W.R.I.T.E. conference organized by Howard Rheingold, 16–18 June 1994, in Vancouver, where the subject was 'the electronic landscape.'

Technology is not always so warmly perceived. Peter Emberley critiques it as a phenomenon that would create uniformity in place of cultural and political openness, one that would replace signs of difference with signs of 'efficiency' (761). Relatedly, John Tagg, in an aside in *Grounds of Dispute*, critiques the 'cyberspace' of the sf writer William Gibson for being a false utopia, and therefore for not being a Borgesian 'place of dissemination' (12).

* Dorothy Seaton ('Post-Colonial') differentiates the 'subversive' politics of *deconstruction* from the more conservative politics of *imperialist* and *counterdiscursive discourse*, using attitudes to land as the sign of political difference – she deems the latter positions conservative to the degree that both assume that discourse has the power to control and familiarize 'land' *even when* they conceptualize land as a site of the unfamiliar and resistant.

† Other commentators have made a similar point, as does Jean-Pierre Richard in *Pages Paysages*. Cf. Bruce Chatwin, who declares that Australian Aboriginal societies 'sing' place – and therefore relationships – into existence, and that place consequently constitutes song. Doris Y. Kadish distinguishes between two forms of semiotic reading of 'description': those that depend on pictorial assumptions (whether decorative or symbolic) and those that expose the non-representational, 'rational' function of descriptive passages about landscape – the one stressing figurative formulation (the garden image, the 'pastoral remnant'), the other stressing social and political outlook (see, e.g., 30–2). See also Brydon, 'Landscape and Authenticity.'

called *Beyond Forget.*[2] The question is: how does a reader read these apparently simple words? 'Forget' (pronounced 'For-zhay') is the name of a small town in Saskatchewan, beyond which (suggests Abley) lie the many realities of prairie that he is trying to recapture, from memory, in prose. But to the anglophone reader, 'Forget' of course reads as the verb 'forget,' the opposite of 'remember.' The title now reads simultaneously in two ways: as *Beyond Forzhay* and *Beyond Forget.* Deliberately it reads place geographically, as space, and also temporarally, as a process of interpretation.[*] Such a title is resonant with implication, hinting at both literature and history. (Even Wordsworth lives allusively in *this* Saskatchewan: 'Our birth is but a sleep and a forgetting,' muses the 'Ode: Intimations of Immortality from Recollections of Early Childhood.') But inferentially, at least, Abley's title also suggests the divided interpretive character of an officially bilingual society. The historical Canadian geographical name to which it directly refers, in the now predominantly anglophone prairie West, is by origin French; the reader is consequently asked to remember that the history of the place is *linguistically* as well as *politically* mixed, francophone as well as anglophone (and now multicultural in other ways as well). History itself, therefore, comes to be seen as a synchronic set of codings, a *palimpsest* (or re-used manuscript page, from which the previous messages have been only partially erased). Maps and names encode in land one shape of history; but the powers of interpretation perennially reconstruct or re-encode this 'one' shape as the reader 'reads' – *sites* and *sights* – the 'page' of place-and-time. '[W]hen you say *place*,' writes the narrator in Dave Godfrey's 'East and/or West,' 'I think *movement*' (*Dark Must Yield* 92; my italics). Each perceptual reconstruction alters the perceived reality.

The English-language vocabulary for characterizing landscape (and people's relationship with land) interconnects with the vocabulary for characterizing language and the use and function of language. This intersection is apparent in many of the terms that have already come into use in these chapters: *cultivation, scene, setting, ground, lines, prospect, range, depiction.* Five more such spatial terms structure the remaining sections of this chapter: *View, Sound, (Re)form, Field,* and *Site.*

---

[*] Paul Carter argues, with reference to Australia, that exploration journals record a progress in time as much as, or perhaps more than, in place. See also Anderson (170–3) on the difference between two kinds of traditional Thai map – those designed to guide a spiritual traveller through a moral journey, and those designed as local (primarily military) guides – and conventional Western maps, with their bird's-eye determination of borders. See also Malouf's interview with Carter.

View

After pictograms and emblem verse, some of the most obvious demonstrations of speech functioning as landscape occur in the work of bp Nichol (as in the closing pages of Book 6 of *The Martyrology*) or in the later work of Earle Birney, where individual poems sometimes take on the visual shape of the 'landscape' they concern themselves with – a public space in Mexico, as in 'Six-Sided Square,' or a series of Canadian 'regions,' as in 'up her can nada,' 'newfoundland,' and 'Alaska Passage.' At other times they reconstruct what readers *understand* by the term *place* by requiring them to rethink the value-laden language that they use to name and represent it. For example, 'Six-Sided Square: Actopan' (see plate 4.3) is an interrupted, serio-comic dialogue, bounded visually by a polyhedron, 'representing' both place (space) and enclosure (language and interpretive attitude). The town 'square' in *this* 'Actopan' is plainly *not* geometrically 'square,' despite the word that is available to name it. By calling it 'six-sided,' Birney breaks out of one set of definitions, but he also encloses with the new dimensions, for six lines or 'sides' actually frame the words on this page. Such 'lines' have their figurative (though not geometrical) 'parallel' inside the speech actions they contain. The metaphoric aspirations of the poet/guide in the poem interact with the limited literalist expectations of the lady tourist to whom the poet/guide speaks; together they demonstrate the way words are constrained by the meanings attached to them and the way meanings are constrained by the function that people attribute to language. What is it, Birney implicitly asks, that words can do? The answer is that they can make poetry, tell truths, articulate all creation; and yet they can also stop change, tell lies, and invoke closure on the mind. People who see language as a stimulus to association and play will keep breaking past the received boundaries of 'fact'; by contrast, people who are determined to be restricted by one version of 'truth,' 'fact,' or 'meaning' may never even realize the extent to which they thus design their own limitations.

Overlapping here are two issues: (1) the ability to 'read the land,' as Grove's narrator claims to be doing in *Over Prairie Trails* (his actions presume in the referential character of speech and in the empirical character of reality), and (2) the ability to see speech itself as a landscape to be shaped. People read place *in* words, and they read place *as* words; they can also read words as place. That is, words have physical dimensions, and occupy space; they can be designed and relocated, to make ornament and to order meaning; they can be at once the subject and the implement of intellectual enquiry, and of aural and visual play; and they can both construct and be a conduit for the set of social attitudes that goes by the general name of 'culture.' Hence, just as the land becomes text, so do text and system become an occupiable territory, open to arrangement and invention, and yet susceptible to similar strokes of presumption and power as those which affected the so-called new continent of North America when European speech enclosed it. They have the power to create 'meaning' and so declare difference; paradoxically they are also vulnerable if a louder or apparently more confident or articulated arrangement of words (or system of values) comes to be accepted as dominant because it conveys – or is deemed to convey – a 'truer,' more 'authentic,' or 'more real' version of meaning, behaviour, relationships, and events.

In the terms that this chapter has so far been using, any colony is susceptible to being overwritten by an imperial language. To use broad political generalizations, Canada and the idea of Canada are vulnerable to the power of the social values embodied in and empowered by American media and American speech; Native and other marginal cultures (or cultures *perceived* as marginal) can be seemingly silenced by European and other majority cultures; women's voices will appear marginal if men's voices are accepted as the norm; one class can dominate another, and its norms of literacy come to seem a universal syntactical and lexical 'standard.' Writers who write *from* such 'categories,' however, frequently find ways to question the categories' legitimacy and to break free of the restrictive verbal paradigms that have come to construct and reconfirm them. Daphne Marlatt's punning, feminist non-linearity in *Ana Historic* (1988), for example, and Jack Hodgins's parodic ironies in *Innocent Cities* (1990) resist the way a dominant culture has historicized female and regional experience as irrelevant. The ironies and the non-linear form, by emphasizing the fragmentation of some structure of language or society (one that was previously conceptualized as unitary or 'whole'), reveal the inadequacies of so-called universal cultural assumptions.

Innocent Cities tells a 'Victorian novel' (i.e., uses a formula of speech) about the arrival of Empire (i.e., a set of nineteenth-century attitudes and preconceptions) in the city of Victoria, BC, and the colony of Victoria, Australia. The names are important, for control over the language of naming is part of the process of asserting cultural dominance. In the course of the book, Native Salish speech is overwritten by Chinook trade jargon; local botanical terms are supplanted by Victorian taxonomies; early residents' ambitions are redirected by the verbal conventions and social proprieties of an imported culture. What was once a place on its own becomes a passive 'region' of another place, a landscape to be read through others' language, as is suggested by a scene describing the 'flotilla of shattered debris' that washes ashore:

empty crates and barrel staves and broken boxes had been flung up onto rocks and wedged between driftwood logs and tangles in the high-tide rows of twisted seaweed. Antwerp. Made in England. California Oleomargarine ... Because the boards had been so brutally smashed, many of the words existed without any context, almost without any meaning. Napkins. Leder. El Dorado. Chlorodyne. Sauterne ... Cider. Kid. Sapone da barba. Waggon. Asphalt Roofing. This same thing was happening ... all up the southwest coastline of the island, printed debris washing in like spawning smelt to leave, where smelt left eggs, a perplexing and untidy deposit of words from every corner of the world. (xv–xvi)

Out of such words, as out of the boards on which they are written, some local characters build their new homes. But the fragmentation, the decontextualization – and then the recontextualization, through the medium of parody – asks that this process of cultural borrowing not be read passively or neutrally, or as 'simple progress,' in the way that conventional histories might suggest. The characters in the novel variously surrender to change or are swallowed up by circumstance; few maintain their illusions, and none remains unscathed. But an active engagement with the *possibility* of communication – even by means of deliberate silence, in the face of conventional and empty speech – can still preserve options for them. One of these options, the novel suggests, is the hope that the language of the future will be free from the biases and limitations inherited from the past.

Equally critical, though using a different narrative strategy and emphasizing female subjectivity, Daphne Marlatt has observed that 'my region, i mean the region i'm writing out of, is not so much place or landscape these days as life as a woman' (Wachtel 13). Her 1988 book that extends this insight, *Ana Historic,* is in one sense set in Vancouver; in another sense it is set inside female consciousness, coding several simultaneous possibilities involving women's past, present, and future history. In the fiction, a contemporary woman named Annie (she is the daughter of Ina and the apparent 'possession' of Richard, and becomes the friend of Zoe, who seems at first to be at the opposite end of her psychological alphabet) seeks to reclaim a woman named Ana Richards from the margins of municipal history; in the process, she also reclaims her own present and future from external control – hence the novel also deconstructs the notion of history itself. Analyzing the force of the phrase '"history says of her,"' the narrating consciousness goes on to observe: 'but when you're so framed, caught in the act, the (f)stop of act, fact – what recourse? step inside the picture and open it up' (56). Here the fractured language – like the de-capitalization of 'i' (an orthographic gesture, an anti-hierarchical political statement) – spells out the need to question the fixity of established conventions about reality and knowledge. The camera-mechanism metaphor suggests only a means to limit exposure; the verbal fracture suggests that control over the picture lies with the subject.

In other words, language – which can be mistakenly identified both with the arbitrariness of a single shutter speed and with the notion of unquestionable 'truth,' linked as it often is with what's sometimes called 'photographic reality'[3] – can work metatextually. By this means, fractured words can reperceive social reality (rather than escape it), just as the 'magic realist' techniques of a painter such as Alex Colville can reperceive reality even though they differ from the techniques of 'conventional realists.' Colville's 1967 acrylic *Pacific*, for example (see plate 4.4), shows the shirtless torso of a man. Though his head is not in the picture, the man appears to be looking through a window at the California coast; he is wearing a wristwatch. On an otherwise bare drafting table in the foreground is a handgun, its physical dimensions emphasized by the ruler that is set into the table-top. The painting is forceful. But its force derives both from the empirical meticulousness of the drawing and from the iconographic juxtaposition of the various items in the room (or, perhaps, the figure's life): watch, *planning table*, headlessness, revolver, and the ocean image/word 'Pacific.' The effect is *tension*, the 'perceptual state' of suspended, unresolved action.

What governs interpretation here are the 'categories' that the viewing person brings to the images: do they overlap and reconfirm each other, or resist integration? Or is a third option possible? Earle Birney's poem 'newfoundland' (which is dedicated to the Newfoundland poet Edwin John [Ned] Pratt) suggests another use of 'categories of view' (see plate 4.5). Here, language functions in one sense verbally, in another as visual form; the relation between these two functions distinguishes between the potential rigidity or stasis of any 'category' in itself and the kinetic vitality of person and voice that the category might contain. The challenge is to see past the frame. In the form the poem took when it was first published, it is a two-colour (red-and-black) print. The two colours highlight the anagrammatical message that is contained in the *letters* (as well as in the implied *geography*, the categorical place, and therefore also in the implied, named, *historical context*) that constructs the word/place/idea 'Newfoundland.' The lines of the poem simply repeat the word *newfoundland* seventeen times, but such a statistical enumeration will not disclose the poetry here; it just describes the surface frame, the appearance. Reading the alternate-colour message (a literal *rubric*, to begin with, and printed in boldface or italic in later editions) pierces this surface, decoding as follows: 'Ned found new land, old fold, and wan wold, found elan, and noun fun, and won an eon; end.' But 'message' by itself is not poetry either; here it leads further, to interpretation. 'Newfoundland,' *in other words*, gives rise to the poet 'Ned,' whose words (emerging from context) articulate the vitality of a particular space and culture. Or – to generalize – cultures create poets, poets create cultures, and language (sometimes oral and performative, and sometimes scored on the plane of the page) is a fluid medium in which this mutual transformation occurs.

Another of Birney's visual poems, 'up her can nada,' is a punning, witty, deliberately rude 'map' of Ontario, using line and word to epitomize all the hostile, self-protective, sexist, and self-righteous attitudes that Birney (or Canadian culture at large) attributes to Ontario's 'Upper Canada' past, figuratively present in Establishment Anglo-Protestant traditions (see plate 4.6). Constructing these attitudes *as a map* is itself part of Birney's critique, for the map *of* 'Upper Canada' articulates in speech and visual design the system of mapping *by* 'Upper Canada' that has given centricity and power to one particular set of social values.[4]

A fourth example finds Birney making self-reflecting speech out of and into the West Coast. The poem 'Alaska Passage' redefines the mountainous territories of the Cordillera visually; before anything else the reader *sees* this poem (see plate 4.7). The 'ranges' are called a 'palimpsest.' By choosing this word, the poet changes the set of attitudes that the conventional observer brings to the 'landscape.' 'up her can nada' parodically adapts conventions; 'Alaska Passage' subverts them by fragmenting the (verbal, visual) assumptions on which they rest. Here, the mountain landscape is no longer to be seen as a (sublime) *fortress barrier*; instead it appears as a folded *page*, not foreign to history but *written on* by history and still moving, 'swimming' past the illusorily still observer. Clearly, 'range' means more than 'mountain'; it implies movement, and it implies reach; Birney's poem suggests, in consequence, that the mind that constructed the mountains as wilderness can also reconstruct them as speech, as a phenomenon not foreign to human experience but intrinsically part of it. All is epitomized by the final line of the poem, which simply reiterates the words 'alaska passage.' But here the words are fragmented on the page; they begin at the ostensible end, with the 'age' of pass*age* – that is, with the potentially debilitating sense of time that is usually conceptualized as unidirectional linear history. They then move on to 'alas' (lifted out of *alas*ka), and hence a debilitating sense of regret or perhaps a failure to liberate self. (Such is Birney's mordant comment on the so-called progress of human life.) But they none the less lead on to 'pass' – the sea *pass*age metaphorically (i.e., verbally) coalescing in this (semantic) landscape with the mountain 'pass' route – offering the promise of transcendence or continuity, even if this continuity might ironically be a promise only to take part in an inconstant cycle of similar discoveries.

Sound

To move from the visual to the aural is to see how tonal control can also function as a medium of social critique. F.R. Scott's 1954 poem 'Laurentian Shield' provides an instructive contrast with 'Alaska Passage.' The difference involves a distinction not just between the two separate land-*forms* but also between two attitudes *associated* with Canadian place – values that particular configurations of land have come to typify, to symbolize. The Coastal Cordillera with its fjords – or '*sounds*' (following on from the images of Captains Cook and Vancouver) – had become a watchword of fearsome Nature, whereas the Canadian Shield had come to epitomize Canada's 'limitless' size and 'untapped' resources, its indeterminate dimensions and echoing solitude. Neither image was concretely fixed in physical reality; both would be challenged by the landscape of speech – in image and in sound. The Birney poems that have already been referred to construct *visual* wordscapes, landscapes-in-language, which parody the received social structures that the culture had been accepting as self-evident truths. Scott constructs *aural* wordscapes, designing space by means of sound, in order to emulate what his generation accepted as the distinctive – or at least as a characteristic – Canadian landscape: its silences, its echoing vastness, the noises and rhythms of nature itself, the idiom and cadence of natural speech.

Yet paradoxes attend this distinction and this vocabulary. Scott's poem is earlier than Birney's and (though it rebelled against certain social injustices in Canadian society, particularly the surrender of 'public wealth' to corporate monopolies) it shows the influence of its engagement with the very conventions it seeks to criticize. Birney's 'Alaska Passage' questions the alienation usually associated with wilderness; Scott's 'Laurentian Shield' reworks the familiar distancing, uninhabited, Group of Seven, non-verbal image of the 'wilderness' landscape. Birney uses the map in 'up her can nada' to query the power relations (the boundary lines, the enclosing structures) that a map conventionally draws; Scott asserts in words the alien speechlessness of the 'typical' Canada:

> Hidden in wonder and snow, or sudden with summer,
> This land stares at the sun in a huge silence
> Endlessly repeating something we cannot hear.
> Inarticulate, arctic,
> Not written on by history, empty as paper,
> It leans away from the world with songs in its lakes
> Older than love, and lost in the miles.   (*Events and Signals* 16)[5]

One of the central paradoxes in Scott's poem – of speaking that which cannot be heard, because the interpretive syntax does not match the expressive syntax – resolves itself only through semantic transformation. Ultimately, says Scott's poem, the 'rock' will have to be turned into 'children.' Yet in such a transformation a reader can hear not just the desire for occupation, but also the presumptiveness of empire. In Scott's work the landscape proves not to be historyless after all. The speaker of the poem presumes in the emptiness and the speechlessness of the land-*before-himself*, and he aspires to rule the future through some form of patriarchal continuity.

One of the features of a later poem, Margaret Atwood's *The Journals of Susanna Moodie* (1970), is that it rejects these presumptions of patriarchy, though it does not minimize their power; for Atwood it is not the rock that is inarticulate but the immigrant–persona–female, whom the patriarchy has conventionally identified with 'land.' Hence the 1852 Mrs Moodie of *Roughing It in the Bush* returns in Atwood's poem no longer as the condescending imperialist; she appears instead as an ordinary person, but as one who is lost on the margins of both conventional civilization and conventional discourse. She can neither interpret a new place through old familiar words nor any longer recognize herself: 'I am a word,' says Atwood's Moodie, 'in a foreign language' (11). If identity is indeterminate, moreover – because speech is controlled by someone else, some external authority of person or convention – then so are the spaces in which people dwell: 'Whether the wilderness / is real or not / depends on who lives there' (13). To recognize that reality inheres in the presumptions of speech suggests further that, for Atwood's Moodie, the external world no longer functions as a referent fixed by dictate or custom but asks instead to be interpreted, read relatively, as a set of shifting signs, an extension of experience and expectation. But is the consequent, verbally constructed landscape itself perceived to be 'articulate' if its terms are not shared within the dominant culture? Can it ever be articulate *and marginal*, or articulate *and subversive* of the dominant terms of construction? These are questions that ask again how speech forms conventionalize power.

Wilfred Watson's earlier poem 'Laurentian Man' (1959) makes clear that this shift from fixed to relative language-landscapes did not take place suddenly in Canadian literary history. Rather, it was part of a slow generational change both in attitudes towards culture and in expectations of the words that construct culture. Why Watson's poem is not better known than it is possibly has something to do with his lexicon, which integrates a complex educated diction with a deliberately irreverent, laconic vernacular. Watson's strategy here is to demonstrate how a religious idiom ('Cain's land') and a Cartesian geographic determinism (the fascination with maps and the 'Shield') *construct* the image of wilderness which they purport merely to *describe*. In Watson's poem, the Laurentian Shield is as barren as any place could be on God's earth, but in Watson's *terms*, 'Canada' is less God's failure than God's challenge. The opening sections emphasize this difference, tonally parodying the version of the national identity that had come by the 1950s to be widely accepted, and that had been directly articulated in Pratt's 'Towards the Last Spike' in 1952. Watson saw this self-image as self-justifying and smug, and he challenged it by questioning its *terms* of self-identification – its Protestant ethic, its image of land:

1.
When indefatigable God decided to make a new man, *homo Canadiensis*
He somewhat dubiously supposed that pulverized
Laurentian Shield would do all right as a corporeal basis,
Because (I give only a few of the Divine Reasons)
Though it's a phlegmatic conservative old-fashioned dust
More than a few centuries dour, without the least vein of humour,
And puritanic to a geologic fault, still,
It reddens with a blush of past granitic fire.

2.
Pioneer in creation, God took a deeper breath than usual,
And said hopefully, let there be life.

The Canadian Shield slept on, as through the ages.
God took a second breath, and cleared his throat.
Let there be *some* life, he hesitated; but the dust was deaf.
Let there be life, or else – God shouted; and at last
Of course there was some life, of a sort.
God rested from this day's labour, quite fatigued.
It's far from good, he said, But then it isn't so bad,
Considering this dense porphyry I've tried to work.

3.
Before him, obvious as a senseless crime, the first Canadian stood gaping
At him, with that magnificent blank complacency,
That awful monotony of face, that face to face
Blankness of mind, all cattle grass and trees, all wood and beef –
Consummatum est, God punned. He all but gave up the ghost,
Self-crucified in a wanton act of creation.
I shall have to make it, he shuddered, a second Eve.
No woman not of Laurentian dust could face this face all her life.

4.
God wept. But still, he thought, brushing away his tears,
It may do yet, if mated to a nice appropriate Eve.
A happy sex life will polish up many rough edges.
It has got a nice big simple decent heart.
I'm not completely sold on brilliancy.
I made the Greek too subtle and too sharp.
The French too polished. The English too poetically glib of tongue.
The Irish too fanciful, always fighting fairies.   (*Poems* 47)

Thus dispensing with others, the poem goes on to seek alternatives to
the Canadian status quo. The new values Watson espouses are relative;
the new landscape is verbal; speech is open to alternative possibilities;
and speech is the territory in which the values change. So he turns to
celebrate the poetic aspirations of Louis Dudek and Irving Layton, poets
whose speech seemed at the time to question the received paradigms of
authority. Only for the conventional were these poets raucous or raw.
Watson saw them otherwise. In *his* Dudek and Layton, 'barbarity'
becomes redefined as 'sophistication' – 'God saw that the rock had
made a great geological leap upward. / It had become, in the new
Canadian, for the first time, quasi-human.' Wonders apparently never

cease, and even St Thomas Aquinas in heaven, Watson avers, is allowed to 'discreetly chuckle' (48–9) at God's uncircumscribed capacities for creation.

Watson's poem was one of several works that in the late 1950s was disputing the precedence of Anglo-Protestant codes in anglophone Canadian culture. The vernacular method is particularly interesting: for this technique constitutes a methodological challenge to the High Anglo cultural conventions of elegant diction, such elegance being a modified extension of the conventional 'elevated diction' that Mackay and Moodie and Goldsmith had been using a century earlier. As used in poetic practice, that is, the vernacular speech redefined the terms that the old versions of landscape had employed to construct the landscape as 'barbaric.' (The word *vernacular* itself comes from a root word meaning the *native-or-homeborn-slave*; to use vernacular speech was to usurp what the powers of rule said was the 'natural' order of things; that is, it was to give precedence to the lower instead of the higher in the terminology of the prevailing system.) Hence Dudek and Layton, in Watson's terms, were 'barbaric' only by the terms of the dominant aesthetic of the time; but such a hierarchy was no more 'natural' than any other. The terms of discrimination could be assigned new priorities, and within his poem Watson uses the the vernacular to reshape the value system within which to define – or 'place' – such categories as those called *barbarity* and *wilderness.*

To substitute 'wilderness' as the 'true' value *in place of* the received forms of custom, attitude, or 'civilization,' however, intrinsically sets up another form of received truth, which in turn invites further questioning. Celebrating wilderness – that is, celebrating all that was 'opposite' to the old recipe for civilization – does not fundamentally alter the distinction on which the old definition was based. It is also likely a romanticized version of reality. In an ebulliently romantic age, a Layton poem will seem invigoratingly fresh, whereas a classically chiselled poem in blank verse, such as Daryl Hine's 'Point Grey' (1968), will seem constricted, subdued. But Hine's classical point, annotated, clarifies even what Watson and Layton and Atwood were attempting to do: questioning the absoluteness of history and of the received terms of expression and evaluation by which a version of history turns into an authority.

It reads in part:

Here, at least, it is a pretty morning,
The first fine day as I am told in months.

I took a path that led down to the beach,
Reflecting as I went on landscape, sex and weather.

...

Sometimes I think the air we breathe is mortal
And dies, trapped, in our unfeeling lungs.

Not too distant the mountains and the morning
Dropped their dim approval on the gesture
With which enthralled I greeted all this grandeur.

...

Though I had forgotten that it could be so simple,
A beauty of sorts is nearly always within reach.   (*Minutes* 37)

Point Grey, of course, the western tip of Vancouver, is the land mass (alluded to in chapter 1) that Captain George Vancouver named after his naval friend Captain George Grey and so claimed for England's (King George's) empire and verbal control. Through measured cadences, Hine changes the terms. Recurrently he interrupts the absolutes of *either/or* propositions with vernacular qualifiers (words such as *at least, I am told, somehow, not exactly*) – hence he leads a modern reader to reread not only the colour of the native land (Point GREY: 'Only the rain makes spectres of the mountains') but also the imperial claim that has in history named the land as it has. In the new context, 'Point Grey' speaks through its literal paradox: Point (the absolute) Grey (the uncertainty) – till a reader recognizes the *punctum indifferens* of classical philosophy, the 'pointless point,' in modern dress. Hine's controlled wit declares here a poetic re-evaluation of history; at the same time it resists any unexamined romantic, nostalgic claims for a 'wilderness civilization.' Yet it has employed vernacular cadences, not used an elaborate elevated diction, in order to do so. Contra-*dictions* abound.

Previous chapters have made use of narrative, paradigmatic, and cumulative strategies of discourse; this chapter is concerned with the processes of 're-reading,' and with some of the ways that the techniques of contrast (shaped in the designs of speech, as *difference, irony, paradox, fragmentation, contradiction, heterotopia*) incorporate many features that were previously found unacceptable in discourse (or 'read' in the landscape).

By refusing the conventional (inherited?) social hierarchies of land and speech (i.e., the valuing of the exploitable over the 'wilderness,' and of elevated diction over the vernacular), the techniques of contrast highlight the potential value of what used to be seen as disparity and can now be 're-read' as a satisfying arrangement in its own right. Those features of speech and landscape that were once deemed 'barren' can now be seen not to be barren *in fact* but barren *only by definition.* Contrast and *contra*-diction – the diction that 'speaks *against*' convention – serve as techniques to resist the past and to reshape the present by suggesting alternative ways of reading the cultural 'landscape.'

In one of the extended 'conversations' that Canadian literary history records, for example, Scott reshapes Pratt, who has reshaped Roberts, who has reshaped Mackay: not in a single sequence of linear developments, but through a complex and contradictory series of permutations and combinations. Birney and Watson reshape what it is that readers understand through Scott and Pratt. The work of Abraham Klein, instructively, allows readers further to reconsider what they understand by Watson.

Klein's highly articulate 1948 poem 'Portrait of the Poet as Landscape' would seem on the surface to be the very example needed here to demonstrate the theme of this chapter, the 'site' or 'space' of speech. For the poet in this poem himself becomes an art object, a design in place, a 'geographical' subject. Further, as an English-speaking socialist Montreal Jew, Klein certainly qualifies as an anglophone exception to the social 'norms' of Upper (and Lower) Canada Anglo-Protestantism: it is from such a source that a challenge to poetic and cultural norms might be expected to come. Is it significant then that 'Portrait' has been lauded – canonized – by critics and anthologists since its appearance? And why was this poem highly praised when Watson's, for example, was largely ignored? Does the difference in response simply derive from the relative length of Watson's work at a time when anthologists in Canada were more readily drawn to short lyrics, perhaps on economic grounds? Or does the difference in response have something more general to do with landscape, language, and value?

In order to define poetry, Klein's poem sets out by dismissing a variety of (other) writers whose grasp exceeds their reach: those who respond like Pavlov's dogs to any stimulus, those who use the voices of others and are merely ventriloquists' dummies, those whose egos make them 'patagonian in their own esteem,' and (significantly) those who cannot distinguish between form and substance, who 'know neither up nor down, mistake the part / for the whole, curl themselves in a comma, / talk technics, make a colon their eyes,' thus distorting what Klein still claims as 'truth,' *whole.* The real poet, Klein goes on, 'seeds illusions,' even if no one appears to listen or applaud:

> Look, he is
> the nth Adam taking a green inventory
> in world but scarcely uttered, naming, praising,
> the flowering fiats in the meadow, the
> syllabled fur, stars aspirate, the pollen
> whose sweet collusion sounds eternally.
> For to praise
>
> the world – he, solitary man – is breath
> to him. Until it has been praised, that part
> has not been. Item by exciting item –
> air to his lungs, and pressured blood to his heart –
> they are pulsated, and breathed, until they map,
> not the world's, but his own body's chart!   (*Complete Poems, Part 2* 638–9)[*]

But clearly, whatever else it is – oracular, prophetic – Klein's poem is not vernacular. This resistance to standard speech in favour of more dense and elliptical patterns – perhaps the incantatory patterns of traditional Hebraic ritual – is neither an intrinsic strength nor an intrinsic flaw, but it is an issue that affects literary history and the conventional evaluation of speech and land, for it raises the question of whether or not there is such a thing as 'natural speech.' If 'value' is a social construct, and 'nature' a paradigm of social perceptions, is language not also a social arrangement? What connection exists, then, between the notion of landscape as a perception open only to those with leisure from the land and the notion of literary art as a form of authority defined by a social register of speech?

As the poet Dennis Cooley observes, in a polemical essay in *Prairie Fire* titled 'The Vernacular Muse in Prairie Poetry': 'It must be difficult, even for the curious, not to perceive vernacular poetry as a failure of imagina-

---

[*]   Zailig Pollock, the editor of this volume, quotes Klein's notebook entry on this poem: 'The modern poet is so anonymously sunk into his environment that, in terms of painting, his portrait is merely landscape' (1001).

tion or intelligence. It hardly offers, it seems, the shock of metaphor or
the challenge of interpretation many of us have come to expect in (good)
poetry. Apparently, vernacular just sits there blinking and naked as a
newborn baby, and (some would have it) just as dumb.' That is, Cooley
goes on, when a set of terms of expression comes to be prized by readers
of many different political persuasions, then those terms – here he lists
*referentiality, unity, high seriousness, linearity, closure, mastery, hierarchy, ingenu-
ity, high-mindedness,* and *systems of overriding belief or structure* – come to
seem absolute rather than socially relative arbiters of art. Other terms
(*fragmentation, inconclusiveness, coarse jesting, uncertainty*) by definition are
consequently (and usually unquestioningly) accepted as inartistic; and
under such conditions readers

can at best be entertained by vernacular poetry, which will seem insignificant by
such standards, immune to the exercise of the hermeneutics in which we have
been so deeply inscribed and by which we have learned to value poetry.

Take the example of W.H. Auden. When he introduced his radical politics into
British poetry, the literary establishment had no difficulty in recognizing and
admiring him as a poet. That's not surprising: Auden's voicing, for all its audacity,
presented no deep affront to accepted discourse. Learned, intelligent, controlled,
it bore all the signs of the literary. It used symbols, drew on myths (especially of
pastoralism and of the apocalypse), observed (however sinuously) conventional
prosody, spoke of serious things, jiggered syntax, built to climaxes, marshalled its
own metaphors, thickened with intricate binaries of meaning, fairly hummed with
literary allusions. Its ironies could easily be forgiven.

Cooley pursues the ramifications of such examples, going on to attack
received 'definitions of the poetic' and also the canonical reputations
to which they lead (171, 178–9).[6] The distinction relates to Klein, for,
in this context, one can appreciate how Klein's versions of social exclusion can be misunderstood and misappropriated, and his (orthodox or
unorthodox) ironies accepted, because the *terms of his expression* were in
tune with the prevalent notion of *approvable poetic discourse.* It is possible
that, in his day, Klein was appreciated immediately not because of what
he was arguing but because (using the vocabulary he did) *he seemed
literary.* It is possible, too, that what he said seemed more radical than
it was.

Paradoxically, it was Anglo-Protestant Watson who challenged the prevailing norms more radically than the Jewish cultural outsider Klein did
– though it is possible of course to so equate 'vernacular' with 'literary'

4.1 *Lacrosse Grounds,* a line engraving by George T. Andrew (15 × 13.6 cm), taken
from an original by Henri Julien (likely of the Montreal lacrosse grounds, and of a
championship game between the Montreal club and the Montreal Shamrocks,
*c.*1881, not long after the new rules had been established by W.G. Beer and others,
and when the game, as a middle-class entertainment, was being advocated as
Canada's 'national sport'). Andrew's engraving (PAC #C83027) depicts a game
of lacrosse together with a stand full of spectators (mostly, but not all, male). In
the foreground, and thus given semiotic priority, lies an open book, with a lock
attached to it; the book (a rule-book?) in turn depicts a game of lacrosse with
(possibly) yet more spectators: a man standing and a boy seated. The positioning
of the book in the engraving thus introduces a tension between the trope of sport
and the trope of the book – that is, between the ostensible egalitarianism of the
'level playing field' and the apparent authority attributed to forms of (self?)
representation.

4.2 Takeo Tanabe's *The Land, 26/72* (acrylic on canvas, 1972, 28 × 40 in., collection Canada Council Art Bank; reproduced courtesy of Takeo Tanabe and the Canada Council Art Bank) dispenses with conventional techniques of perspective, using intersecting shapes and planes of colour to represent *the idea called 'land'* as a field of discourse.

SIX-SIDED SQUARE: ACTOPAN

Do tell me what the ordinary Mex
Madam, there is a plaza in Actopan
where ladies very usual beside most rigid hexagrams
of chili peppers squat this moment
and in Ottomíac gutturals not in Spanish lexicons
gossip while they scratch there in the open

    But arent there towns in Mexico more av—? Dear Madam,
    Actopan is a town more average than mean.
    You may approach it on a sound macadam,
    yet prone upon the plaza's cobbles will be seen
    a brace of ancients, since no edict has forbad them,
    under separate sarapes in a common mescal dream—

        *But someone has to work to make a—*Lady,
        those ladies work at selling hexametric chili,
        and all their husbands, where the zocalo is shady,
        routinely spin in silent willynilly
        lariats from cactus muscles; as they braid they
        hear their normal sons in crimson shorts go shrilly

bouncing an oval basketball about the square—
You mean that all the younger gener—?
I mean this is a saint's day, nothing rare,
a median saint, a medium celebration,
while pigeon-walking down the plaza stair
on tiny heels, from hexahemeric concentration

within the pyramidal church some architect
of Cortés built to tame her antecedents—
You mean that Mexico forgets her histor—? Madam, I suspect
that patterns more complex must have precedence:
she yearns to croon in Harlem dialect
while still her priest to Xipe prays for intercedence.

Actopans all are rounded with the ordinary
and sexed
much as they feel. *You mean—*
they are more hex-
agon and more extraordinary
than even you, dear lady, or than Egypt's queens.

1955

4.3 Earle Birney, 'Six-Sided Square: Actopan.' From *Collected Poems of Earle Birney* by Earle Birney. Used by permission of the Canadian Publishers, McClelland and Stewart, Toronto.

4.4 In Alex Colville's *Pacific* (acrylic polymer emulsion, 1967, 53.3 × 53.3 cm, private collection; © Alex Colville, courtesy of Drabinsky & Friedland Galleries), the meticulousness of 'magic realist' representation highlights the ironic tension between the connotations of the word *Pacific* and the icon of the gun. As the gun is a Browning 1935 (the standard weapon that Colville was issued during the war), the painting has been read as an autobiographical statement about an artist's relation with contemporary violence, particularly in a time and place (California in the 1960s) when weapons were readily accessible and violence common. The perspective (the view of landscape through a window) contrasts with the versions of domesticity and power suggested by plates 2.4 and 3.4, and with the Pachter parody (plate 4.8).

NEWFOUNDLAND
(for E. J. Pratt)

ne w f o u n *d* l a n d
n e w *fo un d* l a n d
ne w f o u n d *la n d*
n e w *fo un* d l a n d
n e w f o u n d *l a n d*
n e w *fo* u n d *l* a n *d*
n e w f o u n d l *a n d*
n e *w* f o u n d l *a n* d
n e *w* f o u n d *l a n d*
n e w *fo un d* l a n d
n e w f o u n d *l a* n d
n e w f o u n d l *a n d*
n e w f o *un* d l a n d
n e w *fo* u *n* d *l a n d*
n e *w* f o u *n* d *l a* n d
n e *w* f o *un* d l a n d
n *e* w f o u n d l a *n d*

St. John's, Newfoundland

184   Land Sliding

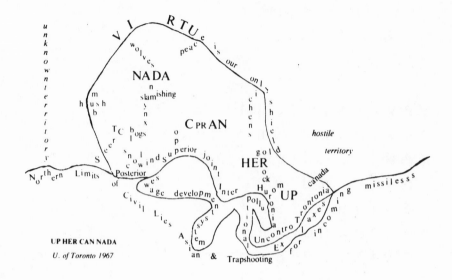

4.6 Earle Birney, 'up her can nada.' From *Collected Poems of Earle Birney* by Earle Birney. Used by permission of the Canadian Publishers, McClelland and Stewart, Toronto.

ka pass age alaska passage ALASKA PASSAGE alaska passage alas

our ship seems reefed
and only the land comes swimming past alaska pass

(one mark of few that men have scribbled
on this lucky palimpsest of ranges)

at times a shake-built shack exchanges
passive stares with Come & Gone
or eyeless waits with stoven side

to slide its bones in a green tide

age alaska passage alaska passage alaska passage alas-ka pass

Alberni Canal 1934/1947/1960

4.7 Earle Birney, 'Alaska Passage.' From *Collected Poems of Earle Birney* by Earle
Birney. Used by permission of the Canadian Publishers, McClelland and Stewart,
Toronto.

4.8 (*pp. 186–9*) Four examples of later twentieth-century reinterpretations of landscape: (*above*) Charles Pachter, *Queen and Bay* (acrylic on canvas panel, 1984, 40 × 50 cm, collection Ray Pladsen, Toronto; reproduced courtesy of Charles Pachter), deals parodically with the verbal language of Toronto street names and the visual language of the Group of Seven; (*right*) Harold Town, *The Great Divide* (oil and lucite on canvas, 1965, 228.6 × 152.4 cm. Art Gallery of Ontario, Toronto; reproduced courtesy of the Executors of the Estate of Harold Town), represents landscape symbolically, the painting lending itself to geographical, political, and sexual readings. (*continued on p. 189*)

4.8 (cont.) (*left*) Otto Rogers, *Black Trees and Cube Sky* (ink and watercolour on vellum paper, 1971, 74.5 × 54.2 cm; collection of the University of Saskatchewan, Saskatoon; photograph by Richelle D. Funk; reproduced courtesy of Otto D. Rogers), produces an elemental landscape out of abstract blocks of black, white, and vivid blue; and (*above*) Ivan Eyre, *Rainy River* (acrylic on canvas, 1978, 195.6 × 167.6 cm; reproduced courtesy of Ivan Eyre, private collection, Toronto; photo: Ernest Mayer, Winnipeg) uses an abstract (perhaps mechanical? perhaps animate?) foreground to draw into question some earlier conventions of landscape representation; what seems 'familiar' about the background (to the observing eye) is 'de-familiarized' by the foreground, and shown to be an artifice or illusion.

4.9 Edward Roper's *Prairie Flowers near Broadview, Assiniboia, N.W.T.* (watercolour and gouache over pencil on laid wove paper, 1887, 51.8 × 31.4 cm; reproduced courtesy of the National Archives of Canada, C-11036), provides a picturesque model (or 'reading') against which to read Robert Kroetsch's poetic 're-reading' of the 'gopher landscape.'

that the terms of critical estimation are skewed again. But Watson's technique was not merely – or consistently – 'vernacular'; he depended to a significant degree for his 'radical' social effect on the juxtaposition of different forms of discourse and on the irreverent disparity he introduced between tone and subject. (In his later poetry he continues his challenge to conventional format by shaping his texts as an unfamiliar aural or visual grid, a grid from which a single voice or multiple voices might break the text free, off the written page and into active performance.)* For approximate visual parallels to this process of challenging convention, one might look to what has happened to landscape in contemporary Canadian painting. Instead of the untravelled Group of Seven bush scenes, one finds the angular patchworks of Joyce Wieland, the abstract colour grids of Jack Bush, the symbolic aerial perspectives of Harold Town, and the apparently realistic landscapes of Ivan Eyre that are altered by the disparities between empirical perceptions and surreal frames. 'Unconventional' media have become familiar. And the Ontario parodies of Charles Pachter – for example, his painting entitled *Queen and Bay*, which punningly literalizes a Toronto street intersection: Queen Street, Bay Street – critique the way Canadian art-viewers have been trained to interpret landscape (the details of bay and sky) in Group of

---

* Constructing the page as a field, a 'paper landscape' on which the arrangement of words is both a visual design and a set of aural directions, is by no means solely a poetic phenomenon or only a contemporary one. Bentley, in 'Let the Blank Whiteness of the Page Be Snow,' comments on a variety of Canadian poets who, prior to the popularity of 'concrete poetry' in the 1970s, associated 'paysage' with 'page,' from Adam Hood Burwell to P.K. Page and A.M. Klein. Turning the idiom around, John Barrell (*Idea of Landscape* 48) also quotes from Hannah More's memoirs concerning a conversation she once had with the eighteenth-century garden designer Capability Brown: 'He told me he compared his art to literary composition. Now there, he said, pointing his finger, I make a comma, and there, pointing to another part (where an interruption is desirable to break the view) a parenthesis – now a full stop, and then I begin another subject.' Barrell goes on to declare: 'It goes without saying, I take it, that the pauses in a sentence, if they are not complexly dictated by the nature of its content, are dictated by it far more than is the content by those pauses' (49) – a position rejected by the writers who treat the page as a field for verbal design. Chambers ('Translation of Antiquity' 369) quotes the same passage from More, arguing that Brown's 'literary' language demonstrates that 'Virgil's *ingentia rura* [the vast countryside and the rural life, associated with labour and justice] and Pliny's *imitatio ruris* [defined as an irregular planting, in combination with ordered plantings, in such a way as to give as much pleasure as a symmetrical planting] had become the syntax of the English landscape, translated from their original texts into the vocabulary of grass and trees.'

Seven brushstrokes.* In Margaret Atwood's story 'Death by Landscape,' collected in *Wilderness Tips* (1991), relatedly, a character surrounds herself with Group of Seven prints, only to have her friend disappear, as the story progresses, into whatever reality it is that this version of landscape comes to represent to her[†] (see plate 4.8). Recurrently these painting strategies require viewers to see differently, to evaluate what they see differently, to re-evaluate how they see. The aural parallel, using vernacular speech, is to modify how a person hears.

---

* As early as 1954, Hugh Kenner had perceived a problem with Group of Seven practices, though in declaring his dissatisfaction he nevertheless reiterated the conventional assumptions about the cultural relation between history and landscape in Canada that these practices served: 'The Group of Seven ... sought their traditions where once upon a time life had demonstrably been lived, by the Indians, the trappers, and the *coureurs du bois* ... The ethos of the frontiersman was stark and taut but in its limited way genuine: to an inhuman environment it gave a vigorously human response. And the discovery of that ethos imparted a vitality to Canadian painting that no Canadian art has enjoyed before or since. The palette, hitherto daubed with the blue-green hazes of neo-Constable farmyards, vibrated with unaccustomed colours ... And with a shudder of triumph, amid horrified academic protest, the Canadian soul achieved its first incarnation.

   'Nobody ever appeared in those pictures, no human form except occasionally a tiny portaging figure hidden by his monstrous canoe. Nobody was needed. The Canadian Face was there right enough, rock of those rocks, bush of those bushes. And because they had so thoroughly succeeded in defining the popular soul up to the point to which it had so far defined itself, the idioms coined by the Group of Seven quickly became clichés to be lithographed on grocers' calendars and bankers' blotters. So that by now the painter who persists in employing these idioms is being no more a pioneer than the poet who traffics in thee's and thou's and red, red roses. He is employing a safely-dictionaried tongue in which he may still say many personal things; but he is not the man who will make the next advance.

   'The primary critical question in Canada today is whether it is yet safe to cut the umbilical cord to the wilderness: whether it is time to conduct a new raid on the inarticulate. The principle relating the fine arts with popular culture may roughly be stated in this way. Popular culture, first of all, never lags behind highbrow culture. Both are strictly contemporary. Popular culture is merely less defined and less articulate. The highbrow depends on the state of the public self-image for his material, and the public depends on the highbrow for its vocabulary. So it is impossible to get ahead of the public. To be "ahead of one's time" means simply to define one's time more sharply than it defines itself' (206–7).

† Adam Shoemaker uses Atwood's 'Death by Landscape' as one example of the way regionalism and the search for a national identity sometimes lead to a disjunction between 'created' national symbols and people's characteristic perceptions of the world in which they live. See also Jonathan Bordo on the link between the Group of Seven's representation of landscape as wilderness (epitomized by Tom Thomson's *The Jack Pine*) and the politics of representing Canada as vacant or uninhabited territory, open to exploitation, a theme extended by Scott Watson's essays.

(Re)form

Now, using the vernacular for reformative purposes has a long history in Canadian letters, and it's a process that sometimes touches directly the question of landscape. Consider Thomas Chandler Haliburton, Tory Loyalist, whose 1836 sequence of *Clockmaker* sketches tried to awaken the Maritime colonists to individual action, by introducing a crass, garrulous Yankee clock pedlar into their midst, one who gulled them and spurred them on in quite unequal measures. Sam Slick, the clockmaker, is full of himself and of Yankee values, values with which Haliburton does not always agree; but Haliburton does admire Sam's anecdotal and political energy, and he uses Sam's *voice* and Sam's *analogies* to pitch his own case for reform. The force of his satire derives in part from its double focus: it assumes a referential reality, a real world to which its words have application, but it behaves as though language were the real world, for speech is the plane on which action occurs. The sketch called 'Sayings and Doings in Cumberland,' for example, concerns itself with a particular instance of political lassitude and a general assumption about human näivety and the capacity of words to reveal it. It opens in an artificial northeastern U.S. dialect, full of flat *a*'s, pronounced *r*'s, syllepsis (*ax* instead of *ask*), and regional verb forms:

'I reckon,' said the Clockmaker, as we strolled through Amherst, 'you have read Hook's story of the boy that one day asked one of his father's guests who his next-door neighbour was, and when he heerd his name, asked him if he warn't a fool. 'No, my little feller,' said he, 'he bean't a fool, he is a most particular sensible man: but why did you ax that 'ere question?' 'Why,' said the little boy, 'mother said t'other day you were next door to a fool, and I wanted to know who lived next door to you.' His mother felt pretty ugly, I guess, when she heerd him run right slap on that 'ere breaker.

'Now these Cumberland folks have curious next-door neighbours, too; they are placed by their location right atwixt fire and water; they have New Brunswick politics on one side, and Nova Scotia politics on t'other side of them, and Bay Fundy and Bay Verte on t'other two sides; they are actilly in hot water; they are up to their cruppers in politics, and great hands for talking of House of Assembly political Unions, and what not. Like all folks who wade so deep, they can't always tell the natur' of the ford. Sometimes they strike their shins agin a snag of a rock; at other times, they go whap into a quicksand, and if they don't take special care they are apt to go souse over head and ears into deep water. I guess if they'd talk more of *rotation*, and less of *elections*, more of them 'ere *dykes*, and less of *banks*,

and attend more to top *dressing*, and less to *re-dressing*, it'd be better for 'em.'
(*Clockmaker* 60)

Built into this passage are the signs of contra-diction: to begin with, the
way the spoken word appears to construct a narrator, Sam, who exists as
some remove from the author. The artifice of this illusion becomes
apparent in a subsequent passage where author and character begin
aurally to coalesce:

'"St John must go ahead, at any rate; you *may*, if you choose, but you must exert
yourselves, I tell you. If a man has only one leg, and wants to walk, he must get
an artificial one. If you have no river, make a railroad, and that will supply its
place ... A bridge makes a town, a river makes a town; but a railroad is bridge,
river, thoroughfare, canal, all in one ..."' (78)

Even though these words are still attributed to Sam, the dialect *cadence*
disappears as Haliburton turns to the reader to make his point didactically, directly, *and in the formal idiom of his class and political intention.* The
vernacular, the 'people's voice,' is given over to instructive anecdote, but
however effective it is as shrewd satire, the vernacular voice (like the
perspective it carries) remains that of the Yankee, the outsider; when
moral and message are to be intoned, Haliburton's speech register shifts
to that of the already established authority. Clearly, Haliburton's conservative idea of social reform belongs to that notion of property that was
referred to in chapter 2 – that is, in championing the building of a
railroad, he is asserting the precedence of economics over political boundary (he is in Nova Scotia, and Saint John is in New Brunswick). The
point here is to recognize not only how much of his argument depends
on land-based metaphor (the *snag*, the *quicksand*, the *deep water*), but also
how much it rests in the political control over speech patterns, in the
seriousness of the wordplay: the punning on *dykes* and *banks*, for example,
or the aural association between *top dressing* and *re-dressing*, or even the
vernacular paradox that a phrase such as 'pretty ugly' contrives. Haliburton was drawing attention to the political force of juxtaposition and
disjuncture, using landscape analogies and speech differences to draw
attention to the institutional causes he personally espoused.
    What many writers of the later twentieth century have attempted to do
is to make such disjuncture their central concern, to turn it into a verbal
field, to make it the ground of associational (as opposed to linear) expression. One of the clearest assertions of this transformation occurs in

Gatien Lapointe's highly charged *Ode au Saint Laurent* (1963), where geography epitomizes Quebec – culturally as well as politically, the two becoming one[7] – and where earth ('la terre') becomes both body and speech ('la parole'):

> Ma langue est d'Amérique
> Je suis né de ce paysage
> J'ai pris souffle dans le limon du fleuve
> Je suis la terre et je suis la parole
> Le soleil se lève à la plante de mes pieds
> Le soleil s'endort sous ma tête
> Mes bras sont deux océans le long de mon corps
> Le monde entier vient frapper à mes flancs
>
> J'entends le monde battre dans mon sang (67)

The implied distinction between the particularities of speech ('parole') and the received conventions of language ('langue') emphasizes the disparity between movement and stasis, the future and the past, authenticity and authority, the body of speech that is the self and the enclosure of words that constitutes empire, political desire, and the status quo.

Writers such as Lapointe are, to revert to Dennis Cooley's argument once more, 'fighting out from under their inscriptions'; they are quarrelling with the received language, as Haliburton was not, though Haliburton was using the vernacular language to quarrel with the political authorities who held power, and with whom he politically (if not necessarily socially) disagreed. Lapointe is objecting to what he perceives as an *anglais* hegemony; Cooley is objecting to the 'hegemony of iambic pentameter,' which, he claims, simply reinforces the received pronunciation of British English. Such received pattern, Cooley goes on, emphasizes fastidious order, 'eliminates from "serious" literature, other than for comic purposes, the drastically elided and, in some of its versions, the emphatic voices of working people' (176).* This distinction between class-

---

* Wilson Harris makes a related point in *The Womb of Space*, when he argues that tourists usually see only what their language predisposes them to see, and that there is more than a superficial significance in the fact that Third World schoolchildren often write poems about snowfalls they have never seen. The notion of the tropics dissolving into a European landscape is both verbal and attitudinal/political, and Harris calls for an enfranchising re-understanding of the language of space.

based language and different *uses* of class-based language affects, as chapter 3 argues, the political cast of regionalism; it also explains why Haliburton, who used dialect form for his social ridicule and indirect political points, but standard speech for his overt lessons in political reform, remains a 'high culture' writer (as Klein does, experimenting within a clearly literary – and received – context) rather than a radical populist.

Field

In *RePlacing*, a 1980 anthology, Dennis Cooley punningly introduces what he hopes to achieve by collecting 'prairie poems' together in one place:

An answer to pentametre and conceit in our bare hands, handling the telltale words. A local pride-poetry in the commonplace, the cows and cars and tall tales in this place. As we say them. As we have our say ... Listening and listing, inventing the inventory. Placing ourselves/our poems in this place. In our name. Remembering the names of our places, remembering our place ... 'I remember' the names and voices, hear them now. Here now, try them, wondering. Earmarked for the Prairies. As if for the first time, putting things in place. (Quoted in *Vernacular Muse* 168)

Or, one might add, releasing the place-ness of things. Beyond Forget.

Cooley traces the contemporary Canadian interest in speech rhythm to the work of the American poet William Carlos Williams, but it is readily apparent that 'vernacular' does not equate exclusively with 'American,' nor with 'prairie'; it has to do with structure and sound, user and usage. In this respect Williams has influenced numerous other writers, in many other places beyond the prairies. Included among them in Canada are Raymond Souster, writing about Toronto streets; George Bowering, writing about the suburbia of self; Robert Kroetsch, composing autobiography 'by field'; Eli Mandel, composing memories of Saskatchewan, India, and South America. More indirectly, Williams has also touched the work of Daphne Marlatt, reinvesting movement in 'Steveston' (1974), or Dennis Cooley in *Fielding* (1983), or Smaro Kamboureli and Lola Lemire Tostevin, reconstructing language as a territory of dislocation in various poems published during the 1980s and 1990s. But basic to the writings of all these poets is a control over cadence. They all rely on the visual spacing of the poem on the page – on line-length, line-position, and background space – to control the speed of the reading (just as musical annotation visually designs rhythms and sequences of sound). Hence the page itself becomes a *field* or a *grid* or a set of *horizons*, on which play the movements of line and syllable and the durations of space and silence.[*]

Spatial 'landscape,'[8] that is, is now constituted by poetry, in the language of poetry, as well as by empirical reality; the old terms of linear cartography acquire another role. (It's more than metaphor, as is indicated by the rhetorical ambivalence of the title image in David Staines's 1986 collection of essays, *The 49th and Other Parallels*; the title's wit depends on the fact that, although the 49th parallel *of latitude* is an international boundary marker only in Western Canada, the term '49th parallel' is used all across Canada as a sign of national political differences – hence in Staines's context the word *parallel* comes to imply 'difference' perhaps more than 'linear likeness' or 'similarity.' Coterminously, the place produces a new meaning for language, and the language preserves some sense of the difference in place.) Composing poetry *by field* constitutes a geography of speech, as the 'Seed Catalogue' section of Robert Kroetsch's *Field Notes* (1981) exemplifies. How do you grow a garden? Kroetsch asks – as one of a cumulative set of variant questions: how do you grow a gardener, a lover, a poet, a shared past, a prairie town? The answer to the last of these questions lies in the form the poet's language takes: the town grows just as the poem does, in language, on the page; in speech, on the land. The poem's town is an image of history (for the town is not a single phenomenon but a series of temporary towns, each momentarily on the landscape). This image is as kinaesthetic as it is visual, occupying rhythm and tempo as well as position on the prairie page.

In one passage, for example, the poem, referring to a gopher, relies on the reader to recall this rodent's quick darting movements and its habit of sitting on its hind legs and surveying the territory before disappearing back into the ground (see plate 4.9). This part of the poem constructs the process of the gopher's movements (and the town's metaphoric mirroring of them) by arranging the tempo of the lines as a series of sharp, sudden (and just as suddenly arrested) twitches:

---

[*]   See also Lionel Kearns, who comments on the way the visual appearance of poetry communicates cadence; in what he calls 'stacked verse,' the setting of the lines of a poem direct the oral performance of it. Relatedly, John Metcalf, writing about style, argues that the placement and the right choice of punctuation marks helps readers to hear, even in conventional prose.

The gopher was the model.
Stand up straight:
telephone poles
grain elevators
church steeples.
Vanish, suddenly: the
gopher was the model.   (*Completed Field Notes* 38)

The rhythms tell of construction and disappearance: the repetitions tell
of the recurrence of the cycle of habitation as new generations of ordinary people attempt again to found a community.

These patterns lead into passages about growing a poet in such an
environment, such a new world 'garden' – passages which advise how to
read the poem and (in the process) how to read the speaking landscape
of a newgrown, still-in-the-making history:

This is a prairie road.
This road is the shortest distance
between nowhere and nowhere.
This road is a poem.

...

As for the poet himself
we can find no record
of his having traversed
the land / in either direction

no trace of his coming
or going / only a scarred
page, a spoor of wording
a reduction to mere black

and white / a pile of rabbit
turds that tells us
all spring long
where the track was

...

We silence words
by writing them down.

...

West is a winter place.
The palimpsest of prairie

under the quick erasure
of snow, invites a flight. (43, 47, 49)

Landscape, or history-in-place (i.e., not 'scenery' in this instance), is for
Kroetsch an act of observant participation, an enactment in local colloquial speech of the character of the life being lived in place. Language and
place thus equate: the poem is a road (a *way, traversed*); the prairie is a
palimpsest (written over and over, subject to erasure); the word is susceptible to silencing inside the authoritarian forms of some version of
other – but it is also capable of voicing, of creating continuity.

The challenge for the poet, embracing simultaneously the potentially
irreconcilable principles of continuity and discontinuity – of re-creation
without linearity – is to avoid containment-by-repetition. Writing out of
place, Kroetsch also writes within various contexts, one of which is
cultural. He responds to other writers, to visual design, to his own
reading; these writings (interpreting the term broadly) become part of
his field. In the case of 'Seed Catalogue,' the poem refers specifically to
rereading Sheila Watson's fiction and observing Hiroshige's *Tokaido*
series of Japanese prints: towards the close of the poem, these become
verbal 'seeds' in Kroetsch's new 'catalogue' of sources. Two forms of
'print' – Watson's Canadian novel *The Double Hook* and Hiroshige's
Japanese visual designs – turn into metaphors of a different kind of
cultivation, one connected to tradition (here both Christian and Shinto,
at a Western crossroads between the explorers' Europe and the Asia they
searched for) but actively free from a blind commitment to it. Thus his
own place becomes 'other,' the home-place alternative to whatever has
already been defined by those whose cultures seem at once more fixed
and more secure:

The double hook:
The home place.

The stations of the way:
the other garden

Flourishes.
Under absolute neglect. (45–6)

Many other contemporary writers have also enquired into the otherness of self, though not always with the same degree of celebration that Kroetsch brings to the art of the margin. Among them are Al Purdy, Alice Munro, Basil Johnston, Rudy Wiebe, John Newlove, Beatrice Culleton, Rohinton Mistry, Claire Harris, Joy Kogawa, Lucy Ng, and Jim Wong-Chu. Repeatedly, the character of marginality is constructed through a process of 'rereading' the textual landscapes of other writers, especially those with history or lineage on their side, or those already established in some international canon. For example, Culleton and Newlove (in *April Raintree* and 'The Pride,' respectively) have both tried to reach past the terms of official history – the version of Canada that emphasizes the 'civilizing' power of European 'occupation' – to question why conventional literary metaphor designs the Native peoples as an absence in the country, a dying race, the past rather than the future. But the differing perspectives and language of these two writers declare their different backgrounds and literary intentions. Where Newlove writes formally, out of a decent desire for cross-cultural communication in the present,[9] Culleton writes in the vernacular, out of the personal experience of racial and social prejudice. Newlove tries to celebrate what might come from the past, Culleton to reform the present by resisting the past, and the two positions do not yet meet.

The poems of Purdy and the stories of Munro, by contrast, deal more directly with the lineage of European settlement, especially in Ontario – yet here the European past does not constrain either writer to avoid the Canadian vernacular. Both writers use colloquial rhythms effectively, in part to emphasize that inertia and nostalgia, whatever appeal they might hold for individual people or for whole communities, do not stop time and therefore do not keep social change from happening. By way of example, Munro's 'Chaddeleys and Flemings' (its two parts first published separately, in 1978 and 1979, in slightly different form) and Purdy's 'The Country North of Belleville' (from *The Cariboo Horses*, 1965) both deal with the past, both deal with time, and both rely on repetitions and silences as a way of characterizing the effects of change on the lives of communities and individuals. In Munro's story, set in western Ontario, the repetitions tell of annual cycles of work and of generational cycles of inheritance and departure; the silences tell of absences and oppositions, dislocation and the active process of forgetting, of making marginal. A different marginality informs the empirical and metaphorical Country North of Belleville that Purdy's poem alludes to; this country is, of course, the territory that Mrs Moodie could never quite control, the country that Atwood's Moodie wanders in anew, and the generational ghosts that occupy Purdy's poem – another region in time, perhaps – are thus rooted in Canadian literary practice as well as in the Ontario landscape. But just as Kroetsch discovers part of himself through rereading Watson, so Purdy discovers self by rooting speech and culture in place, *in the reading of place*; intrinsically, through the *action* of his own poem, he also tells how the Old World's preconceptions gradually fade as the dominant working measure of aesthetic propriety.

But any new practice acquires the patina of propriety to the degree that it becomes conventional; so with the presumed virtue of 'open form' or 'ordinary' speech. The need to avoid solipsism (a different kind of challenge in this context) is an issue which the opening of George Bowering's novel *Burning Water* (1980) directly addresses. The self, says the text, shapes everything. And the 'George' who is the narrator declares his identity with geography and history – that is, with both George Vancouver and King George the Third. The narrative parody in Bowering's book undermines this claim just as it undermines the historical and geographical 'claims' through which European explorers and politicians declared authority over Canada. This parody also undermines a number of the cultural claims (for example, the virtue of referentiality or the pre-eminence of realism) that various literary schools have used to declare their own importance. But how does a reader judge this literary practice: sympathetically (as cleverness, or play)? or unsympathetically (as pretension)? or is there some other way?

That the novel's title is an oxymoron should be advance warning about this text; it sees history and autobiography as arbitrary systems, accidents of occasion, without any direct or unquestionable claim on reality or 'truth.' The prose that results from this premise (or pre-emptive conclusion) is at once serious about art and comic in its tonal intent; the narrator claims that his subject (George Vancouver, George the Third, George the Self) is narrative:

So I began to plan a novel, about us, about the strange fancy that history is given and the strange fact that history is taken. Without a storyteller, George Vancouver is just another dead sailor.

How could I begin to tell such a story? I asked myself. Books do have beginnings, but how arbitrary they can be. In 1792, for instance, some English ships appeared out of the probable fog off the west coast of North America, where Burrard Inlet is now, but in the late sixties of the twentieth century I was staring at the sea from Trieste and composing verse about those European mariners visiting the western claims of British North America. ('prologue')

The 'probable fog' is an apt medium for hypothesis, and useful to remember when hypotheses (as they often do) take on the trappings of unassailable truth. Challenging the rigidities of cultural 'origin,' Bowering's text resists conventional (or predetermined) paradigms of heroism, culture, and civilization, and it rewrites the fictions of history as historical fictions. A metatext, it provides a map of its own reading, and by analogy suggests that Canadian society is another metatext, one which invites the 'reader' to participate actively in the process of constructive reinterpretation. Perhaps one sign of this activity happening is that some readers of Bowering's text have questioned the process that permits his 'I' to become their 'we' in the first place: isn't it (despite the literary parody) another version of imperial claiming? they ask. Doesn't the construction of Native figures in the text, for example, continue to marginalize Natives, and therefore doesn't the text reiterate the very social paradigms it purports to deconstruct? One reply takes the form of another question: Doesn't this protest continue to assume that literary *representation* is equivalent to social *reality*? To which there is a further response: But if you belong to the social group that is in reality being marginalized, how can you not see a conventional representation as an expression of the attitudes that are perpetuating the existing margins – and in any event, isn't that what colonial–imperial debates are all about, including the one that leads Bowering to parody the heroic narratives of the age of sail? Power and permission are at issue: who holds the power? who gives permission? and what are the consequences and processes of change?

Site

In some ways it would be convenient to end at this juncture, with language reconstituting self as self reclaims language. But clearly, any claim upon self, however mobile the landscape, creates new margins even if (or as) it erases old ones. Gender, race, multiculturalism, class, belief: other limits to the myths of possession always thrust language into flux again. Consider the instance of Eli Mandel. A Jew from Saskatchewan who in his later years lived and wrote in urban Toronto, Mandel was not unaware of region and nation; much of his writing – as in *Out of Place* (1977) – is concerned with reconceiving the meaning of 'Estevan, Saskatchewan' (a national/regional home place), and at the same time with questioning the kind of nationalism that led to the Holocaust, and consequently to destruction, violence, and exile. Yet Mandel was also aware of the degree to which places and ideas, constructed in words, are extensions of the 'other' landscapes of the mind: *Auschwitz* and *Estevan* are both 'beyond Toronto' if not 'beyond forget.' What matters is the poet's awareness of Otherness, the world of not-self. But because the Other is still always restrained and limited by the names that the self imposes upon it, 'civilization' confronts 'wilderness' once more. 'My country is not a country / but winter,' writes Mandel in 'Envoi' (*Stony Plain* 96), translating the refrain from Gilles Vigneault's popular song 'Mon pays, ce n'est pas un pays, c'est l'hiver' (*Vieux mots* 13) – and the old familiar metaphor of a land of ice and snow comes back again into Canadian literature. This time, however, the topocentric metaphor functions no longer to *contain* a nation, but rather to challenge the authority of what has come to be known as 'disinformation' (inaccurate information promulgated as truth). As Dennis Cooley writes, the shapes of speech redefine the value of the meaning that readers attach to the shapes of authority.

In the 1980s, that is, 'national*ism*' came to be seen as a 'problem,' as an emotional precursor to imperial claim (which could be couched in political or in other terms: tribal, ethnic, gender-bound) and hence a 'site' of some form of 'violence.' Mandel's poem 'The Madwomen of the Plaza de Mayo' set in Buenos Aires at the time of Argentina's authoritarian autocratic Generals, provides an example; it conceptualizes 'a soldier' as 'a man who is not a man, / A fence, a spike' (*Life Sentence* 52). In other words, when authority comes to be dehumanized, it declares (even insists on) hurtful boundaries, because such boundaries serve the authority in place: they scapegoat others, create victims, and concoct the illusion that such actions and boundaries are normal. In the Argentina of the Generals, the system achieves this end, temporarily, by proclaiming the 'others' to be 'mad'; it is the mothers of the 'desaparecidos' (the disappeared ones, the Generals' political victims), mothers who actively and silently protest against the government, in a public city square, who are the so-called madwomen of Mandel's title. The authoritarian system thus skews the scales of normality and reason: for who is mad here, and who in such a world is permitted to be sane? Mandel's poem resists both the ease and the paralysis of silent acquiescence. The poem's rhetorical gaps, its resistant political silences, argue for the continuity of the community that violent forms of national*ism* (not therefore to be confused with nation*hood*) recurrently attempt to organize and control.

Such violence is not alien to Canada (as Timothy Findley's and Margaret Atwood's fictions, for example – *The Wars, Headhunter, The Handmaid's Tale* – make clear). Hence Mandel's poem also argues that whatever land people live in is larger than property, larger than region, larger than a name on a map ('Canada,' 'Buenos Aires'), and larger than the idea of place in a theory of closed nationalism. Global military threats, global technologies, and global ecological damage affect everyone. So when we read landscape, we read another text; our family finally is a human family, and our land the earth we severally share.

While these are nice-sounding words, and even a laudable aspiration, they nevertheless do not take into account the force of custom, the idiosyncrasies of human behaviour, the competitive will to power that draws many people into war (even in the name of love), or the ease with which a dominant culture generalizes its own ambition into a normative pattern for the world. Hence while contemporary writing has (1) repeatedly been a site of social resistance, it has also (2) repeatedly been a site for the expression of an artificial cultural uniformity; and neither of these critical generalizations in isolation will adequately convey the temper of the 1980s and 1990s.

In Canadian writing, the spirit of resistance frequently shows up in works that are set abroad – cultural nationalism proving not to be a barrier against the technologies of travel, mass media, and instantaneous electronic communication. At one extreme are the numerous examples of social abuses in other countries, that come in for moral critique from temporary tourists and find their way into poetry and prose. Of another order entirely are the aesthetic experiences of place and politics, as in the work of P.K. Page. Lorraine M. York, writing about Page's painting, poetry, and autobiographical writings, for example, explains how Page 'arranges her artistic career in terms of travel' ('Home Thoughts' 325). A place called 'Canada' thus functions as a 'place of retrospective,' whereas places called 'Brazil' and 'Mexico' function as aesthetic equivalents of 'day' and 'night.' With a lowercase 'b,' moreover, a place called 'brazil' is transformed from a mappable country into a condition of sensitivity – Page herself wonders if this 'brazil' might have happened anywhere. For her, it constitutes a process of transformation, one that requires the artist to reconsider the conventions of artistry and their relation to insight and observation. The terms of place here are aesthetic; the conditions and conventions of creativity, however, are both psychological and political.

Works by writers such as Rohinton Mistry, Claire Harris, and Lucy Ng make clear that social discrimination is not merely a fact of life *elsewhere*, but also a condition of some people's experience *inside Canada*. In their writings, it is *Canada-as-the-'other'-place* that comes in for critique, and *Canada-as-home* that becomes the site of social resistance. For these writers, the experience of Canada-as-other stems from their own immigrant experience or that of their family, from their observation of cultural discrimination in action, and from their recognition of viable cultural alternatives. 'Swimming Lessons,' the final story in Mistry's *Tales from Firozsha Baag* (1987), for example, connects the isolating experiences of a young male Parsi immigrant in Toronto with the numerous kinds of exclusion (the bullying related to class and sexuality, and to economics and ethnicity) that had been practised in the Bombay of his youth. The spatial metaphors (travel, emigration, swimming distances, home) insist that place is a process, a site of change. And so is the literary page. In *Drawing Down a Daughter* (1992), relatedly, a poem addressed to a fictional daughter, Trinidad-born Claire Harris's narrator insists on the reality of spatial and cultural differences, and relates them to gender politics:

> Girlchild   i wish you something to be passionate
> about   someone to be passionate with   a father for instance
> natural opponent of any right thinking girl
>
> and where the hell is yours
>
> i'm telling you   Girl   you have to watch men
> you leave the islands to come to Canada
> you meet the man in Canada
> he's born in Canada   his grandfather's born in Canada
> you marry him in Canada
> now he wants to live in the islands! (23)

The vernacular here expresses Trinidad rhythms, but Trinidad rhythms *in dislocation*: the idiom insists on a politics of refusal as well as a politics of adaptation. Implicitly, the poem asks what the 'national language' of Canada is, at a time when the cultural vocabulary is in flux. Who is a natural citizen, and who is 'naturalized'? And is there *a place* for someone new?*

Lucy Ng handles idiom in a markedly different way from Harris (less oral and anecdotal, more imagistic). In a suite called 'The Sullen Shapes of Poems,' she writes about her parents' immigration to Canada and about the character of her own inheritance, growing up not as an immigrant, but as the child of immigrants, in a double place and culture:

> It must have been a relief after Hong Kong and
> Trinidad (mere islands) to find yourself in the
> wide expanse called Canada: British Columbia,
> thick fir trees, mountains solid as the back of
> your hand. You could buy a house, a piece of
> land, plant yourself firmly in the North American
> soil. Sometimes you even forgot this was the
> second mainland you called home. (161)

Historically and sociologically, this transition was less easy than it sounds.

---

* The entire *canadas* issue of *semiotext(e)* deals with border conditions, hence with differences between open and covert social expression. Jody Berland comments on the spatial ramifications of meteorological practice by alluding to the recurrence of the landscape trope in Canada – finding it to have been a historically effective means of aestheticizing and confirming *as natural* a 'white' (not only 'snow-bound') and otherwise illogical identity (29). This 'illogicality' is read here as the consequence of not devising national or cultural boundaries in accordance with topography, but there is no intrinsic reason why topography should be the prime determiner of social or cultural organization. 'Ethnic difference' – a marker of one such potential cultural boundary, designating both inclusion and exclusion – is, of course, also a problematic term. Asserting 'difference' can sometimes exclude people generally (or artists in particular) from mainstream recognition; conversely, it can also function as a strategy to validate an otherwise insecure identity – an identity often *made insecure* by mainstream social practice – or to assert the intrinsic value of a specific group or belief or custom or expression that varies from the mainstream. Clearly, the 'mainstream' (another problematic term) can itself change, blending with, without co-opting or totally assimilating, the 'other.' In the very process of mainstream acceptance, however, the category 'ethnic difference' is also likely rewritten, for the fact (especially the fact of bilateral) 'acceptance' removes the essential oppositionality on which any politics of 'necessary difference' relies. But if 'acceptance' erases, rather than comes to terms with, the paradigms of difference, then the cultural mainstream has not yet recognized that, in social practice, 'acknowledgment' and 'accepting equivalence in value' are not the same. See also Crosby, on the 'construction of the imaginary Indian.'

In the poem, words such as *wide, solid, house, land,* and *plant firmly* suggest
a smooth adaptation and ready accommodation, but Asian immigrants to
Canada did not find a uniform welcome among either European or First
Nations communities (as Gabrielle Roy's story 'Where Will You Go, Sam
Lee Wong?' and Lee Maracle's story 'Yin Chin' both testify). When, in
Ng's text, the 'solid' words run up against the qualification 'Sometimes,'
the poem reveals elliptically the competing forces of tradition and discrimination.* The 'sullen shape of poems' becomes apparent in the
language and in the space created by the disrupted sequence. And as
place (a geography of two 'homes') becomes text, so text becomes place
(a site of disjuncture, a site for critique):

> Chinese cafe, grocery, laundry – skipping rope
> rhymes – you want something different for me.
> Poet? you say. What's that? You recall Li Po
> drunk under the white moon, chasing her cold
> reflection in the river. His body skimming and
> sinking, the blue and white robes twisting
> brushstroke of calligraphy on water,
>
> You gave me these: a river, a boat,
> a bridge. The sullen shapes of poems. (168)

Acts of resistance do not have to be loud to be effective or heard; they
have only to insist, as this poem does, on options.†

---

* Relatedly, Audrey Kobayashi argues that English-language poetry among the *Nisei* and
Sansei (second- and third-generation Japanese Canadians), particularly that of
Takeo Nakano, recurrently adopts conventional Japanese vernacular forms (haiku,
tanka) to construct the moral landscape associated with Japan, in order that the Canadian landscape (a site of internment during the Second World War, which is the
explicit social subject of much contemporary Japanese Canadian writing) might in
turn be invested with moral properties.
† Various art forms can express plural social options. Cf. the effect of artist Paul
Wong's 1992 autobiographical video presentation called *Chinaman's Peak: Walking the
Mountain*. The title itself constructs the dual heritage Wong wants to recognize and
record; it refers both to a particular Canadian landscape and to a particular Chinese
custom. The video thus *rereads* the conventional map of the Rocky Mountains against
a traditional Chinese ritual, the ritual of honouring ancestors called 'Walking the
Mountain' (in Mandarin: *guo-shan*). The geographical name 'Chinaman's Peak,' a
mountain near Banff, alludes to the Chinese workers who constructed the Canadian
Pacific Railway through Kicking Horse Pass. Among other things, this 'rereading'

But options can sometimes be illusory, and illusions of difference (or similarity) can be marketed, for whatever reason, sometimes converting a radical position (at any point on a political spectrum) into a conventional fashion. 'Art' can be co-opted for advertising, for example. Film can manipulate 'real' settings into real facsimiles, as when movies and TV series filmed in Vancouver (e.g., *The X-Files, Sirens, The Accused, The Never Ending Story, Rumble in the Bronx, Jumanji, Stakeout*) or Toronto (e.g., *Due South, The Freshman, The Kidnapping of the President, Little Man Tate, Moonstruck, To Die For*) use scenes in these cities to 'represent' Seattle, New York, Pittsburgh, Washington, and numerous other places – even fictional ones. And 'language' can be co-opted as a status marker. Signs of commercial uniformity show up in product names, mass-media programming, formula fiction, publishers' sense of 'safe' market products, and numerous other venues; in the world described by ad copy, 'landmark' accomplishments are apparently the norm, not the exception.

That this uniformity affects language, and specifically the language that is used to characterize land, is perhaps most obvious in the character of urban change between the 1950s and the 1990s and the new nomenclature of suburban real estate. This change is, in part, the subject of George Bowering's meditation on young poets' ambitions and older poets' memories, 'The Great Grandchildren of Bill Bissett's Mice,' in *Urban Snow* (1992). The poem alludes to the Vancouver of 1958, when Bowering, Lionel Kearns, Fred Wah, Frank Davey, Gladys Hindmarch, Red Lane, Bill Bissett, Jamie Reid, and several others were arriving in town, seeking to be writers 'who mattered,' looking (as the poem puts it) for 'the water ... / This wet dark Vancouver looked / like the latest thing. It was mysterious and open, this / waterfront. It was not far from Hamburg and Burma. / It was instructive. // (It was romantic.)' (98–9).

> Daphne Marlatt was here as a girl. She saw them coming;
> They came from small towns and no towns in the in-
> terior from the north and the island.
>
> They came with their solitary dreams, looking for a
> page to write something entirely new on.

---

reinserts the Chinese railway workers into an honourable place in Canadian history; it also contrasts with the early CPR advertising brochures which saw the Rockies only in relation to Swiss pictoriality and the philosophic sublime. See also Heesok Chang.

But I came from the British Empire. I was a girl in
Conrad country. I was born into colonial British, a
language my mother gave me and tried to keep
herself, here, next to the deep trees, the dark
between the trees and the hearts of these people.

I grew up wanting to learn the language of this place.   (99–100)

'We decided,' he adds, 'to write a city and call it Vancouver,' focusing on
'Yew Street' in 'Kits':

All the streets named after trees would plunge steep
into Kitsilano's tidy bay. Pine Street. Chestnut. Maple.
Yew trees are for poets in graveyards; we all know
that. All these tree streets are lined with expensive
condos now. Two decades ago they offered cheap
housing and warehousing for students and out of
work marijuana boys and girls. How ignorant
Vancouver was, how innocent.

Nowadays how can you avoid a voice, says
You got water. You got mountain views. You got
valuable real estate. (101–2)

The poem goes on somewhat plaintively to try to recapture the energy of
youth, to say that the 1958 desire for a local voice was 'a good idea after
all' (111), especially in view of the changes in fashion and value that at
once affect poetry and property, language and land,[10] shaping the 'land-
office' sensibility in yet another guise.

What Bowering's poem implicitly recognizes, and commercial advertising openly articulates, is the way the 1990s enterprise of land sales fuses
town planning with social status. For example, the real estate pages of the
Saturday, 3 October 1992, issue of the Vancouver *Sun* newspaper provide
these instances of new housing developments advertising their names and
seeking purchasers and tenants: Queen Anne Green, Regent's Gate, St
James House, Orchard Hill, Foxborough Hills, Parkgate, Murrayville
Glen, Tiffany Ridge, Blossom Park, Belmont Ridge, Westwood Place,
Forest Edge, Highpoint Gardens, Summit Pointe, Meadow View, Vista
Ridge, and Hyland Grove (which claims 'It's the location' [C16], presum-
ably echoing the old real estate adage that 'Location Is Everything').

While these names all draw directly on land terminology, there is little about any of them that suggests (as 'Kitsilano,' 'Port Moody,' and 'Coquitlam' do) historical or geographical specificity (though even they displaced the Squamish and Musqueam words that once named sites in the vicinity of 'Vancouver': *Whoi-Whoi*, for example, or *Ulksen*, or *Snauq*). The names of the new housing developments project instead the aura of being computer-generated for their semiotic value, for the resonance of power and position that they carry with them from a given social hierarchy. Paradoxically, for the generation of the 1990s – who sometimes claim to be committed to the future, ecological internationalism, and political 'correctness' – such terms promise a guaranteed lifestyle by reinscribing the presumed status and elegance of Englishness (or, in the case of 'Pointe,' an artificial Frenchness): humourlessly, they draw on the discourse of old empires – which is precisely the language that Bowering's generation, celebrating in the vernacular the 'Kitsilano' waterfront, was attempting to free itself from.

Related examples show up in some paradigms of immigrant settlement in other Vancouver suburbs: the Fraser River delta region, for example, which is now called the city of Richmond. (The name 'Richmond,' of course, echoes the name of the 2,000-acre deer park near London, England, that was established by King Charles I; and 'Fraser' is named after the Scots explorer and river navigator Simon Fraser; but Richmond was once called 'Lulu Island,' named in 1862 by Colonel Moody, after Miss Lulu Sweet, an actress in the first touring company to visit BC, before which it was the site of several camps used by Halkomelem-speaking peoples).* This

---

* See G.P.V. and Helen Akrigg, and Bruce Macdonald. 'Richmond' is not named immediately after its English namesake, but after 'Richmond Farm,' established in the nineteenth century by an Australian immigrant to Canada, who named it after a favourite place in Australia, which in turn was named after the English park. Cf. J.M. Bumsted on Toronto suburban development in the postwar years. Fritz Steele also makes the point that the 'localization' of suburb names is disappearing as generic names come into use in certain schools of urban planning; the point is reiterated in other contexts by Thomas J. Schlereth; by Caroline Mills, esp. in a section called 'We're Selling a Lifestyle'; and by Allan Pred, who in *Lost Words and Lost Worlds* writes of the way that *official names* place under erasure what he calls 'popular geography' (which exists in the vocabulary that local residents have for local places). Scott Watson writes of a separate but related practice when he speaks of the 'urban semiotic' of such visual artifacts as Jeff Wall's *Landscape Manual* of the 1970s, which deliberately tried to record local ordinariness as unspectacular, and hence to counter pictorializing conventions ('Defeatured Landscape'); see also Seamon, on the tensions that derive from an art of postmodern politics.

area attracted in 1992 a high proportion of home-buyers who had recently immigrated from Hong Kong. One reason adduced for this tendency is that the district name translates appealingly into Cantonese (*fu-gwai-men* = 'gateway to riches'),* perhaps indirectly reiterating the traditional Cantonese name for Canada (adapted from the term developed on the California gold fields), 'Gold Mountain' (*gumshan*). Each wave of new immigrants, apparently, seeks security in the familiar terms of the old culture, and each new generation of aspiring landowners seeks validation (and invisibility?)¹¹ by accepting the values coded semiotically in the status quo. How then, can one say that literature connects, either symbolically or mimetically, with 'real life' – and read literature as a site of demurral – if the real people who constitute the society are so clearly embracing the blandness of market generalities? It is the absolute that is misleading here. Clearly literature is not just a site of social critique; it is also a site of reconfirming the status quo, a practice which perhaps has most attraction for those who aspire to current forms of power (or elegance, or fashion); and it is a site in which 'new' and 'old' traditions perennially interact, often productively, as in the society itself.

* Consultation with Richmond real estate sales offices, February 1993. An alternative reading (and likely a folk etymology) is suggested by Daphne Bramham, reporting for the Vancouver *Sun*: 'The word Richmond sounds like rich-man, which some Chinese believe makes it a lucky place. And *feng shui* experts – who practise the art of determining whether a location will bring luck or at least no ill fortune – say Richmond's location is lucky because on a map it appears to be placed at the mouth of a dragon's head' (9 March 1993, A1, no sources named). The mention of *feng shui*, however (a South China system of geomancy, on which see Walters), is a useful reminder that the European 'landscape' terminology that has been prevalent in discussions of Canada (*prospect, wilderness, picturesque, sublime*) is not the only terminology that can be used. Indeed, much new housing in Vancouver and elsewhere in Canada in the 1990s is being built with the principles of *feng shui* in mind. Within the terms of this system, the world is read by its shape as distinct from its component substance. The five elemental 'shapes' are called *earth* (which refers to flat-topped structures, including flat roofs, not simply to things made from earth, such as plateaus), *metal* (referring to rounded, dome-shaped structures, the word *metal* coming from an association with the shape of coins), *fire* (pointed structures, such as spires), *wood* (columnar, pillar-shaped structures, not just those made of wood), and *water* (complex structures and undulating landscapes, those that have no shape but can take on any shape). The 'dragon' is one of four beasts (the others are bird, tiger, and tortoise) that are, respectively, associated with directions (east, south, west, north), movement (right, backwards, left, forwards), and seasons (spring, summer, autumn, winter) for structures that are south-facing. The effort of *feng shui* masters is to ensure that the elements are harmoniously arranged so as to ensure prosperity and good fortune for those who dwell in such structures and in the neighbourhood of land-shapes that resemble them.

Land Sliding

This chapter has argued that literature in Canada has recurrently used a 'land' discourse while probing a contrast between received language and vernacular language, and that this contrast in turn articulates a shifting contact line between groups that hold and assert power and those that don't but want to. Race, religion, gender, region, sexuality, property possession, profit, ecological conservatism: each of these concerns uses slightly different terms of social division, or promises slightly different forms of reconciliation. The voices, that is, of a resistant and oppositional art in Canada characteristically use the vernacular – 'the people's speech' – but the aim of such resistance is more often to partake in power than to erase power itself. The imperial naming words do not disappear, nor does the principle of power (and therefore of distinction) that these words represent. In a society, moreover, in which every generation has grown up and renewed itself through immigration, each wave of new people (and new writers) has sought to participate in this trans-formational process, thus continuing through time the dialogue between two forms of language. To ask who the new people are, at any time, is to clarify what has been taken as 'mainstream' and 'normative,' and to ask what the new resistance is and where its voices are coming from.

At any given time, consequently, one might argue that an 'indigenous' English language is in existence in Canada, and that it can be perceived in anglophone Canadian literature; but it does not follow that those with social and cultural power will necessarily choose to use a popular dis-course, nor that (even if they do use it, in speech, say) they will use it as an arbiter of cultural value, nor that (among those who do use the ver-nacular as a measure of worth) the speech of the middle class, the speech of the working class, and the '*literary* vernacular' will be identical or precisely coincide. Mrs Moodie's diction, for instance, was once consid-ered 'high art.' In her revisions of the periodical sketches that she collect-ed as *Roughing It in the Bush*, she elevated the diction of a number of vernacular passages,[12] and reinforced a number of racial stereotypes (leaving, for example, some 'comic' passages in 'dialect'), in order to solidify her appeal to the then-current arbiters of taste. Ironically her version of the tasteful (shaped in England before she emigrated) had been overtaken in England by social change and new styles by the time she expressed it in print some years after her arrival in Canada; her style would also be superseded in Canada when the language of, for example, newspaper reportage became more of a cultural norm than the language of 'polite society' fiction and Established Church rhetoric. Discourse also changes whenever oppositional values, such as those articulated through urban slang and gender correctness, are severally given value. Such changes do not necessarily mean a decline in sophistication, or in the capacity of ordinary people to appreciate abstract ideas, or in the willingness of literature to express them. (For one thing, such a generalization would conveniently ignore the earthiness of many works accepted as literary classics, from Ovid and Algonquin tales to Shakespeare and Swift; for another, it would ignore the revolutions represented by the work of Burns, Wordsworth, and – in Canada – Alexander McLachlan, which in their day, however formal they might sound by the 1990s, espoused *as literary* the language of ordinary people.) Nor does linguistic change necessarily guarantee greater sophistication. It likely does mean, however, that the nature of sophistication is itself always in the process of being redefined, at least in part to give value to the attitudes and aspirations that are expressed in common speech.

In the present, as in any other time, these attitudes are susceptible to manipulation – which may be what the marketing of suburban housing-estate names intends, and may (in a different register) be what literary histories, canonizing one work or author and excluding another, repeatedly attempt. It is all very well to observe that Birney, Bowering, and Kroetsch, say, have used vernacular oppositional techniques in their poetry and prose in order to question the received values, the unexamined priorities, of a canonical Canadian Literature. But how accessible is their work to the people for whom (in some sense at least) they implicitly claim to write? for whose values they declare themselves to be spokesmen? Why, if the Canadian people can severally hear their own voices in the oppositional literature of Marlatt and Kroetsch and Harris, are they collectively persuaded by the voices of other people – by the American voices of the mass media (TV sitcom, fundamentalist rhetoric, popular song: some of this language, of course, crafted by Canadian writers) or by the Establishment voices of the advertising industry?

One answer would be that the transnational voices of media and industry *are* the true voices of the contemporary working classes. This answer, cynical and passive, is simplistic. A second answer would observe that, for the majority of Canadians, the page is becoming obsolete as a site of social resistance, and that the new sites are aural and visual, in the market itself or on tape and disc and computer screen. This answer is naïve: it accepts print and screen as mutually exclusive rather than as complementary media; the Internet has already come to be troped in the language of land, as an 'information superhighway,' and the computer screen, like the page before it, can after all be printed out both in 'portrait' and 'landscape' formats. A third answer would fasten on the processes of rhetorical persuasion, noting that mass appeals to 'ordinary discourse' construct markets *and have themselves also been marketed* – honed by market research for the Empire of Commerce – hence they can in turn be read as the latest medium of imperial discourse rather than as the unmediated voice of common desire that they so earnestly pretend. This answer does not mean that no answer is possible. It suggests, rather, that a belief in *fixed* answers is likely 'mis*placed*'; and that human behaviour, in Canada as elsewhere, changes, resisting categorical enclosure; and that no uniform set of social or literary values will satisfy all citizens or all readers, just as no rigid hierarchy of values will work always, for all people, in all places. The more immediate challenge for most people might well be to find ways of negotiating competing desires – but with what results, to what end? An open society? A national language? An open society is one in which people enjoy several concurrent options – all of them fulfilling, none of them detrimental to others – and where they have the liberty and opportunity to choose among them: but such 'ideal aspirations' have a way of turning into fixed systems with rigid margins, systems sometimes as dangerous as they can be powerful. And a 'national language' might well be one of the notions that inhibits freedom rather than guarantees it; for words can also be dangerous and powerful. One of the reasons, of course, that establishments find words powerful is that they can be used to confirm existing authority – and one of the reasons they find words dangerous is that literature sometimes gives alternative aspirations an effective voice.

Out of the cadence of their own experience – the rhythms of nature, community, and human expression – all people construct the priorities that give their lives value. The value system they decide on, the 'language' they choose to speak, is intrinsically committed to evaluative distinctions; it can never be wholly free from bias and the past. But it is not exempt from change. Hence to *read the land* in Canada is not simply to observe patterns of ownership and exploitation, or divisions of measurement and authority, or imported paradigms of garden and wilderness, but also to listen to the succession of ways by which the society has moved 'beyond forget' and attempted to speak its own values. Reading the 'land sliding,' in consequence, reveals more than a geography of emptiness, power, and commercial productivity. It reveals the sites of choice and change. And these in turn reveal the presence of value in the strategies of connection that a people who call themselves 'Canadian' devise to live by, and the presence of value in the metaphoric landscapes – the strategies of communication – that their artists, listening to experience, design.

Notes

Land-Forms: An Introduction

1 Lefebvre has directly influenced most of the spatial theorists who have published since. Among them are such writers as Ian Buchanan, who emphasizes Lefebvre's insistence on the connection between space and historical practice; Pierre Bourdieu, who in part argues the connection between social space and the genesis of 'classes'; David Harvey; Edward Soja; Derek Gregory; and Doreen Massey. Harvey and Soja both argue a Marxist position. Harvey insists that as the existence of money shapes space and time (165), space becomes a usable commodity (177) in power exchanges, and that spatial practices (whether material, perceptual, or imaginative) all constitute discourses of accessibility, appropriation, and domination (262). Soja further emphasizes the degree to which historicism relegates spatial relations to an intellectual margin (15), by insisting that historicism fails to take sufficiently into account the principle that Soja considers axiomatic: that is, that space is not simply a superficial materiality but primarily a set of power relations (7). Derek Gregory draws on Lefebvre, Soja, Harvey, and other theorists – Jean Baudrillard, Walter Benjamin, Michel De Certeau, Michel Foucault, Anthony Giddens, Jürgen Habermas, and Edward Said among them – to survey the multiple presumptions that have underlain geographical practice, and to probe (and in the long run champion) its humanist possibilities. Soja critiques Giddens, and chastises Foucault for being too much a historian (19). Foucault, for his part, insists that society cannot be explained by an appeal to 'fundamental' issues, origins or foundations, but that society consists of 'reciprocal relations' and 'perpetual gaps between intentions' (247). Doreen Massey, in turn, critiques Soja and Harvey, primarily for failing to take women's views adequately into account;

see, for example, 'Flexible Sexism.' See also Grossberg and the seven essays
collected in the special *Geography and Postmodernism* issue of *Environment and
Planning D: Society and Space.*

2 See also Stoddart, who examines the place, within the discipine, of biology,
discovery, evolution, and other systems and theories.

3 See, for example, Godlewska and Smith, 3.

4 Jonathan Crush also comments on post-colonial responses to space; see esp.
334–7.

5 See Massey, 'Political Place of Locality Studies.'

6 Linda Hutcheon is one among many contemporary critics who resist this
term. In 'Frye Recoded: Postmodernity and the Conclusions' [referring,
i.e., to Frye's two 'Conclusions' to the *Literary History of Canada*: the first to
the one-volume first edition, and the second to the third volume of the
second edition], Hutcheon attempts to reconfigure the term in the light of
postmodern literary practice.

7 D.E.S. Maxwell reiterates the now familiar argument that the North American
forest is like the European cathedral, averring that landscape 'word-portraits,'
in settler societies such as Canada, the United States, and Australia, function symbolically to assert possession or title. Richard Cavell's insights in
'Theorizing Canadian Space' are particularly helpful in rereading this position. By drawing on the theories of Lefebvre, Soja, Foucault, Cosgrove,
Marshall McLuhan, and others, Cavell demonstrates the relevance of postmodern theories of geography and deconstructivist theories of architecture
to an understanding of 'heterotopia' and Canadian cultural space. Examining Arthur Erickson's architectural designs and Bill Reid's sculpture (con-
joined in the Chancery, the Canadian Embassy complex in Washington,
DC), Cavell questions the contemporary validity of Northrop Frye's modernist theories of 'structure' and space (and what they imply about a
'homogeneous' conception of 'Canada').

Chapter 1: Landing

1 See, for example, Blaut, who examines the relation between doctrines of
racial and climatological 'superiority' and political expansion; and the
essays in Godlewska and Smith, *Geography and Empire*. Smith also reviews the
politics of geographers' profession, with reference to works by Edward Said,
Aijaz Ahmad, and Mary Louise Pratt, in 'Geography, Empire and Social
Theory.' On the relation between metaphors of place and space, concepts
of masculinity, and definitions of cultural excellence, see During.

2 See also Schama's *Landscape and Memory* and the two books by Yi-Fu Tuan,

which examine the attitudes that different societies attach to the environment, the codes they use to configure them, and such topics as body space
(experience), mythical space, architectural space, and notions of 'home-
land.' Cf. Mingay's *A Social History of the English Countryside*, which contains
substantial data on income, dinners, disease, and other related details.
Fitter's *Poetry, Space, Landscape* argues that representations of landscape,
from ancient Greece to the European Renaissance, can be explained only
with reference to the cultural values that pertain in particular societies and
at particular historical moments; also drawing on Freud, however, Filter
hypothesizes that four 'matrices of perception' (11) – *ecological, cosmographic,
analogical,* and *technoptic* (appeals, respectively, to human needs for subsis-
tence and security, a current world-order, comparative paradigms that affect
interpretation, and 'art') – recurrently, though variously, govern the kinds
of gratification that people at any time derive from landscapes. Also relevant are E.H. Gombrich's comments on the psychology of pictorial representation (as in the coding and interpretation of photography, maps, and
painting) in such works as *Art and Illusion*, esp. 'From Light into Paint'
(33–62), and *The Image and the Eye*, esp. 'Mirror and Map: Theories of Pictorial Representation' (173–214).

   In addition to the works of theory already cited, a considerable body of
writing in geography that bears on the reading of 'landscape' is sometimes
specifically linked with 'literature.' Marc Brosseau (who draws attention to
the early influence on anglophone geographies of the tradition of 'espace
vécu' – space *as experienced*, 'true-to-life' space – as developed by such
French geographers as Armand Frémont) reviews trends in the field of
what has come to be known as 'literary geography,' as do Allen Noble and
Ranesh Dhussa. Some commentators, such Ronald Bordessa and J. Douglas
Porteous, seek paradigms of interdisciplinary usage. Porteous, using the
work of Malcolm Lowry as the chief example, proposes a structural model
that would distinguish four categories of relationship with land (inside/
home; outside/home; inside/away; outside/away). The four contributors to
'Literary Landscapes – Geography and Literature,' edited by Sandberg and
Marsh, allude to literature's function as fact, symbol, and message for the
geographer, to the city in Canadian writing (the notion of 'urban landscape' – referring variously to planning concepts, visual features, and sociological distribution patterns – is further touched on in *The Changing Social
Geography of Canadian Cities*, ed. Bourne and Ley), and to women's voice in
prairie literature. C.L. Salter and W.J. Lloyd, in *Landscape in Literature*, suggest ways of reading landscape (by which they mean all land uses, from
scenery and farm to trash heap and gas station 'garden') for its 'signatures'

(signatures of settlement, sacred space, behavioural and transportation signatures, and so on). Nigel Thrift, in 'Landscape and Literature,' a letter to the editor of *Environment and Planning A*, rejects Salter in particular, and all attempts in general to read literary texts for geographical evidence, or as 'geography'; Thrift also, however, assumes that the function of literary criticism is to effect some sort of 'transcendental' understanding of words.

Literary critics, for their part, also deal in taxonomies, often reading 'landscape' simply as 'setting,' as do Leonard Lutwack in *The Role of Place in Literature*, E.W. Gilbert in 'The Idea of the Region,' and Gillian Tindall in *Countries of the Mind*. Tindall, for example, focuses on Thomas Hardy's 'Wessex' and Charles Dickens's fictional 'London,' treating them conventionally as *real* (or at least *realized*) 'places.' Gilbert identifies 'region' simply as a political unit, and consequently construes writers such as Hardy, Arnold Bennett, and George Eliot to be bounded by the agricultural or industrial interests of particular British *counties*. Lutwack attempts to chart categories of literary uses of place and 'placelessness,' focusing on Melville and American nationalism. Thrift's later 'Literature, the Production of Culture and the Politics of Place' (1983) draws on Adorno and other cultural philosophers to argue a closer relation between the politics of reading literature (his examples include John Fowles and First World War writing) and the politics of reading 'place' through literary artifacts. Douglas C.D. Pocock's 'Geography and Literature,' with a more detailed bibliography, surveys existing commentary (to 1988) on the relation of setting, character, plot, and context to geographical study, closing with the suggestion that looking at landscape makes structuralists of us all.

3 On Native cultures in Canada, see, for example, Dickason, and Morrison and Wilson, eds. Further comments on the constructedness of the idea of nature, including essays by John Barrell and Yi-Fu Tuan, can be found in Kemal and Gaskell.

4 The subject of Native mapping has been much discussed. See, for example, Heidenreich and D. Wayne Moodie. See also Kane's comments on the spirituality of the Peterborough Petroglyphs and maps of mythtime in Canada and Australia, and his reading of the Haida poet John Sky's myth of three worlds as a 'map' of kinship and creative power. Ian Baucom, by contrast (see esp. 22–3), analyzes map making (especially in a postmodern age) as an imperialist project, one that tries to make space conform to a theory of origins, and (quoting Baudrillard to the effect that a map substitutes a sign of the real for the real itself) reveals a nostalgia for 'presence' in a time of 'displacement.'

5 For an account of the 'marvels and legends' and 'monstrous races' that

European historians repeatedly associated with foreign lands – they date at least as far back as the fifth century B.C. – see Dickason, *Myth of the Savage*, and Woodward 330–3. Cf. Scott Watson, 'Race, Wilderness.'

6 On the influence of trickster stories on contemporary writing, see Davidson.

7 Rev. from *Gatherings* II, ed. Armstrong, 29. See also Damm's comments on colonialism, identity, and the character of indigenous literature ('Says Who'), and Brian Maracle's reclamation of his heritage (3) as an Iroquois on 'Great Turtle Island' (North America).

8 Ong further observes that oral cultures are 'aggregative' rather than 'analytic,' 'participating' rather than 'objectively distanced,' 'situational' rather than 'abstract,' and characteristically 'conservative,' 'agonistic' or polemical, marked by features of verbal 'redundancy' or repetition, and 'homeostatic' or concerned with a present social balance. His terms and distinctions are in some dispute. See also Durant. For further technical commentary on oral and written forms, see Halliday. See also Macaulay, who reviews current literature on the subject; identifies a number of semantic and organizational strategies affecting discourse; and then examines the way these strategies apply to forms of narrative, argument, instruction, and description. Dennis Tedlock discusses the importance of the voice and freedom from the page; Ron Scollon and Suzanne Scollon address issues of orality associated with children's storytelling; Ward Parks discusses the relation between oral forms and dialogic theory, making the point that 'oral tradition' is available to most modern critics in written form; Peter Dickinson argues that oral features function in 'fourth world' texts as deliberate narrative strategies, which implicitly if not explicitly question the forms of power assumed by the existing majority; and Harvey Graff examines the sociological implications of the idea of 'literacy' in nineteenth-century Ontario, tracing connections between literacy and the social idoleogy of Christian morality. Graff cites Egerton Ryerson, John Strachan, and John William Dawson, among others, arguing that the function of educational organization and curriculum, with its emphasis on a particular kind of literacy, is to valorize a particular set of 'intellectual tastes and pleasures' (34) and therefore a particular kind of social hegemony – and that the 'myths' that even now attend the presumptions of universal literacy must be questioned.

9 Ramusio's (Venetian dialect) Italian version of this and the preceding passage reads this way: 'Noi ci accostammo a loro con le barche, e la mett[t]emmo in un'altro porto piu verso ponente una lega che detto fiume di San Iacomo, qual credo che sia un de miglior porti del modo [mondo], e fu chiamato il porto di Iacques Carthier. Se la terra fosse cosi buona, come vi sono buoni porti, sarebbe un gran bene, ma ella non si debbe

chiamar terra nuova, anzi sassi e grebani salvatichi, e proprii luoghi da
fiere, percioche in tutta l'Isola di Tramontana io non viddi tanta terra che
se ne potesse caricar un carro, e vi smontai in parecchi luoghi, e all' Isola
di Bianco Sabbione non v'è altro che musco, e piccioli spini dispersi,
secchi, e morti, e in somma io penso che questa fia la terra che Iddio dette
a Caino' (436).

10 On Native literature and Natives in literature, see Monkman, Goldie, King
et al., Petrone, New (*Native Writers*), and Armstrong (*Looking*).

11 See McGregor (challenged by MacLaren ['McGregor Syndrome']), Cook
('Imagining'), and Kline, who focuses on attitudes to power and the roles
of women.

12 On the relation between travel, contact, and representation, see, for example, Todorov, Greenfield, and Greenblatt. On the codes of empire used at
the empire's frontier, or 'contact zone,' see Mary Louise Pratt. On American travellers' representations of Canada, see Doyle.

13 Robert Lawson-Peebles argues that American revisionary attitudes towards
'wilderness' were part of the sociopolitical rejection both of England and of
the English resistance to seeing the 'new' landscape positively; related ideas
are expressed in Leo Marx's 'The American Revolution.' Tamara Plakins
Thornton also observes that the conventional American notion that the
farmer was the true republican served a hierarchical political model.

14 Simon Pugh usefully surveys garden conventions and the extensive literature on this subject. On the relation between garden conventions and classical aesthetics, see also Plumwood, Chambers, and Hunt (*Gardens and the
Picturesque*). English-language Canadian garden writing has been anthologized by von Baeyer and Crawford. Relatedly, the common use of the term
'garden' to refer to a hockey arena – Toronto's 'Maple Leaf Gardens,' for
example – at once draws on the term's original meaning ('enclosure') and
in some measure domesticates a contact sport.

15 See McKinsey for an analysis (with extensive visual examples) of the changing symbolic meaning associated with representations of the Falls, from the
seventeenth to the nineteenth century. See also Osborne, York ('"Sublime
Desolation"'), Kettner and Tamminga, Simpson-Housley and Norcliffe (esp.
Ramsay 158–70), Coates (who draws examples from Elizabeth Hale's 'picturesque' paintings of the countryside near Ste Anne), and Paikowsky. Graeme
Wynn strongly critiques not the premise, but the depth of analysis achieved
in the Simpson-Housley and Norcliffe anthology, in 'For the Birds.'
    The sociologist Rob Shields (esp. 117–61) examines the tension between
received perceptions of Niagara Falls (as sublime wilderness) and the popular construction of the Falls as the 'honeymoon capital of the world,' using

the dichotomy as one example of the process whereby people on the margins of power use 'difference' or 'Otherness' to reconceptualize space. He writes of the 'century-long exchange' between elite and popular culture in representing Niagara Falls: 'An alternative geography begins to emerge from the margins which challenges the self-definition of "centres", deconstructing ... universalised and homogeneous spatialisation ... to reveal ... a cartography of fractures which emphasises the relations between differently valorised sites and spaces sutured together under masks of unity such as the nation-state' (278).

Patrick McGreevy emphasizes a further aspect of the 'sublime' response to Niagara; observing that 'to read any landscape is to read a text of metaphors, or more precisely a text of synecdoches' (80), he focuses particularly on death imagery (the brink, the plunge, the abyss) and its connection with nineteenth-century Christian belief and economic individualism. Drawing on the writings of McGreevy and others, Karen Dubinsky emphasizes the sexuality of descriptions of Niagara, using a 'sex and gender-conscious analysis' (64) to examine the tourist industry associated with the Falls. See also Irwin.

16 See 'Samuel Hearne,' 'Grandest Tour,' 'Franklin Expedition,' and 'Palliser and Hind Survey'; cf. Belyea on Franklin. Two articles by Dorothy Seaton argue that 'strangeness' or 'the other' is often defined as 'non-discursive,' 'awaiting language,' and that 'land' (the site of actual confrontation or encounter) is often used as a textual sign of the territorial discourses of both imperial and post-colonial agendas; Seaton reads the 'novel' as a site of conflict over meaning and value, and defines 'field' as the discursive range of 'conflictive, undecidable meaning' as opposed to a monolithic or 'totalising system' of meaning ('Colonising Discourses' and 'Land and History'). See also Ryan, and Andrews.

17 The consequences of this distinction for Canadian literary criticism is the subject of Leon Surette's 'Here Is Us.' Margery Fee also considers how literary styles reflect conceptual responses to landscape.

18 Barrell distinguishes between the aesthetic presumptions of eighteenth-century art and poetry (with special reference to James Thomson, John Dyer, and John Clare) and the conventions of eighteenth-century writers on agriculture, who were preoccupied with the question of the 'enclosure' of 'uncultivated land' (94). Susan Glickman examines Thomas Cary's 1789 Quebec poem 'Abram's Plains' against the conventions of eighteenth-century topographical discourse established by Pope, Denham, and Thomson, to describe a 'pastoral yet imperial, peaceful yet predatory Britain' (503). Stafford (*Voyage into Substance* ch. 5) notes how the prospect,

the extensive landscape, came to be associated not only with distance but also with a freedom from limits, thus serving social and economic aspirations as well as aesthetic fashion.

19 See also Mary Lu MacDonald for a response to Cook ('Imagining') and an analysis of *positive* Canadian literary views of nature.

Chapter 2: Land-Office

1 Although cartography is often treated as though it were intrinsically documentary and unassailably objective, several studies have addressed the power and tendentiousness of mapping strategies. See, for example, Monmonier, who illustrates the techniques of distortion and weighting; Buisseret, on the metaphor of the *grid* 'as a net cast over the intractable Americas' (867); and the *On Maps and Mapping* issue of *artscanada*, including Warkentin's 'Discovering the Shape of Canada.' Several of Aritha van Herk's essays deal with the relation between space, mapping, metaphor, and gender: see *A Frozen Tongue*, esp. 25–34, 54–68, 127–38. See also Huggan, and Jackson.

2 For further detail, see New, *Dreams* 178–9.

3 Cf. Graff on 'literacy' and the social values of nineteenth-century Ontario.

4 See Hart 65. Samples of such posters can be seen at the Glenbow Museum in Calgary.

5 See Hall, Titley, and Dragland. Dragland speaks of 'absence,' that is, the cultural space that negates the value of some cultural constituent (153), and of 'the habit of superiority' that characterizes the discourse of Indian Affairs (106 ff.).

6 See, for example, Binnie-Clark's personal narrative, *Wheat & Woman*.

7 The editors of Roberts's *Collected Poems* quote (406) from Elsie Pomeroy's 1943 biography, *Sir Charles G.D. Roberts*, on the classical elegiac measure used here ('alternating hexameter and pentameter lines ... , so popular with Ovid').

8 Cf. Elaine Yee Lin Ho, 'Of Laundries and Restaurants: Fictions of Ethnic Space.'

9 Cf. Elizabeth Grosz, 'Bodies – Cities.'

10 For studies of the impact of technology on pastoral ideals, and of the forms of capitalist production as determiners of priorities in social relations, see Leo Marx (*The Machine in the Garden*), and Raymond Williams (*The Country and the City*). On Canadian industrial and urban estate planning, see Norcliffe, and Caulfield.

11 See also Kreisel's 1968 essay, 'The Prairie: A State of Mind.'

12 Cf. Dennis Lee on the concepts of earth and world, in *Savage Fields*.
13 See, for example, Kolodny; Higonnet and Templeton, whose work is illustrated with several woodcuts showing how women's bodies were often
treated as cartographic territories; Bondi and Domosh; and several of the
essays anthologized by Godard and by Neuman and Kamboureli. Simon
Ryan examines the gendering implicit in exploration discourse. The relation between space and gender is also the subject of much sociological
literature, as when Linda McDowell sees capitalism as a system that associates masculinity with centres of production and femininity with suburbs of
reproduction. Daphne Spain argues for a reciprocity between space and
status, noting that space plays a role in establishing and maintaining 'gender stratification' and that 'spatial segregation' (in architectural design,
segregated schoolrooms, urban housing, and separate workplaces) creates
'more than ... a physical distance; it also affects the distribution of knowledge women could use to change their position in society' (xiv). Cf. J.B.
Harley, 'Maps, Knowledge, and Power.' Barbara Stafford, in *Voyage into
Substance*, by contrast, associates the idea of landscape 'penetration' with
the seventeenth-century faith in objective empiricism. See also Brydon, 'No
(Wo)man Is an Island,' a critique of the 'master-narrative' of nationalism,
read in relation to images of women and the 'body politic' associated with
them; and Ross Gibson, 'Geography and Gender,' a Lacanian account of
the psychological iconography of the Australian cultural landscape (Adam
as explorer, the rock outcrop and the isolated tree as a phallic *axis mundi*).
What French feminist theorists such as Hélène Cixous and Luce Irigaray
have called the phallogocentrism of the aesthetic preoccupation with outcrop (protuberance) and house (erection) is alluded to also by Stafford,
and by van Herk ('Women Writers').

Chapter 3: Landed

1 For further discussion of the concept of 'home,' see Bhabha, and Massey
('Woman's Place').
2 W.J. Keith's *Literary Images of Ontario* draws on a wide range of examples of
Ontario writing, from pioneer journals and the poems of Charles Sangster
to the work of Alice Munro and Dennis Lee; Keith comments on the range
of categorizing adjectives – from 'prosaic' to 'lovely' (97) – that writers have
brought to Ontario landscapes; on such recurrent motifs as Indians, trees,
farm life, and small town; and on the construction of Ontario as a 'region'
(differentiating 'Toronto' from other locales). The variety of techniques
used in characterizing the regional identity of Toronto is also one of the

subjects addressed by Michael Hough. James Reaney ('Ontario Culture')
and Michael Peterman ('Ontario': 'Ontario surely is a poem, a spatial song
of multifaced landscape' 3–4) have examined the role of local lore and
popular culture in conventionalizing regional attitudes. Commentaries on
James Reaney and John Richardson, especially, have used the term 'Sou-
westo' to mark Southwestern Ontario as an identifiable region separate
from the rest of the province. The term is attributed to the painter Greg
Curnoe (see Duffy 130, 153). Curnoe's own *Deeds/Abstracts* traces the extended history of a specific London (Ontario) lot (38 Weston Street, sub-lot
7, Registered Plan #312, in Westminster Township), from the time of the
Neutral Indians through several generations of working-class 'European'
ownership, in order to probe the relation between 'deeds' (property
claims) and 'misdeeds' and occupation (the particularities, as distinct from
the generalities, of local history and culture). Allan Smith observes that Ontario literature has selectively and sequentially defined *prosperity* as the avail-
ability of land, defined *woods* as balm for the soul, defined *north* as a symbol
of future development, and defined *wild* as a recreational resource for an
urban population. Patricia Jasen examines the role that versions of wilderness played in establishing the Ontario tourist industry.
3 The poetry of Carmelita McGrath provides a different representation of
  Newfoundland's cold-climate landscape; in 'If the Land Has Memory,' for
  example, the land is the *body* – on which is written the *palimpsest* of human
  dreams. For further discussion of Newfoundland regionalism, see
  O'Flaherty, and Overton. The North constitutes another region that has
  attracted substantial comment. See, for example, Mandel ('Inward,
  Northward Journey'); Moss (*Enduring Dreams*); Wiebe (*Playing Dead*);
  Mitcham (*Northern Imagination*); Atwood (*Strange Things*); and the special
  Representing North issue of *Essays on Canadian Writing*, edited by Sherrill
  Grace. For further comments on 'nordicity' – the construction of 'North' in
  Canada and the social construction of Canada as 'the true north strong and
  free' – see Shields (*Places on the Margin* 162–206) and Warwick (*Long
  Journey*).
4 On Maritime regionalism, see Keefer; Davies; and Ennals and Holdsworth.
5 On recurrent structural paradigms in Canadian short fiction, see Bonheim.
6 On the house motif, see Jackel; Holdsworth; and Bachelard; for Bachelard,
  the trope of the house (tower to hut) in phenomenology suggests shelter,
  self, and the power to be vigilant. (Eli Mandel's comments on Harris treat
  the landscape as a phenomenological 'house.') Cf. E.D. Blodgett on prairie,
  town, settlement patterns, and geometry, in *Configuration*, esp. 187–218. For
  further discussion of prairie regionalism, see Friesen; Ricou (*Vertical Man,*

'Meadowlark'); Harrison; van Herk ('Woman Writers,' which argues that the conventional perspective that defines aesthetic images of the prairie is male, but that there are ways to subvert conventions); Rees; and Jordan.

7 For further discussion of BC regionalism, see Pritchard; New ('Continent'); Madoff, who speaks of three 'grammars of nature'; Barbour; Barman; Brayshaw; Cole; Linsley ('Painting'); and Ricou ('of British Columbia Writing'). Ricou ('Dumb Talk') also studies the relation between Native cultural forms (e.g., the pictogram) and BC literature. British Columbia has also figured in the conceptualization of 'ecotopianism' – a collectivist movement that imagines the North American west coast, from California to Alaska, as a separate political region, one that would be environmentally conscious and culturally 'free' from the existing, militaristic nation-state. (See Brown, and Sarasohn.) The development of 'ecocriticism,' relatedly, has followed primarily on the publication of books by Karl Kroeber and Lawrence Buell, and Glen Love's articles in *Western American Literature* provide an introduction to this approach to reading. See also the work of Raglon and Scholtmeijer, Gayton (*Landscapes*), and Richard H. Grove; Grove argues that environmentalism has its origins in responses to colonial expansion.

8 Beth Watzke argues that regionalism expresses itself not strictly through the specifics of physical geography but more in the body of attitudes that is associated with local places.

9 See also York, 'Better Nature.'

10 On ways in which the idea of Northness and the image of the Canadian Shield have been used to construct a version of national identity, see, respectively, Berger ('True North') and Cole Harris ('Myth of the Land').

11 *Heartland and Hinterland*, edited by L.D. McCann, for example, exemplifies a recurrent geographic construction; J.M.S. Careless's *Frontier and Metropolis* expresses a parallel historical binarism; the opening essay in D.M.R. Bentley's *Gay]Gray Moose* ('Preamble' 1–13) furnishes an example from literary criticism, one that attempts to distinguish between 'baseland' and 'hinterland' techniques and preoccupations. Sandra Djwa, in 'New Soil,' discusses the influence of the 'resonant symbolic language' (15) of the Group of Seven on the work of Pratt, Scott, Smith, and W.W.E. Ross. George Woodcock, in 'There are no universal landscapes,' observes the 'regionalist' (37) and analogical character of the Group of Seven's representations of land, contrasting their work with that of Paul Kane and Jack Shadbolt.

12 Ralph Heintzman considers the relation between Quebec and Creighton's *Empire*; W.H. New, in 'Great-River Theory,' comments on imperial rhetoric and examines further the relation between Creighton and MacLennan.

13 On some of the English literary analogues associated with river imagery, see Colwell, Herendeen, and Schama.

14 Several of the essays collected in Berry and Acheson bear on this connection, particularly those by Richard Preston, who draws on Mildred Schwartz's *Politics and Territoriality* (a sociological work that tends to equate 'regions' in Canada with political units, i.e., the provinces), by the geographer Peter Crabb, and by the literary critic Victor Konrad; and a commentary on social psychology, structuralism, and Marxism by Matthews and Davis, which disputes the Marxist argument made by Ornstein, Stevenson, and Williams – that is, that 'class' is not 'geographical.' Other essays in Berry and Acheson's book examine drama; fiddle music; stock auction speech; marketing strategies; and the work of Kroetsch, Wiebe, Anne Hébert, and others, as signs of regional character in Canada. See also Winks, who probes culture, geography, economics, and 'situational factors' as influences that construct American regions, and warns against the dangers of insularity and the tendency, sometimes, for myths of region to turn into 'vital lies' (35). Barry Cooper examines what he calls the 'Loyalist heartland' (211) base that underlies conventional definitions of 'Canada' – epitomized for Cooper by the work of Northrop Frye – and traces regional resentments (and the articulation of regional alternatives) in large part to unitary 'Loyalist' generalizations.

15 Cf. Homi Bhabha on borders and homogeneity, throughout *The Location of Culture*. A.N. Ebeogu, writing primarily about African literature, clearly summarizes nineteenth-century notions of nationalism, applicable beyond Africa. See also Anderson; Womack, who argues that the 'picturesque' was used as a technique for contriving an arbitrary sense of a Scottish national past that paradoxically served the cause of political federation with England; and Green, who focuses on the design of Paris as a demonstration of class values and imperial power.

16 For other relevant comments on regionalism see Matthews, Melnyk, and Westfall.

17 See Raymond Williams, *Culture*, for an introductory discussion of the dialectics of social systems; and see Lawson for a survey of the way 'place' has shifted in post-colonial critical discourse from a sign of universality to a sign of difference. Commentary on social and cultural change is not, of course, a phenomenon only of the last decades of the twentieth century. Lewis Mumford, in *The City in History*, cites Ralph Waldo Emerson's 1836 comment to the effect that the new scales of space in the nineteenth century will turn roads into streets and regions into neighbourhoods (430).

18 Laurence drew directly on O. Mannoni's *Prospero and Caliban* in 1960; but see also Mudimbe.

Chapter 4: Landscape

1 See, for example, Barthes, *Elements of Semiology.* Relatedly – in, for example, *The Responsibility of Forms* – Barthes has written on photography as part of a general examination of the forms of representation and of the ways in which people understand 'representations.'

2 Other recent works with metaphorical titles that link land and language include Steve McCaffery's *North of Intention,* Timothy Findley's *Inside Memory,* Patricia Smart's *Writing in the Father's House,* Diane McGifford, ed., *The Geography of Voice,* Helen Humphreys's *The Perils of Geography,* and M. Nourbese Philip's *Frontiers.* John Moss, in 'Landscape, Untitled,' uses the landscape metaphor to reflect on the reality of words; while the Irish poet Seamus Heaney, also drawing on the geographic metaphor, refers in *The Place of Writing* to the unstable role of place in the creative imagination, mentioning that 'place' can variously conceptualize source, exile, liberation, and distraction, among other sensibilities. Of related interest is J. Hillis Miller's *Topographies,* which – reflecting on Dickens, Heidegger, Derrida, and others – reads place-naming as performance, a way of making a site into a figure, the product of writing (4).

3 On photographic images in Canadian fiction, especially the work of Timothy Findley, and on the violence of photographic representation, see, for example, Kröller, and Sims. Cf. Ross Gibson on Australian film ('Camera natura').

4 On the use of the map as a semiotic trope in literature, see Huggan, whose *Territorial Disputes* contains an extensive supplementary bibliography. See also Jackson, whose *Maps of Meaning* uses changes in the mapping of ghetto, gang territory, gay bar, and other streetscapes as signs of a changing social ideology and therefore as a linguistic process.

5 Sandra Djwa reads the poem sympathetically, as a socialist credo influenced by Stephen Spender's 'The Making of a Poem' (*Politics* 225–8).

6 See also Cmiel on American popular speech.

7 See also the special *Cartographies* issue of *Etudes françaises.*

8 For a general guide to the subject of 'spatial form,' see Cavell.

9 See the poet's subsequent comments on 'The Pride,' after the poem had been politically critiqued, in his interview with Jan Bartley, esp. 150.

10 For further identifications between language and place, see also Bowering's

'Vancouver as Postmodern Poetry,' and Derksen's 'Sites Taken as Signs.'
11 Cf. Daphne Marlatt, 'Entering In'.
12 On editorial changes, and on J.W.D. Moodie and Richard Bentley's sepa-
    rate contributions to the manuscript, see Peterman, and Thurston.

Works Cited

Aberdeen, Lady [Ishbel Gordon, Marchioness of Aberdeen and Temair].
Through Canada with a Kodak. 1893. Introd. Marjory Harper. Toronto: U
Toronto P, 1994.

Abley, Mark. *Beyond Forget: Rediscovering the Prairies*. Vancouver: Douglas &
McIntyre, 1986.

Agnew, John. 'Representing Space: Space, Scale and Culture in Social Science.'
Duncan and Ley 251–71.

Akrigg, G.P.V., and Helen Akrigg. *British Columbia Place Names*. Victoria: Sono
Nis, 1986.

Alexander, David G. 'Canadian Regionalism: A Central Problem.' *Atlantic Cana-
da and Confederation: Essays in Canadian Political Economy*. Comp. Eric W.
Sager, Lewis R. Fischer, and Stuart O. Pierson. Toronto: Memorial U and
U Toronto P, 1983. 44–50.

Allan, Andrew. 'A Description of the Great Falls, of the River Saint John, in
the Province of New Brunswick.' Daymond and Monkman 1: 62–3.

Anderson, Benedict. *Imagined Communities: Reflections on the Origin and Spread of
Nationalism*. Rev. ed. London: Verso, 1991.

Andrews, Malcolm. *The Search for the Picturesque: Landscape Aesthetics and Tourism
in Britain, 1760–1800*. Stanford: Stanford UP, 1989.

Aristotle. *A New Aristotle Reader*. Ed. J.L. Ackrill. Oxford: Clarendon, 1987.

Armstrong, Jeannette. ed. *Gatherings II*. Penticton, B.C.: Theytus, 1992.

– *Looking at the Words of Our People: First Nations Analysis of Literature*. Penticton,
B.C.: Theytus, 1993.

– *Slash*. Penticton, B.C.: Theytus, 1990.

Ashcroft, Bill, Gareth Griffiths, and Helen Tiffin, eds. *The Post-colonial Studies
Reader*. London & New York: Routledge, 1995.

Atwood, Margaret. 'Death by Landscape.' *Wilderness Tips*. Toronto: McClelland & Stewart, 1991. 107–29.
– *The Handmaid's Tale*. Toronto: McClelland & Stewart, 1985.
– *The Journals of Susanna Moodie*. Toronto: Oxford UP, 1970.
– *Life Before Man*. Toronto: McClelland & Stewart, 1979.
– *The Robber Bride*. Toronto: McClelland & Stewart, 1993.
– *Surfacing*. Toronto: McClelland & Stewart, 1972.
– *Strange Things: The Malevolent North in Canadian Literature*. Oxford: Clarendon, 1995.
– *Survival*. Toronto: Anansi, 1972.
Aubin, Robert Arnold. 'Old Lands and New,' *Topographical Poetry in XVIII-Century England*. New York: MLA, 1936. 194–224, 291–3.
Avis, Walter S., ed. *A Concise Dictionary of Canadianisms*. Toronto: Gage, 1973.
Bachelard, Gaston. *The Poetics of Space*. Trans. Maria Jolas. Boston: Beacon, 1964.
Baird, Irene. *Waste Heritage*. 1939. Toronto: Macmillan, 1973.
Barbour, Douglas. 'Notes Towards an Identification of Regionalism in Canadian Poetry,' in Berry and Acheson 569–77.
Barman, Jean. 'The West Beyond the West: The Demography of Settlement in British Columbia.' *Journal of Canadian Studies* 25.3 (Fall 1990): 5–18.
Barnes, Trevor J., and James S. Duncan, eds. *Writing Worlds: Discourse, Text & Metaphor in the Representation of Landscape*. London & New York: Routledge, 1992.
Barrell, John. *The Idea of Landscape and the Sense of Place, 1730–1840*. Cambridge: Cambridge UP, 1972.
Barthes, Roland. *Elements of Semiology* [1973]. Trans. Annette Lavers and Colin Smith. New York: Hill & Wang, 1991.
– *The Responsibility of Forms* [1964]. Trans. Richard Howard. Berkeley: U California P, 1991.
Bartley, Jan. 'An Interview with John Newlove.' *Essays in Canadian Writing* 23 (Spring 1982): 135–56.
Bate, Jonathan. *Romantic Ecology: Wordsworth and the Environmental Tradition*. London & New York: Routledge, 1991.
Baucom, Ian. 'Dreams of Home: Colonialism and Postmodernism.' *Research in African Literatures* 22.4 (Winter 1991): 5–27.
Beer, W.G. *Lacrosse: The National Game of Canada, Containing the Laws of the Game as Recently Amended*. Montreal: Dawson, 1879.
Bell, David, and Gill Valentine, eds. *Mapping Desire*. London & New York: Routledge, 1995.
Belyea, Barbara. 'Captain Franklin in Search of the Picturesque.' *Essays on Canadian Writing* 40 (Spring 1990): 1–24.

Bentley, D.M.R. *The Gay/Grey Moose: Essays on the Ecologies and Mythologies of Canadian Poetry, 1690–1990.* Ottawa: U Ottawa P, 1992.
- 'Introduction.' *Quebec Hill.* By J. Mackay. London, ON: Canadian Poetry Press, 1988. xi–xlvii.
- 'Let the Blank Whiteness of the Page Be Snow,' *Gay/Grey Moose,* 201–16.
Berger, Carl. *The Sense of Power.* Toronto: U Toronto P, 1970.
- 'The True North Strong and Free.' *Nationalism in Canada.* Ed. Peter Russell. Toronto: McGraw-Hill, 1966. 3–26.
Berland, Jody. 'Remote Sensors: Canada and Space.' *semiotext(e)* 6.2 (1994): 28–35.
Bermingham, Ann. *Landscape and Ideology: The English Rustic Tradition.* Berkeley: U California P, 1986.
Berry, Reginald, and James Acheson, eds. *Regionalism and National Identity.* Christchurch: Assoc. for Canadian Studies in Australia and New Zealand, 1985.
Bevis, William. 'Native American Novels: Homing In.' *Recovering the Word.* Ed. Brian Swann and Arnold Krupat. Berkeley: U California P, 1987. 598–9.
Bhabha, Homi. *The Location of Culture.* London & New York: Routledge, 1994.
Billings, Robert, comp. 'Regionalism and Internationalism,' *Waves* 11.2–3 (1983): 37–46.
Binnie-Clark, Georgina. *Wheat & Woman.* 1914. Introd. Susan Jackel. Toronto: U Toronto P, 1979.
Birney, Earle. *The Collected Poems of Earle Birney.* Toronto: McClelland & Stewart, 1975.
Blaut, J.M. *The Colonizer's Model of the World: Geographical Diffusionism and Eurocentric History.* London: Guilford, 1993.
Blodgett, E.D. *Configuration.* Toronto: ECW, 1982.
Bly, Robert. *Iron John.* New York: Addison-Wesley, 1990.
Bondi, L., and M. Domosh. 'Other Figures in Other Places: On Feminism, Postmodernism and Geography.' *Environment and Planning D: Society and Space* 10.2 (April 1992): 199–214.
Bonheim, Helmut. *The Narrative Modes.* Cambridge: D.S. Brewer, 1982.
Booth, Annie L., and Harvey M. Jacobs. 'Ties That Bind: Native American Beliefs as a Foundation for Environmental Consciousness.' *Environmental Ethics* 12.1 (Spring 1990): 27–43.
Bordessa, Ronald. 'Moral Frames for Landscape in Canadian Literature.' Simpson-Housley and Norcliffe 58–70.
Bordo, Jonathan. 'Jack Pine – Wilderness Sublime or the Erasure of the Aboriginal Presence from the Landscape.' *Journal of Canadian Studies* 27.4 (Winter 1992–3): 98–128.

Bourdieu, Pierre. *Language & Symbolic Power.* Ed. John B. Thompson, trans. Gino Raymond and Matthew Adamson. Cambridge: Polity, 1992.

Bourke, Lawrence. 'A Place in History: The Ash Range, Landscape and Identity.' *Westerly* 1 (Autumn 1993): 17–24.

Bourne, Larry P., and David F. Ley, eds. *The Changing Social Geography of Canadian Cities.* Montreal: McGill–Queen's UP, 1993.

Bowering, George. *Burning Water.* Toronto: General, 1980.

– 'Reaney's Region.' *A Way with Words.* Ottawa: Oberon. 37–53.

– *Urban Snow.* Vancouver: Talonbooks, 1992.

– 'Vancouver as Postmodern Poetry.' *Colby Quarterly* 19.2 (June 1993): 102–18. Rpt. in Delany 121–43.

Bramham, Daphne. 'Building boom follows successful mall for Asians.' *Vancouver Sun,* 9 March 1993. A1.

Brayshaw, Christopher. *Out of the Garden: The Contemporary British Columbia Landscape.* Richmond, BC: Richmond Art Gallery, 1996.

Brooke, Frances. *The History of Emily Montague.* 1769. Ed. Mary Jane Edwards. Ottawa: Carleton UP, 1985.

Brossard, Nicole. *L'Amèr* [1977]. Trans. Barbara Godard as *These Our Mothers.* Toronto: Coach House, 1983.

Brosseau, Marc. 'Geography's Literature.' *Progress in Human Geography* 18 (1994): 333–53.

Brown, R.M. 'New Regionalism in America.' Robbins, Frank, and Ross 37–96.

Brydon, Diana. 'Landscape and Authenticity.' *Dalhousie Review* 61.2 (Summer 1981): 278–90.

– 'No (Wo)man Is an Island: Rewriting Cross-Cultural Encounters in the Canadian Context.' *Kunapipi* 15.2 (1993): 48–56.

Buchan, John [Lord Tweedsmuir]. *Sick Heart River.* 1941. Ed. & introd. by David Daniell. Oxford: Oxford UP, 1994.

Buchanan, Ian. 'Lefebvre and the Space of Everyday Life.' *Southern Review* 27.2 (June 1994): 127–37.

Buckler, Ernest. *The Mountain and the Valley.* Toronto: McClelland & Stewart, 1961.

– *Ox Bells and Fireflies.* 1968. Toronto: McClelland & Stewart, 1974.

Buell, Lawrence. *The Environmental Imagination: Thoreau, Nature Writing, and the Formation of American Culture.* Cambridge, MA, & London: Belknap/Harvard UP, 1995.

Buisseret, David. 'Maps and Power – or – Something Nasty in the Glovebox.' *Queen's Quarterly* 100.4 (Winter 1993): 861–8.

Bumsted, J.M. 'From Don Mills to Paradise Crescent: Home Sweet Suburb: The great post-war migration,' *The Beaver* (October/November 1992): 26–33.

Bunce, Michael. *The Countryside Ideal: Anglo-American Images of Landscape.* London & New York: Routledge, 1994.

Burgin, Victor. 'The City in Pieces.' *New formations* 20 (Summer 1993): 33–45.

Burke, Edmund. *A Philosophical Enquiry into the Origin of Our Ideas of the Sublime and Beautiful.* 1757. Ed. Adam Phillips. Oxford & New York: Oxford UP, 1990.

Burn, Ian. *Dialogue: Writings in Art History.* North Sydney: Allen & Unwin, 1991.

Buss, Helen M. 'Women and the Garrison Mentality: Pioneer Women Autobiographers and Their Relation to the Land.' *Re(dis)covering Our Foremothers.* Ed. Lorraine McMullen. Ottawa: U Ottawa P, 1990. 123–36.

Buttimer, Anne. 'Home, Reach, and the Sense of Place.' *The Human Experience of Space and Place.* Ed. Anne Buttimer and David Seamon. London: Croom Helm, 1980. 166–87.

Callaghan, Morley. *Stories.* Toronto: Macmillan, 1959.

– *Such Is My Beloved.* 1957. Toronto: McClelland & Stewart, 1969.

Careless, J.M.S. *Frontier and Metropolis: Regions, Cities and Identities in Canada before 1914.* Toronto: U Toronto P, 1989.

Carr, Emily. *Klee Wyck.* Toronto: Oxford UP, 1941.

Carruthers, Mary. *The Book of Memory: A Study of Memory in Medieval Culture.* Cambridge: Cambridge UP, 1990.

– *The Witness and the Other World: Exotic European Travel Writing, 400–1600.* Ithaca & London: Cornell UP, 1988.

Carter, Paul. *The Road to Botany Bay: An Exploration of Landscape and History.* Chicago: U Chicago P, 1987.

Cartier, Jacques. *Navigations to Newe Fraunce.* 1580. Readex Microprint, 1966.

Cartographies. Special issue of *Etudes françaises* 21.2 (1985).

Castro, Brian. 'Heterotopias: Writing and Location.' *Australian Literary Studies* 17.2 (1995): 178–83.

Caulfield, Jon. 'Augurs of 'Gentrification': City Houses of Four Canadian Painters.' Simpson-Housley and Norcliffe 187–202.

Cavell, Richard. 'Spatial Form.' *Encyclopedia of Contemporary Literary Theory.* Ed. Irene R. Makaryk. Toronto: U Toronto P, 1993. 629–31.

– 'Theorizing Canadian Space: Postcolonial Articulations.' *Canada: Theoretical Discourse/Discours théoretiques.* Ed. Terry Goldie and Carmen Lambert. Montreal: Assoc. for Canadian Studies, 1994. 75–104.

Chadbourne, Richard, and Hallvard Dahlie, eds. *The New Land: Studies in a Literary Theme.* Waterloo, ON: Wilfrid Laurier UP, for the Calgary Institute for the Humanities, 1978.

Chambers, Douglas D.C. 'The Translation of Antiquity: Virgil, Pliny, and the Landscape Garden.' *University of Toronto Quarterly* 60.3 (Spring 1991): 354–73.

Chang, Heesok. 'Allegories of Community: Chinese-Canadian Art in Vancouver.' Delany 217–41.

Chatwin, Bruce. *The Songlines*. Markham, ON: Viking Penguin, 1987.

Cixous, Hélène. *The Newly Born Woman* [1975]. Trans. Betsy Wing. Minneapolis & London: U Minnesota P, 1993.

Clark, Lovell. 'Regionalism? or Irrationalism?' *Journal of Canadian Studies* 13.2 (Summer 1978): 119–24.

Cmiel, Kenneth. *Democratic Eloquence: The Fight over Popular Speech in Nineteenth-Century America*. New York: William Morrow, 1990.

Coates, Colin M. '"Like the Thames towards Putney": The Appropriation of Landscape in Lower Canada.' *Canadian Historical Review* 74.3 (September 1993): 317–43.

Coates, Ken S., and Robin Fisher, eds. *Out of the Background: Readings on Canadian Native History*, 2d ed. Toronto: Copp-Clark, 1996.

Coffin, David R. *Gardens and Gardening in Papal Rome*. Princeton: Princeton UP, 1991.

Cole, Douglas. 'The Intellectual and Imaginative Development of British Columbia.' *Journal of Canadian Studies* 24.3 (Fall 1989): 70–9.

Colomina, Beatriz, ed. *Sexuality & Space*. Princeton Papers on Architecture 1. Princeton: Princeton Architectural P, 1992.

Colwell, Frederic S. *Rivermen: A Romantic Iconography of the River and the Source*. Montreal: McGill–Queen's UP, 1989.

Combe, William. *Doctor Syntax's Three Tours*. London: Chatto & Windus, [1878?].

Conly, Verena Andermatt. *Hélène Cixous*. Toronto: U Toronto P, 1992.

Connor, Ralph. *Black Rock; A Tale of the Selkirks*. Toronto: Westminster, 1898.

Cook, Ramsay. 'Imagining a North American Garden: Some Parallels and Differences in Canadian and American Culture.' *Canadian Literature* 103 (Winter 1984): 10–23.

– *The Regenerators*. Toronto: U Toronto P, 1985.

Cooley, Dennis. *Fielding*. Saskatoon: Thistledown, 1983.

– 'The Vernacular Muse in Prairie Poetry.' *Prairie Fire* [1986–7]. Rpt. in *The Vernacular Muse*. Winnipeg: Turnstone, 1987. 167–222.

Cooper, Barry. 'The West: A Political Minority.' *Minorities and the Canadian State*. Ed. Neil Nevitte and Allan Kornberg. Oakville, ON: Mosaic P, 1985. 203–20.

Cosgrove, Denis E. *Social Formation and Symbolic Landscape*. London: Croom Helm, 1984.

Cosgrove, Denis E., and Stephen Daniels, eds. *The Iconography of Landscape*. Cambridge: Cambridge UP, 1988.

Coupland, Douglas. *Microserfs*. Toronto: HarperCollins, 1995.

Crabb, Peter. 'Regionalism and National Identity: Canada and Australia.' Berry and Acheson 19–32.

Creighton, Donald. *The Empire of the St. Lawrence*. Rpt. of *The Commercial Empire of the St. Lawrence* 1937. Toronto: Macmillan, 1956.

Cronon, William. 'A Place for Stories: Nature, History, and Narrative.' *Journal of American History* 78.4 (1992): 1347–76.

Crosby, Marcia. 'Construction of the Imaginary Indian.' Douglas 267–91.

Crush, Jonathan. 'Post-Colonialism, De-colonization, and Geography.' Godlewska and Smith 333–50.

Culleton, Beatrice. *In Search of April Raintree*. Winnipeg: Pemmican, 1983.

Curnoe, Greg. *Deeds/Abstracts: The History of a London Lot*, ed. Frank Davey. London: Brick, 1995.

Damm, Kateri. *my heart is a stray bullet*. Cape Croker, ON: Kegedonce P, 1993.

– 'Says Who.' Armstrong, *Looking*, 9–26.

Daniels, Stephen, and Denis Cosgrove. 'Spectacle and Text: Landscape Metaphors in Cultural Geography.' Duncan and Ley 57–77.

Davidson, Arnold E. *Coyote Country: Fictions of the Canadian West*. Durham, NC, & London: Duke UP, 1994.

Davies, Gwendolyn. 'The Song Fishermen: A Regional Poetry Celebration.' *Studies in Maritime Literary History, 1760–1930*. Fredericton: Acadiensis, 1991. 163–73.

Daymond, Douglas, and Leslie Monkman, eds. *Literature in Canada*. 2 vols. Toronto: Gage, 1978.

de Certeau, Michel. 'Spatial Stories.' *The Practice of Everyday Life* [1980]. Trans. Steven Rendall. Berkeley: U California P, 1984. 115–30.

Delany, Paul, ed. *Vancouver: The Postmodern City*. Vancouver: Arsenal Pulp P, 1994.

de la Roche, Mazo. *Jalna*. Boston: Little, Brown, 1927.

de Lauretis, Teresa. *Alice Doesn't: Feminism, Semiotics, Cinema*. Bloomington: Indiana UP, 1984.

Deleuze, Gilles, and Félix Guattari. *A Thousand Plateaus: Capitalism and Schizophrenia* [1980]. Trans. Brian Massumi. Minneapolis: U Minnesota P, 1987.

– *What Is Philosophy?* [1991]. Trans. Hugh Tomlinson and Graham Burchell. New York: Columbia UP, 1994.

Derksen, Jeff. 'Sites Taken as Signs: Place, the Open Text, and Enigma in the New Vancouver Writing.' Delany 144–61.

Dickason, Olive Patricia. *Canada's First Nations: A History of Founding Peoples from Earliest Times to the Present*. Toronto: McClelland & Stewart, 1992.

– *The Myth of the Savage*. Edmonton: U Alberta P, 1984.

Dickinson, Peter. '"Orality in Literacy": Listening to Indigenous Writing.' *Canadian Journal of Native Studies* 14.2 (1994): 319–40.

Dionne, René. 'Les études littéraires régionales.' *Revue d'histoire littéraire du Québec et du Canada français* 14 (1987): 135–43.

Diprose, Rosalyn, and Robyn Ferrell, eds. *Cartographies: Poststructuralism and the Mapping of Bodies and Spaces.* North Sydney: Allen & Unwin, 1991.

Djwa, Sandra. '"A New Soil and a Sharp Sun": The Landscape of a Modern Canadian Poetry.' *Modernist Studies* 2.2 (1977): 3–17.

– *The Politics of the Imagination: A Life of F.R. Scott.* Toronto: McClelland & Stewart, 1987.

Douglas, Stan, ed. *Vancouver Anthology: The Institutional Politics of Art.* Vancouver: Talonbooks, 1991.

Doyle, James. 'From Conservative Alternative to Vanishing Frontier: Canada in American Travel Narratives, 1799–1899.' *Canadian Review of American Studies* 5.1 (Spring 1974): 26–35.

Dragland, Stan. *Floating Voice: Duncan Campbell Scott and the Literature of Treaty 9.* Concord, ON: Anansi, 1994.

Dubinsky, Karen. '"The Pleasure Is Exquisite but Violent."' *Journal of Canadian Studies* 29.2 (Summer 1994): 64–88.

Duffy, Dennis. *A World under Sentence: John Richardson and the Interior.* Toronto: ECW, 1996.

Duncan, James, and David Ley, eds. *Place/Culture/Représentation.* London & New York: Routledge, 1993.

Duncan, Sara Jeannette. 'The Veritable West.' *Sara Jeannette Duncan: Selected Journalism.* Ed. Thomas E. Tausky. Ottawa: Tecumseh, 1978. 79–81.

Durant, Alan. 'The Concept of Secondary Orality.' *Dalhousie Review* 64.2 (Summer 1984): 332–53.

During, Simon. 'Transporting Literature: Relations between Metropolitan and Colonial Literary Cultures During the Settlement Period.' *Shakespeare's Books: Contemporary Cultural Politics and the Persistence of Empire.* Ed. Philip Mead and Marion Campbell. Parkville, Victoria: U Melbourne English Dept, 1993. 50–78.

Ebeogu, A.N. 'African Literature: Regional, National and Ethnic Imperatives.' *Ariel* 14.2 (1983): 21–33.

Emberley, Peter. 'Places and Stories: The Challenge of Technology.' *Social Research* 56.3 (Autumn 1989): 741–85.

Ennals, Peter, and Deryck Holdsworth. 'Vernacular Architecture and the Cultural Landscape of the Maritime Provinces: A Reconnaisance.' *Acadiensis* (1981). Rpt. in Wynn, *People,* 177–95.

Fairbanks, Carol. *Prairie Women.* New Haven & London: Yale UP, 1986.

Falkiner, Suzanne. *Wilderness* and *Settlement.* The Writer's Landscape series. East Roseville, NSW: Simon & Schuster, 1992.

Fee, Margery. 'Romantic, Modern, Post-modern: Ways of Writing the Canadian Landscape.' *American–Canadian Studies* [Taejon, Korea] 4 (1995): 161–76.

Findley, Timothy. *Headhunter.* Toronto: HarperCollins, 1993.

– *Inside Memory.* Toronto: HarperCollins, 1990.

– *The Wars.* Toronto: Clarke Irwin, 1977.

Fisher, Robin. 'Judging History: Reflections on the Reasons for Judgment in *Delgamuukw v. B.C.*' *BC Studies* 95 (Autumn 1992): 43–54. Rpt. in Coates and Fisher 391–401.

Fisher, Robin, and Hugh Johnston, eds. *From Maps to Metaphors: The Pacific World of George Vancouver.* Vancouver: U British Columbia P, 1993.

Fitter, Chris. *Poetry, Space, Landscape: Toward a New Theory.* Cambridge & New York: Cambridge UP, 1995.

Fladmark, Knut. *British Columbia Prehistory.* Ottawa: National Museums of Canada, 1986.

Foucault, Michel. *The Order of Things: An Archeology of the Human Sciences.* Trans. Alan Sheridan-Smith. New York: Random House, 1970.

– 'Space, Knowledge, and Power.' Trans. Christian Hubert. *The Foucault Reader.* Ed. Paul Rabinow. New York: Pantheon, 1984. 239–56.

Franklin, John. *Sir John Franklin's Journals & Correspondence.* Ed. Richard C. Davis. Toronto: Champlain Society, 1995.

Frémont, Armand. *La Région, espace vécu.* Paris: Presses universitaires de France, 1976.

Friesen, Gerald. 'The Prairies as Region: The Contemporary Meaning of an Old Idea.' *River Road: Essays on Manitoba and Prairie History.* Winnipeg: U Manitoba P, 1996. 165–82.

Frye, Northrop. *The Bush Garden.* Toronto: Anansi, 1971.

Fuller, Peter. 'The Geography of Mother Nature.' Cosgrove and Daniels. 11–31.

Gayton, Don. *Landscapes of the Interior: Re-Explorations of Nature and the Human Spirit.* Gabriola Island, BC: New Society, 1996.

– *The Wheatgrass Mechanism: Science and Imagination in the Western Canadian Landscape.* Saskatoon: Fifth House, 1990; 2d ed. 1992.

Geertz, Clifford. *Local Knowledge: Further Essays in Interpretive Anthropology.* New York: Basic, 1983.

Geography and Postmodernism. Special issue of *Environment and Planning D: Society and Space* 10.1 (February 1992).

Gibson, Edward M. '"Where Is Here?" The Uses of Geography in English-Canadian Literature.' *Studies in Canadian Regional Geography: Essays in Honor of J. Lewis Robinson.* B.C. Geographical Series 337. Ed. Brenton M. Barr. Vancouver: Tantalus Research, 1984. 132–49.

Gibson, Graeme. *Perpetual Motion.* Toronto: McClelland & Stewart, 1982.

Gibson, Ross. 'Camera natura: Landscape in Australian Feature Films' [1983].

Rpt. in *Australian Cultural Studies: A Reader.* Ed. John Frow and Meaghan Morris. Urbana & Chicago: U Illinois P, 1993. 209–21.

– 'Geography and Gender.' *South of the West: Poscolonialism and the Narrative Construction of Australia.* Bloomington & Indianapolis: Indiana UP, 1992. 82–110.

Gilbert, E.W. 'The Idea of the Region.' *Geography* 45 (1960): 157–75.

Gilpin, William. *Three Essays: On Picturesque Beauty, On Picturesque Travel, and On Sketching Landscape.* London: R. Blamire, 1792.

Glickman, Susan. 'Canadian Prospects: *Abram's Plains* in Context.' *University of Toronto Quarterly* 59.4 (Summer 1990): 498–515.

Globe and Mail [Toronto]. 11 December 1995; 30 March 1996.

Godard, Barbara, ed. *Gynocritics/Gynocritiques.* Toronto: ECW, 1987.

Godfrey, Dave. *Dark Must Yield.* Erin, ON: Press Porcépic, 1978.

Godlewska, Anne, and Neil Smith, eds. *Geography and Empire.* Oxford & Cambridge, MA: Blackwell, 1994. 'Introduction: Critical Histories of Geography,' 1–8.

Goldie, Terry. *Fear and Temptation.* Montreal: McGill–Queen's UP, 1989.

Goldman, Marlene. 'Earth-quaking the Kingdom of the Virgin.' *Canadian Literature* 137 (Summer 1993): 21–38.

Goldsmith, Oliver. *The Rising Village.* 1825 & 1834. Ed. Michael Gnarowski. Montreal: Delta Canada, 1968.

Gombrich, E.H. 'From Light into Paint.' *Art and Illusion.* Washington: Pantheon, 1960. 33–62.

– 'Mirror and Map: Theories of Pictorial Representation.' *The Image and the Eye.* Oxford: Phaidon, 1982. 173–214.

Grace, Sherrill. 'Quest for the Peaceable Kingdom: Urban/Rural Codes in Roy, Laurence, and Atwood.' *Women Writers and the City: Essays in Feminist Literary Criticism.* Ed. Susan Merril Squier. Knoxville: U Tennessee P, 1984. 193–209.

– ed. Representing North. Special issue of *Essays on Canadian Writing* 59 (1996).

Graff, Harvey J. *The Literacy Myth: Literacy and Social Structure in the Nineteenth-Century City.* New York: Academic P, 1979.

Grant, George Monro, ed. *Picturesque Canada.* 2 vols. Toronto: Beldon Bros., 1882.

Green, Nicholas. *The Spectacle of Nature: Landscape and Bourgeois Culture in Nineteenth-Century France.* Manchester: Manchester UP, 1990.

Greenblatt, Stephen. *Marvellous Possessions: The Wonder of the New World.* Chicago: U Chicago P, 1991.

Greenfield, Bruce. *Narrating Discovery: The Romantic Explorer in American Literature, 1790–1855.* New York: Columbia UP, 1992.

Greenhill, Pauline. *True Poetry: Traditional and Popular Verse in Ontario.* Montreal: McGill–Queen's UP, 1989.

Gregory, Derek. *Geographical Imaginations.* Oxford & Cambridge, MA: Blackwell, 1994.

Gross, Alan G. *The Rhetoric of Science.* Cambridge, MA, & London: Harvard UP, 1990.

Grossberg, Lawrence. 'The Space of Culture, the Power of Space.' *The Post-Colonial Question: Common Skies, Divided Horizons.* Ed. Ian Chambers and Lydia Curtie. London: Routledge, 1996. 169–88.

Grosz, Elizabeth. 'Bodies–Cities.' Colomina 241–53.

Grove, Frederick Philip. *In Search of Myself.* Toronto: McCourt, 1949.

– *Over Prairie Trails.* 1922. Toronto: McClelland & Stewart, 1991.

– *A Search for America.* 1927. Toronto: McClelland & Stewart, 1991.

Grove, R.H. *Green Imperialism: Colonial Expansion, Tropical Island Edens, and the Origins of Environmentalism, 1600–1860.* Cambridge & New York: Cambridge UP, 1995.

Haliburton, Thomas Chandler. *The Clockmaker.* [1836]. Toronto: McClelland & Stewart, 1993.

Hall, D.J. *Clifford Sifton.* 2 vols. Vancouver: U British Columbia P, 1981, 1985.

Halliday, M.A.K. 'Spoken and Written Modes of Meaning.' *Comprehending Oral and Written Language.* Ed. Rosalind Horowitz and Jay Samuels. San Diego: Academic P, 1987. 55–82.

Hamer, David. *New Towns in the New World: Images and Perceptions of the Nineteenth-Century Urban Frontier.* New York: Columbia UP, 1990.

Harding, Brian, and Ellen Harding. 'Looking Forward; Looking Backward: American and Canadian Scenery in the 1830s.' *British Journal of Canadian Studies* 8.2 (1993): 163–79.

Harley, J.B. 'Maps, Knowledge, and Power.' Cosgrove and Daniels 277–312.

Harley, J.B., and David Woodward, eds. *Cartography in Prehistoric, Ancient, and Medieval Europe and the Mediterranean.* The History of Cartography I. Chicago & London: U Chicago P, 1987.

Harris, Claire. *Drawing Down a Daughter.* Fredericton: Goose Lane, 1992.

Harris, Cole. 'The Emotional Structures of Canadian Regionalism.' *The Challenges of Canada's Regional Diversity.* Toronto: Canada Studies Foundation, 1981. The Walter L. Gordon Lecture Series [1980–1], 5: 9–30.

– 'The Myth of the Land in Canadian Nationalism.' *Nationalism in Canada,* ed. Peter Russell. Toronto: McGraw-Hill, 1966. 27–43.

Harris, Wilson. *The Womb of Space.* Westport, CT: Greenwood, 1983.

Harrison, Dick. *Unnamed Country.* Edmonton: U Alberta P, 1977.

Hart, E.J. *The Selling of Canada: The CPR and the Beginnings of Canadian Tourism.* Banff: Altitude, 1983.

Harvey, P.D.A. *Medieval Maps.* Toronto & Buffalo: U Toronto P, 1991.

Harvey, David. *The Urban Experience.* Baltimore: Johns Hopkins UP, 1989.

Hayman, Robert. '[The Pleasant Life in Newfoundland].' Anthologized in *The Oxford Book of Canadian Verse in English.* Ed. Margaret Atwood. Toronto: Oxford UP, 1982. 1.

Heaney, Seamus. *The Place of Writing.* Atlanta: Scholars P, 1989.

Heidenreich, Conrad. 'The Natural Environment of Huronia and Huron Seasonal Activities.' Wynn, *People,* 42–55.

Heintzman, Ralph. 'Political Space and Economic Space: Quebec and the Empire of the St. Lawrence.' *Journal of Canadian Studies* 29.1 (Summer 1994): 39–63.

Herendeen, Wyman H. *From Landscape to Literature: The River and the Myth of Geography.* Pittsburgh: Duquesne UP, 1986.

Hiebert, Paul. *Sarah Binks.* Toronto: Oxford UP, 1947.

Highway, Tomson. *The Rez Sisters.* Saskatoon: Fifth House, 1988.

Higonnet, Margaret, and Joan Templeton, eds. *Reconfigured Spheres: Feminist Explorations of Literary Space.* Amherst: U Massachusetts P, 1994.

Hine, Daryl. *Minutes.* New York: Atheneum, 1968.

Ho, Elaine Yee Lin. 'Of Laundries and Restaurants: Fictions of Ethnic Space.' *Wasafiri* 21 (Spring 1995): 16–19.

Hodgins, Jack. *Innocent Cities.* Toronto: McClelland & Stewart, 1990.

– *The Invention of the World.* 1977. Toronto: McClelland & Stewart, 1994.

Hoffmann, Gerhard. 'Postmodern Culture and Indian Art.' *In the Shadow* 257–331.

Holdsworth, Deryck. 'Revaluing the House.' Duncan and Ley 95–109.

Hopwood, Victor. 'Explorers by Land to 1867.' *Literary History of Canada.* Ed. Carl Klinck, Alfred G. Bailey, Claude Bissell, Roy Daniells, Northrop Frye, and Desmond Pacey, 2d ed. Toronto: U Toronto P, 1976. 1: 19–53.

Horwood, Harold. 'Men Like Summer Snow.' *Stories from Pacific and Arctic Canada,* ed. Andreas Schroeder and Rudy Wiebe. Toronto: McClelland & Stewart, 1974. 230–7.

Hough, Michael. *Out of Place: Restoring Identity to the Regional Landscape.* New Haven & London: Yale UP, 1990.

Huggan, Graham. *Territorial Disputes: Maps and Mapping Strategies in Contemporary Canadian and Australian Fiction.* Toronto: U Toronto P, 1994.

Humphreys, Helen. *The Perils of Geography.* London, ON: Brick Books, 1995.

Hunt, John Dixon. *The Figure in the Landscape: Poetry, Painting, and Gardening during the Eighteenth Century.* Baltimore & London: Johns Hopkins UP, 1976.

– *Gardens and the Picturesque: Studies in the History of Landscape Architecture.* Cambridge, MA, & London: MIT P, 1992.

Hunter-Duvar, John. *De Roberval.* Excerpted in Daymond and Monkman, 1: 225–6.

Hutcheon, Linda. 'Frye Recoded: Postmodernity and the Conclusions.' *The Legacy of Northrop Frye*, ed. Alvin A. Lee and Robert D. Denham. Toronto: U Toronto P, 1994. 105–21.

Hutchison, Bruce. *The Unknown Country.* 1942. Rev. ed. Toronto: Longmans, Green, 1948.

In the Shadow of the Sun: Perspectives, ed. Canadian Museum of Civilization. Hull, PQ: CMC, 1993.

Irwin, William. *The New Niagara: Tourism, Technology, and the Landscape of Niagara Falls, 1776–1917.* State College, PA: Penn State UP, 1996.

Jackel, Susan. 'The House on the Prairies.' *Canadian Literature* 42 (Autumn 1969): 46–55.

Jackson, Peter. *Maps of Meaning: An Introduction to Cultural Geography.* London: Unwin Hyman, 1989.

Jasen, Patricia. *Wild Things: Nature, Culture, and Tourism in Ontario, 1790–1914.* Toronto: U Toronto P, 1995.

Jefferys, Charles William. *The Picture Gallery of Canadian History.* 3 vols. Toronto: Ryerson, 1942, 1945, 1950.

Jiles, Paulette. *Sitting in the Club Car Drinking Rum and Karma-Kola: A Manual of Etiquette for Ladies Ccrossing Canada by Train.* Winlaw, BC: Polestar, 1986.

Johnston, Basil. *Tales the Elders Told: Ojibway Legends.* Toronto: Royal Ontario Museum, 1981.

Jordan, David M. *New World Regionalism: Literature in the Americas.* Toronto: U Toronto P, 1994.

Kadish, Doris Y. *The Literature of Images.* New Brunswick, NJ, & London: Rutgers UP, 1987.

Kaiser, Rudolf. 'Chief Seattle's Speech(es): American Origins and European Reception.' *Recovering the Word: Essays on Native American Literature.* Ed. Brian Swann and Arnold Krupat. Berkeley: U California P, 1987. 497–536.

Kamboureli, Smaro. *In the Second Person.* Edmonton: Longspoon, 1985.

Kane, Sean. *Wisdom of the Storytellers.* Toronto: Broadview, 1994.

Kattan, Naïm. 'Le thème de l'espace dans la littérature canadienne-française.' Chadbourne and Dahlie. 121–32.

Kearns, Lionel. 'Notes on the Stack.' *Tish* 16 (14 December 1962). Rpt. in *Tish No. 1–19.* Ed. Frank Davey. Vancouver: Talonbooks, 1975. 337–9.

Keefer, Janice Kulyk. *Under Eastern Eyes: A Critical Reading of Maritime Fiction.* Toronto: U Toronto P, 1987.

Keith, W.J. *Literary Images of Ontario.* Toronto: U Toronto P, 1992.
- *The Poetry of Nature.* Toronto: U Toronto P, 1980.
- *Regions of the Imagination.* Toronto: U Toronto P, 1986.
Kemal, Salim, and Ivan Gaskell, eds. *Landscape, Natural Beauty and the Arts.* Cambridge: Cambridge UP, 1993.
Kenner, Hugh. 'The Case of the Missing Face.' *Our Sense of Identity.* Ed. Malcolm Ross. Toronto: Ryerson, 1954. 203–8.
Kertzer, J.M. 'L'Avarice de la Terre.' *Canadian Poetry* 5 (Fall/Winter 1979): 124–7.
Ketterer, David. *Canadian Science Fiction and Fantasy.* Bloomington: Indiana UP, 1993.
Kettner, J.D., II, and M.J. Tamminga, curators. *The Beautiful, the Sublime, and the Picturesque: British Influence on American Landscape Painting.* St Louis: Washington UP, 1984.
King, Thomas. Interview. Lutz 107–16.
- 'Introduction.' *All My Relations: An Anthology of Contemporary Canadian Native Prose.* Toronto: McClelland & Stewart, 1990. ix–xvi.
- 'The One About Coyote Going West.' *One Good Story, That One.* Toronto: Harper Perennial, 1993. 65–80.
King, Thomas, Cheryl Carver, and Helen Hoy, eds. *The Native in Literature.* Toronto: ECW, 1987.
Kirby, William. *The Golden Dog* 1877. Abridged. Toronto: McClelland & Stewart, 1969.
Klein, A.M. *Complete Poems, Part 2: Original Poems, 1937–1955, and Poetry Translations.* Ed. Zailig Pollock. Toronto: U Toronto P, 1990.
Kline, Marcia B. *Beyond the Land Itself: Views of Nature in Canada and the United States.* Cambridge, MA: Harvard UP, 1970.
Kobayashi, Audrey. 'Structured Feeling: Japanese Canadian Poetry and Landscape.' Simpson-Housley and Norcliffe 243–57.
Kolodny, Annette. *The Lay of the Land.* Chapel Hill: U North Carolina P, 1975.
Konrad, Victor, 'Symbolic Landscapes of Nationalism and Regionalism in Canada.' Berry and Acheson 515–24.
Kowaleski, Michael. 'Writing in Place: The New American Regionalism.' *American Literary History* 6.1 (Spring 1994): 171–83.
Kreisel, Henry. *The Almost Meeting and Other Stories.* Edmonton: NeWest, 1981.
- 'The Prairie: A State of Mind.' 1968; Rpt. in *Contexts of Canadian Criticism.* Ed. Eli Mandel. Chicago & London: U Chicago P; Toronto: U Toronto P, 1971. 254–66.
Kroeber, Karl. *Ecological Literary Criticism: Romantic Imagining and the Biology of Mind.* New York: Columbia UP, 1994.

– *Retelling/Rereading: The Fate of Storytelling in Modern Times.* New Brunswick, NJ: Rutgers UP, 1992.

Kroetsch, Robert. 'Seed Catalogue.' *Completed Field Notes.* Toronto: McClelland & Stewart, 1989. 32–51.

– 'Unhiding the Hidden.' *The Lovely Treachery of Words.* Toronto: Oxford, 1989. 58–63.

Kröller, Eva-Marie. 'The Exploding Frame.' *Journal of Canadian Studies* 16.3–4 (1981): 68–74.

Lamb, W. Kaye, ed. and introd. *The Journals and Letters of Sir Alexander Mackenzie.* Toronto: Macmillan, 1970.

Landscape. Special issue of *Meanjin* 47.3 (Spring 1988).

Lapointe, Gatien. *Ode au Saint Laurent.* 1983. Trois-Rivières: Editions du Zephyr, 1985.

Laurence, Margaret. *A Bird in the House.* Toronto: McClelland & Stewart, 1974.

– *The Diviners.* 1974. Toronto: McClelland & Stewart, 1975.

– *The Fire-Dwellers.* Toronto: McClelland & Stewart, 1969.

Lawson, Alan. 'Countries of the Mind: Place as Value in Canadian and Australian Critical Discourse.' Berry and Acheson 579–86.

Lawson-Peebles, Robert. *Landscape and Written Expression in Revolutionary America.* Cambridge: Cambridge UP, 1988.

Leacock, Stephen. *Sunshine Sketches of a Little Town.* 1912. Toronto: McClelland & Stewart, 1989.

Lebowitz, Andrea Pinto, ed. *Living in Harmony: Nature Writing by Women in Canada.* Victoria, BC, & Custer, WA: Orca, 1996.

Le Dantec, Denise, and J.-P. Le Dantec. *Reading the French Garden: Story and History,* trans. Jessica Levine. Cambridge: MA: MIT P, 1990.

Lee, Dennis. *Savage Fields.* Toronto: Anansi, 1977.

Leer, Martin. 'From Linear to Areal: Suggestions Towards a Comparative Literary Geography of Canada and Australia.' *Kunapipi* 12.3 (1990): 75–85.

Lefebvre, Henri. *The Production of Space* [1974]. Trans. Donald Nicholson-Smith. Oxford & Cambridge, MA: Blackwell, 1991.

LePan, Douglas. 'Some Observations on Myth and Legend – Irish and Canadian.' *Transactions of the Royal Society of Canada* 4th ser. 17 (1979): 85–97.

– *The Wounded Prince and Other Poems.* London: Chatto & Windus, 1948.

Linsley, Robert. 'Landscape and Literature in the Art of British Columbia.' Delany 193–216.

– 'Painting and the Social History of British Columbia.' Douglas 225–45.

Liversidge, M.J.H. 'Sriking 'a native note': C.W. Jefferys and Canadian Identity in Landscape Painting.' *British Journal of Canadian Studies* 9.1 (1994): 64–71.

Livingstone, David N. *The Geographical Tradition.* Oxford & Cambridge, MA: Blackwell, 1992.

Love, Glen. 'Et in Arcadia Ego: Pastoral Theory Meets Ecocriticism.' *Western American Literature* 27.3 (1992): 195–207.

– 'Revaluing Nature: Toward an Ecological Criticism.' *Western American Literature* 25.3 (1990): 201–15.

Lutwack, Leonard. *The Role of Place in Literature.* Syracuse: Syracuse UP, 1984.

Lutz, Hartmut. Interview with Thomas King. *Contemporary Challenges: Conversations with Canadian Native Authors.* Saskatoon: Fifth House, 1991. 107–16.

Lynes, Jeanette, and Herb Wylie. 'Regionalism and Ambivalence in Canadian Literary History.' *Open Letter* 9.4 (Fall 1995): 117–27.

Macaulay, Marcia. *Processing Varieties in English: An Examination of Oral and Written Speech across Genres.* Vancouver: U British Columbia P, 1990.

Macdonald, Bruce. *Vancouver: A Visual History.* Vancouver: Talonbooks, 1992.

MacDonald, J.E.H. 'Scandinavian Art.' *Northward Journal* 18–19 (November 1980): 9–35.

MacDonald, Mary Lu. 'The Natural World in Nineteenth-Century Canadian Literature.' *Canadian Literature* 111 (Winter 1986): 48–65.

Mackay, J. 'Quebec Hill or Canadian Scenery.' 1797. Rpt. in *Three Early Poems from Lower Canada.* Ed. Michael Gnarowski. Montreal: Lawrence M. Lande, 1969.

Mackenzie, Alexander. *The Journals and Letters of Sir Alexander Mackenzie.* Ed. W. Kaye Lamb. Cambridge: Hakluyt Society, 1970.

MacKenzie, John M. *Imperialism and the Natural World.* Manchester: Manchester UP, 1990.

MacLaren, Ian. 'The Aesthetic Mapping of Nature in the Second Franklin Expedition.' *Journal of Canadian Studies* 20.1 (1985): 39–57.

– 'Aesthetic Mapping of the West by the Palliser and Hind Survey Expeditions, 1857–1859.' *Studies in Canadian Literature* 10.1–2 (1985): 24–52.

– 'The Grandest Tour: The Aesthetics of Landscape in Sir George Back's Exploration of the Eastern Arctic, 1833–1837.' *English Studies in Canada* 10.4 (1984): 436–56.

– 'The McGregor Syndrome,' *Canadian Poetry* 18 (Spring/Summer 1986): 118–30.

– 'Samuel Hearne and the Landscape of Discovery.' *Canadian Literature* 103 (Winter 1984): 27–40.

MacLennan, Hugh. *Barometer Rising.* New York: Duell, Sloan and Pearce, 1941.

– *Two Solitudes.* 1945. Toronto: Macmillan, 1967.

MacLulich, T.D. 'The Explorer as Hero.' *Canadian Literature* 75 (Winter 1977): 61–73.

Madoff, Mark S. 'Hewers of Wood: Politics and Poetical Landscape in British Columbia.' Berry and Acheson 485–93.

Malouf, David. 'Space, Writing and Historical Identity.' *Thesis Eleven* 22 (1989): 92–105.

Mandel, Eli. 'The Inward, Northward Journal of Lawren Harris.' *artscanada* [Myth and Landscape issue] 222–3 (October/November 1978): 17–24.

– *Life Sentence.* Toronto & Victoria: Press Porcépic, 1981.

– 'Romance and Realism in Western Canadian Fiction.' *Another Time.* Erin, ON: Press Porcépic, 1977. 54–67.

– *Stony Plain.* Erin, ON: Press Porcépic, 1973.

– 'Writing West: On the Road to Wood Mountain.' *Another Time* 68–78.

Mannoni, O. *Prospero and Caliban: The Psychology of Colonization.* Trans. Pamela Powesland. 2d ed. New York: Praeger, 1964.

Maracle, Brian. *Back on the Rez: Finding the Way Home.* Toronto: Viking, 1996.

Maracle, Lee. 'Yin Chin.' *Sojourner's Truth and Other Stories.* Vancouver: Press Gang, 1990. 65–72.

Marlatt, Daphne. *Ana Historic.* Toronto: Coach House, 1988.

– 'Entering In: The Immigrant Imagination.' *Canadian Literature* 100 (Summer 1984): 219–23.

– *Steveston.* Vancouver: Talonbooks, 1974.

Marx, Leo. 'The American Revolution and the American Landscape.' *The Pilot and the Passenger: Essays on Literature, Technology, and Culture in the United States.* New York: Oxford UP, 1988. 315–36.

– *The Machine in the Garden.* 1964. New York: Oxford UP, 1967.

Massey, Doreen. 'Flexible Sexism.' *Space, Place, and Gender* 212–48.

– 'The Political Place of Locality Studies.' *Space, Place, and Gender* 125–45.

– *Space, Place, and Gender.* Minneapolis: U Minnesota P, 1994.

– 'A Woman's Place.' *Space, Place, and Gender* 191–211.

Matthews, Ralph. *The Creation of Regional Dependency.* Toronto: U Toronto P, 1983.

Matthews, Ralph, and J. Campbell Davis. 'Is Regionalism Dead? Confronting Recent Interpretations of Regionalism in Canada.' Berry and Acheson 339–52.

Maxwell, D.E.S. 'Landscape and Theme.' *Commonwealth Literature: Unity and Diversity in a Common Culture.* Ed. John Press. London: Heinemann Educational, 1965. 82–9.

McCaffery, Steve. *North of Intention.* New York: Roof; Toronto: Nightwood, 1986.

McCann, L.D., ed. *Heartland and Hinterland.* 2d ed. Scarborough, ON: Prentice-Hall, 1987.

McClung, Nellie. *In Times Like These.* Introd. Veronica Strong-Boag. Toronto: U Toronto P, 1972.

McDowell, Linda. 'City and Home.' *Sexual Divisions: Patterns and Processes.* Ed. Mary Evans and Clare Ungerson. London: Tavistock, 1983. 142–63.

McGifford, Diane, ed. *The Geography of Voice: Canadian Literature of the South Asian Diaspora.* Toronto: TSAR, 1992.

McGrath, Carmelita. 'If the Land Has Memory.' *Signatures: Newfoundland Women Artists and Writers.* Ed. Carmelita McGrath. St John's: Killick, 1996. 14–17.

McGreevy, Patrick. 'Reading the Texts of Niagara Falls: The Metaphor of Death.' Barnes and Duncan 56–72.

McGregor, Gaile. *The Wacousta Syndrome: Explorations in the Canadian Langscape.* Toronto: U Toronto P, 1985.

McKay, Ian. *The Quest of the Folk: Antimodernism and Cultural Selection in Twentieth-Century Nova Scotia.* Montreal & Kingston: McGill–Queen's UP, 1994.

McKenna, Katherine M.J. *A Life of Propriety.* Montreal & Kingston: McGill–Queen's UP, 1994.

McKillop, A.B. *Contours of Canadian Thought.* Toronto: U Toronto P, 1987.

McKinsey, Elizabeth. *Niagara Falls, Icon of the American Sublime.* Cambridge: Cambridge UP, 1985.

McLachlan, Alexander. *The Poetical Works of Alexander McLachlan.* 1900. Introd. Margaret Fulton. Toronto: U Toronto P, 1974.

McNaughton, Trudie, ed. *Countless Signs: The New Zealand Landscape in Literature.* Auckland: Reed Methuen, 1986.

Meinig, D.W. *The Interpretation of Ordinary Landscapes.* New York: Oxford, 1979.

Melnyk, George. *Radical Regionalism.* Edmonton: NeWest, 1981.

Metcalf, John. 'Punctuation as Score.' *Kicking Against the Pricks.* Toronto: ECW, 1982. 95–116.

Miller, J. Hillis. *Topographies.* Stanford: Stanford UP, 1995.

Mills, Caroline. 'Myths and Meanings of Gentrification.' Duncan and Ley 149–70.

Mingay, G.E. *A Social History of the English Countryside.* London: Routledge, 1991.

Mistry, Rohinton. *Tales from Firozsha Baag.* Markham, ON: Penguin, 1987.

Mitcham, Allison. *The Northern Imagination: A Study of Northern Canadian Literature.* Moonbeam, ON: Penumbra, 1983.

– *Prophet of the Wilderness: Abraham Gesner.* Hantsport, NS: Lancelot, 1995.

Mitchell, W.O. *Who Has Seen the Wind.* 1947. Toronto: Macmillan, 1972.

Moi, Toril. *Sexual/Textual Politics.* London & New York: Methuen, 1985.

Monkman, Leslie. *A Native Heritage.* Toronto: U Toronto P, 1981.

Monmonier, Mark. *How to Lie with Maps.* Chicago & London: U Chicago P, 1991.

Moodie, D. Wayne. 'Indian Map-Making.' Wynn, *People,* 56–67.

Moodie, Susanna. *Letters of a Lifetime.* Ed. Carl Ballstadt, Elizabeth Hopkins, and Michael Peterman. Toronto: U Toronto P, 1985.

- *Life in the Clearings versus the Bush.* 1853. Ed. Robert L. McDougall. Toronto: Macmillan, 1959.

- *Roughing It in the Bush.* 1853. Ed. Carl Ballstadt. Ottawa: Carleton UP, 1988.

Moodie, Susanna, and J.W. Moodie, eds. *The Victoria Magazine, 1847–1848.* Vancouver: U British Columbia Library, 1968.

Moore, Henrietta L. *Space, Text and Gender: An Anthropological Study of the Marakwet of Kenya.* Cambridge: Cambridge UP, 1986.

Morrison, R. Bruce, and C. Roderick Wilson, eds. *Native Peoples: The Canadian Experience.* Toronto: McClelland & Stewart, 1986.

Moss, John. *Enduring Dreams: An Exploration of Arctic Landscape.* Concord, ON: Anansi, 1994.

- 'Landscape, Untitled.' *Essays on Canadian Writing* 29 (Summer 1984): 26–47.

Motut, Roger. 'From Ploughshares to Pen: Prairie Nostalgia.' Chadbourne and Dahlie 61–78.

Mudimbe, V.Y. *The Invention of Africa: Gnosis, Philosophy, and the Order of Knowledge.* London: James Currey; Bloomington & Indianapolis: Indiana UP, 1988.

Mulhallen, Karen. 'Schaferscapes/Wolfbound: Twelve Notes Toward a New View of Camping.' *Descant* 26.1 (Spring 1995): 133–76.

Mumford, Lewis. *The City in History: Its Origins, Its Transformation, and Its Prospects.* New York: Harcourt, Brace, 1961.

Munro, Alice. 'Chaddeleys and Flemings.' *The Moons of Jupiter.* Toronto: Macmillan, 1982, 1–35.

- *Dance of the Happy Shades.* Toronto: McGraw-Hill Ryerson, 1968.

- *Friend of My Youth.* 1990. Toronto: Penguin, 1991.

Murray, Heather. 'Metaphor and Metonymy, Language and Land in Swamp Angel.' *WLWE* 25.2 (Autumn 1985): 241–52.

Naipaul, V.S. *The Enigma of Arrival.* New York: Viking Penguin, 1987.

Nakano, Takēo, with Leatrice Nakano. *Within the Barbed Wire Fence: A Japanese Man's Account of His Internment in Canada.* Toronto: U Toronto P, 1980.

Neuman, Shirley, and Smaro Kamboureli, eds. *A Mazing Space.* Edmonton: Longspoon/NeWest, 1986.

New, W.H. *Dreams of Speech and Violence.* Toronto: U Toronto P, 1987.

- 'The Great-River Theory: Reading MacLennan and Mulgan.' *Essays on Canadian Writing* 56 (Fall 1995): 162–82.

- ed. *Native Writers and Canadian Writing.* Vancouver: U British Columbia P, 1990.

- 'A Piece of the Continent, A Part of the Main: Some Comments on B.C. Literature.' *BC Studies* 67 (Autumn 1985): 3–28.

Newlove, John. *The Fat Man: Selected Poems, 1962–1972*. Toronto: McClelland & Stewart, 1977.

Ng, Lucy. 'The Sullen Shapes of Poems.' *Many-Mouthed Birds*, Ed. Bennett Lee and Jim Wong-Chu. Vancouver: Douglas & McIntyre, 1991. 161–8.

Nichol, bp. *The Martyrology. Book 6 Books, 1978–1985*. Toronto: Coach House, 1987.

Noble, Allen G., and Ranesh Dhussa. 'Image and Substance: A Review of Literary Geography,' *Journal of Cultural Geography* 10.2 (Spring/Summer 1990): 49–65.

Norcliffe, Glen. 'In a Hard Land: The Geographical Context of Canadian Industrial Landscape Painting.' Simpson-Housley and Norcliffe 71–85.

Northey, Margot. *The Haunted Wilderness: The Gothic and Grotesque in Canadian Fiction*. Toronto: U Toronto P, 1976.

Novak, Barbara. *Nature and Culture: American Landscape and Painting, 1825–1875*. New York: Oxford UP, 1980.

O'Flaherty, Patrick. *The Rock Observed*. Toronto: U Toronto P, 1979.

Olsson, Gunnar. *Lines of Power/Limits of Language*. Minneapolis & Oxford: U Minnesota P, 1991.

Ondaatje, Michael. *In the Skin of a Lion*. Toronto: McClelland & Stewart, 1987.

Ong, Walter. *Orality and Literacy*. London & New York: Methuen, 1982.

On Maps and Mapping. Special issue of *artscanada* 188–9 (Spring 1974).

Orbell, Margaret. *The Natural World of the Maori*. Photographs by Geoff Moon. Auckland: Collins, 1985.

Ornstein, Michael, H. Michael Stevenson, and A. Paul Williams. 'Region, Class and Political Culture in Canada.' *Canadian Journal of Political Science* 13.2 (June 1980): 229–71.

Osborne, Brian S. 'The Iconography of Nationhood in Canadian Art.' Cosgrove and Daniels 162–78.

Overton, James. 'A Newfoundland Culture?' *Journal of Canadian Studies* 23.1–2 (Fall 1990): 5–18.

Paikowsky, Sandra. 'Landscape Painting in Canada.' *Profiles of Canada*. Ed. Kenneth G. Pryke and Walter C. Soderlund. Toronto: Copp Clark Pitman, 1992. 336–62.

Paradis, Andrea, ed. *Out of This World Canadian Science Fiction & Fantasy Literature*. Ottawa: Quarry/National Library of Canada, 1995.

Parks, Ward. 'The Textualization of Orality in Literary Criticism.' *Vox intexta: Orality and Textuality in the Middle Ages*. Ed. A.N. Doane and Carol Braun Pasternack. Madison: U Wisconsin P, 1991. 46–61.

Peterman, Michael. 'Susanna Moodie (1803–1885).' *Canadian Writers and Their Works*, Fiction series 1. Ed. Robert Lecker, Jack David, and Ellen Quigley. Downsview, ON: ECW. 63–104.

- 'Ontario: Ours to Discover.' *Journal of Canadian Studies* 20.1 (Spring 1985): 3–4.
Petrone, Penny. *Native Literature in Canada: From the Oral Tradition to the Present.* Toronto: Oxford UP, 1990.
Philip, M. Nourbese. *Frontiers: Essays and Writings on Racism and Culture.* Stratford, ON: Mercury, 1992.
Pile, Steve, and Nigel Thrift, eds. *Mapping the Subject: Geographies of Cultural Transformation.* London & New York: Routledge, 1995.
Pinder, Leslie Hall. 'To the Fourth Wall.' in *Vancouver Forum: Old Powers, New Forces.* Ed. Max Wyman. Vancouver: Douglas & McIntyre, 1992. 19–51.
Plumwood, Val. 'Plato and the Bush: Philosophy and the Environment in Australia.' *Meanjin* 49.3 (Spring 1990): 524–36.
Pocock, Douglas C.D. 'Geography and Literature.' *Progress in Human Geography* 12 (1988): 87–102.
Polk, James. *Wilderness Writers.* Toronto: Clarke Irwin, 1972.
Pollock, Griselda. *Vision and Difference: Femininity, Feminism and Histories of Art.* London & New York: Routledge, 1988.
Pope, Alexander. *Poetical Works.* Ed. Herbert Davis. Oxford: Oxford UP, 1978.
Porteous, J. Douglas. 'Literature and Humanist Geography.' *Area* 17.2 (June 1985): 117–22.
Pratt, E.J. *Complete Poems Part 2.* Ed. Sandra Djwa and R.G. Moyles. Toronto: U Toronto P, 1989.
- *E.J. Pratt on His Life and Poetry.* Ed. Susan Gingell. Toronto: U Toronto P, 1983.
Pratt, Mary Louise. *Imperial Eyes: Travel Writing and Transculturation.* London & New York: Routledge, 1982.
Pred, Allan. *Lost Words and Lost Worlds.* Cambridge: Cambridge UP, 1990.
- 'Place as Historically Contingent Process: Structuration and the Time-Geography of Becoming Places.' *Annals of the Association of American Geographers* 74.2 (June 1984): 279–97.
- 'Structuration and Place: On the Becoming of Sense of Place and Structure of Feeling.' *Journal for the Theory of Social Behaviour* 13.1 (March 1983): 45–68.
Preston, Richard. 'Regionalism and National Identity: Canada.' Berry and Acheson 3–11.
Pritchard, Allan. 'West of the Great Divide.' *Canadian Literature* 94 (Autumn 1982): 96–112, and 102 (Autumn 1985): 36–53.
Pugh, Simon. *Garden–Nature–Language.* Manchester: Manchester UP, 1988.
Purdy, Al. 'Ave Imperator.' *Canadian Literature* 73 (Summer 1977): 86.
- *The Cariboo Horses.* Toronto: McClelland & Stewart, 1965.
Raglon, Rebecca, and Marian Scholtmeijer. 'Shifting Ground: Metanarratives, Epistemology, and the Stories of Nature.' *Environmental Ethics* 18 (1996): 19–38.

Ramsay, Ellen. 'Picturing the Picturesque.' Simpson-Housley and Norcliffe 158–70.

Ramusio, Giovanni. *Terzo volume della navigationi et viaggi raccolto gia da M. Gio. Battista Ramusio.* Venice, 1565.

Reaney, James. 'Ontario Culture and – What?' *Canadian Literature* 100 (Spring 1984): 252–7.

Redbird, Duke. *We Are Metis.* Willowdale, ON: Ontario Metis and Non-status Indian Assoc., 1980.

Rees, Ronald. *New and Naked Land: Making the Prairies Home.* Saskatoon: Western Producer Prairie, 1988.

Regis, Pamela. *Describing Early America: Bartram, Jefferson, Crèvecoeur, and the Rhetoric of Natural History.* De Kalb: Northern Illinois UP, 1992.

Reid, Bill, and Robert Bringhurst. *The Raven Steals the Light.* Vancouver & Toronto: Douglas & McIntyre, 1984.

Reid, Martine. 'In Search of Things Past, Remembered, Retraced, and Reinverted.' *In the Shadow* 71–92.

Richard, Jean-Pierre. *Pages Paysages.* Paris: Editions du Seuil, 1984.

Richler, Mordecai. *The Apprenticeship of Duddy Kravitz.* Boston & Toronto: Little, Brown, 1959.

Ricou, L.R. 'Dumb Talk.' *BC Studies* 65 (Spring 1985): 34–47.

– 'The Meadowlark Tradition: popular verse of the Canadian Prairie.' *Essays on Canadian Writing* 18–19 (Summer-Fall 1980): 161–8.

– *Vertical Man/Horizontal World.* Vancouver: U British Columbia P, 1973.

– 'The Writing of British Columbia Writing.' *BC Studies* 100 (Winter 1993–4): 106–20.

Ridington, Robin. *Trail to Heaven: Knowledge and Narrative in a Northern Native Community.* Vancouver & Toronto: Douglas & McIntyre, 1988.

Ringuet [Philippe Panneton]. *Trente Arpents* [1938]. Trans. Felix and Dorothea Walter as *Thirty Acres.* Toronto: McClelland & Stewart, 1989.

Robbins, William G., Robert J. Frank, and Richard E. Ross, eds. *Regionalism and the Pacific Northwest.* Corvallis: Oregon State UP, 1983.

Roberts, Sir Charles G.D. *The Collected Poems of Sir Charles G.D. Roberts,* Ed. Desmond Pacey and Graham Adams. Wolfville, NS: Wombat, 1985.

– *The Last Barrier and Other Stories.* Toronto: McClelland & Stewart, 1958.

Rose, Gillian. 'Making Space for the Female Subject of Feminism.' Pile and Thrift 332–54.

Rosen, Charles. *The Romantic Generation.* Cambrdige, MA: Harvard UP, 1995.

Ross, Malcolm. *The Impossible Sum of Our Traditions.* Toronto: McClelland & Stewart, 1988.

Ross, Sinclair. *As For Me and My House.* 1941. Toronto: McClelland & Stewart, 1989.

Roy, Gabrielle. *Bonheur d'occasion* [1945]. Trans. Alan Brown as *The Tin Flute*. Toronto: McClelland & Stewart, 1989.

– 'Where Will You Go Sam Lee Wong?' *Garden in the Wind* [*Un jardin au bout du monde*, 1975]. Trans. Alan Brown. Toronto: McClelland & Stewart, 1977. 49–104.

Roy, Patricia. *Vancouver: An Illustrated History*. Toronto: James Lorimer & National Museum of Man, 1980.

Rutherford, Anna, ed. *Populous Places: Australian Cities and Towns*. Sydney: Dangaroo, 1992.

Ryan, Simon. 'Exploring Aesthetics: The Picturesque Appropriation of Land in Journals of Australian Exploration.' *Australian Literary Studies* 15.4 (October 1992): 282–93.

– 'Voyeurs in Space: The Gendered Scopic Regime of Exploration.' *Southerly* 1 (1994): 36–49.

Salter, C.L., and W.J. Lloyd. *Landscape and Literature*. Washington: Assoc. of American Geographers, 1976.

Sandberg, L. Anders, and John S. Marsh, eds. 'Literary Landscapes – Geography and Literature.' *Canadian Geographer* 32.3 (1988): 266–76.

Sarasohn, David. 'Regionalism, Tending toward Sectionalism.' Robbins, Frank, and Ross 223–36.

Schama, Simon. *Landscape and Memory*. Toronto: Random House, 1995.

Schlereth, Thomas J., ed. *Cultural History and Material Culture: Everyday Life, Landscapes, Museums*. Ann Arbor & London: UMI, 1990.

Schwartz, Mildred. *Politics and Territoriality: The Sociology of Regional Persistence in Canada*. Montreal & Kingston: McGill–Queen's UP, 1974.

Scollon, Ron, and Suzanne B.K. Scollon. 'Cooking It Up and Boiling It Down: Abstracts in Athabaskan Children's Story Retellings.' *Coherence in Spoken and Written Discourse*. Ed. Deborah Tannen. Norwood, NJ: ABLEX, 1984. 173–97.

Scott, Duncan Campbell. 'Poetry and Progress.' Rpt. in S.L. Dragland, *Duncan Campbell Scott: A Book of Criticism*. Ottawa: Tecumseh, 1974. 7–27.

Scott, F.R. *Events and Signals*. Toronto: Ryerson, 1954.

– *F.R. Scott: Selected Poems*. Toronto: Oxford, 1966.

Scott, J.M. *The Land that God Gave Cain*. Harmondsworth: Penguin, 1933.

Seamon, Roger. 'Uneasy in Eden: Jeff Wall and the Vancouver Syndrome.' Delany 242–56.

Seaton, Dorothy. 'Colonising Discourses: The Land in Australian and Western Canadian Exploration Narratives.' *Australian–Canadian Studies* 6.2 (1989): 3–14.

– 'Land and History: Inter-Discursive Conflict in Voss.' *Australian and New Zealand Studies in Canada* 4 (Fall 1990): 1–14.

– 'The Post-Colonial as Deconstruction: Land and Language in Kroetsch's *Badlands.' Canadian Literature* 128 (Spring 1991): 77–89.

Shields, Rob. *Places on the Margin: Alternative Geographies of Modernity.* London & New York: Routledge, 1991.

Shoemaker, Adam. 'Landscapes and Mindscapes, Regionalism and Nationalism in Canadian and Australian Culture.' *Re-Siting Queen's English.* Ed. Gilliam Whitlock and Helen Tiffin. Amsterdam & Atlanta: Rodopi, 1992. 117–29.

Shortridge, James R. 'The Emergence of 'Middle West' as an American Regional Label.' *Annals of the Association of American Geographers* 74.2 (1984): 209–20.

Silk, J. 'Beyond Geography and Literature.' *Environment and Planning D: Society and Space* 2.2 (April 1984): 151–78.

Silko, Leslie Marmon. 'Landscape, History, and the Pueblo Imagination.' *Antaeus* 57 (Autumn 1986): 83–94.

Simpson-Housley, Paul, and Glen Norcliffe, eds. *A Few Acres of Snow: Literary and Artistic Images of Canada.* Toronto: Dundurn, 1992.

Sims, Peter. 'Photography "in Camera."' *Canadian Literature* 113–14 (Summer/ Fall 1987): 145–66.

Smart, Patricia. *Writing in the Father's House: The Emergence of the Feminine in the Quebec Literary Tradition.* Toronto: U Toronto P, 1991.

Smith, A.J.M. *Collected Poems.* Toronto: Oxford UP, 1962.

Smith, Allan. 'Farms, Forests and Cities: The Image of the Land and the Rise of the Metropolis in Ontario, 1860–1914.' *Old Ontario: Essays in Honour of J.M.S. Careless,* Ed. David Keane and Colin Read. Toronto & Oxford: Dundurn, 1990. 71–94.

Smith, Neil. 'Geography, Empire and Social Theory.' *Progress in Human Geography* 18.4 (1994): 491–500.

Soja, Edward. *Postmodern Geographies: The Reassertion of Space in Critical Social Theory.* London & New York: Verso, 1989.

Spain, Daphne. *Gendered Space.* Chapel Hill: U North Carolina P, 1992.

Spettigue, Douglas. *FPG: The European Years.* Ottawa: Oberon, 1973.

Sprat, Thomas. *History of the Royal Society of London.* 1667. Ed. Jackson I. Cope and Harold Whitmore Jones. St Louis: Washington UP, 1958.

Stacey, Robert. 'A Contact in Context: The Influence of Scandinavian Landscape Painting on Canadian Artists Before and After 1913.' *Northward Journal* 18–19 (November 1980): 9–56.

Stafford, Barbara Maria. *Voyage into Substance: Art, Science, Nature, and the Illustrated Travel Account, 1760–1840.* Cambridge, MA: MIT P, 1984.

Staines, David, ed. *The 49th and Other Parallels: Contemporary Canadian Perspectives.* Amherst: U Massachusetts P, 1986.

Steele, Fritz. *The Sense of Place.* Boston: CBI, 1981.

Stich, K.P. 'Grove's New World Bluff.' *Canadian Literature* 90 (Autumn 1981): 111–23.

Stoddart, David R. *On Geography and Its History.* Oxford: Basil Blackwell, 1992.

Stratford, Philip. 'Quebec Landscape Poetry in French and English: A Song for Two Voices, Not Necessarily a Duet.' *Multiple Voices: Recent Canadian Fiction.* Ed. Jeanne Delbaere. Sydney: Dangaroo, 1990. 161–74.

Sun [Vancouver]. 3 October 1992.

Surette, Leon. 'Here Is Us: The Topocentrism of Canadian Literary Criticism.' *Canadian Poetry* 10 (Spring/Summer 1982): 44–57.

Tacey, David J. *Edge of the Sacred: Transformation in Australia.* North Blackburn, Victoria: HarperCollins, 1995.

Tagg, John. *Grounds of Dispute: Art History, Cultural Politics and the Discursive Field.* London: Macmillan, 1992.

Talbot, Steve. '"Sacred Mother Earth" – Indians and the Land.' *Gulliver: Deutsch-englische Jarbucher* 17 (1985): 53–70.

Taylor, C.J. 'Legislating Nature: The National Parks Act of 1930.' *To see ourselves/ to save ourselves: Ecology and culture in Canada.* Ed. Rowland Lorimer, Michael McGonigle, Jean-Pierre Revéret, and Sally Ross. Montreal: Assoc. for Canadian Studies, 1991. 125–37.

Tedlock, Dennis. 'Toward an Oral Poetics.' *New Literary History* 8.3 (Spring 1977): 507–19.

Teyssot, Georges. 'Heterotopias and the History of Spaces.' Trans. David Stewart. *Architecture and Urbanism* 10.121 (1980): 79–100.

Thomas, Clara, and John Lennox. 'Grove's Maps.' *Essays on Canadian Writing* 26 (Summer 1983): 75–9.

Thomas, Keith. *Man and the Natural World.* London: Allen Lane, 1983.

Thompson, David. *Travels in Western North America, 1784–1812.* Ed. Victor G. Hopwood. Toronto: Macmillan, 1971.

Thomson, Edward William. *Old Man Savarin and Other Stories.* New York & Boston: Crowell, 1895.

Thornton, Tamara Plakins. *Cultivating Gentlemen: The Meaning of Country Life among the Boston Elite, 1785–1860.* New Haven: Yale UP, 1989.

Thrift, Nigel. 'Landscape and Literature.' *Environment and Planning A* 10 (1978): 347–49.

– 'Nature, the Production of Culture and the Politics of Place.' *Antipode* 15.1 (1983): 12–24.

Thurston, John. 'Rewriting Roughing It.' *Future Indicative.* Ed. John Moss. Ottawa: U Ottawa P, 1987. 195–204.

Tindall, Gillian. *Countries of the Mind: The Meaning of Place to Writers*. London: Hogarth, 1991.

Tippett, Maria, and Douglas Cole. *From Desolation to Splendour: Changing Perceptions of the British Columbia Landscape*. Toronto: Clarke Irwin, 1977.

Titley, E. Brian. *A Narrow Vision: Duncan Campbell Scott and the Administration of Indian Affairs in Canada*. Vancouver: U British Columbia P, 1986.

Todorov, Tzvetan. *The Conquest of America: The Question of the Other* [1982]. Trans. Richard Howard. New York: Harper & Row, 1984.

Tolstoy, Leo. 'How Much Land Does a Man Need?' 1886. *Stories and Legends*. Trans. Louise and Aylmer Maude. New York: Pantheon, [1946]. 45–66.

Tostevin, Lola Lemire. *The Color of Her Speech*. Toronto: Coach House, 1982.

Traill, Catharine Parr. *The Canadian Settler's Guide*. 1855. Toronto: McClelland & Stewart, 1969.

Trollope, Frances. *Domestic Manners of the Americans*. 1832. Ed. Donald Smalley. New York: Alfred A. Knopf, 1949.

Tuan, Yi-Fu. *Space and Place: The Perspective of Experience*. Minneapolis: U Minnesota P, 1977.

– *Topophilia: A Study of Environmental Perception, Attitudes, and Values*. 1974. Rev. ed. New York: Columbia UP, 1990.

Turner, Graeme. *National Fictions: Literature, Film, and the Construction of Australian Narrative*. 2d ed. St Leonards, NSW: Allen & Unwin, 1993.

Vancouver, George. *A Voyage of Discovery to the North Pacific Ocean, and round the World*. 1798. Amsterdam: N. Israel; New York: Da Capo, 1967.

van Herk, Aritha. *A Frozen Tongue*. Sydney: Dangaroo, 1992.

– *No Fixed Address*. Toronto: McClelland & Stewart, 1986.

– *Places Far from Ellesmere: A Geografictione: explorations on site*. Red Deer, AB: Red Deer College P, 1990.

– 'Woman Writers and the Prairie: Spies in an Indifferent Landscape.' *Kunapipi* 6.2 (1984): 15–25.

Vigneault, Gilles. 'Mon pays.' *Avec les vieux mots*. Ottawa: Editions de L'Arc, 1964. 13.

von Baeyer, Edwinna, and Pleasance Crawford, eds. *Garden Voices: Two Centuries of Canadian Garden Writing*. Toronto: Random House, 1995.

Wachtel, Eleanor. 'An Interview with Daphne Marlatt.' *Capilano Review* 41 (1986): 4–13.

Wadland, John Henry. *Ernest Thompson Seton: Man in Nature and the Progressive Era, 1880–1915*. New York: Arno, 1978.

Waiser, Bill. *Park Prisoners: The Untold Story of Western Canada's National Parks, 1915–1946*. Saskatoon: Fifth House, 1995.

Wakefield, Edward Gibbon. *The Collected Works of Edward Gibbon Wakefield.* Ed. M.F. Lloyd Prichard. Auckland: Collins, 1969.

Walters, Derek. *The Feng Shui Handbook.* London & San Francisco: Thorsons, 1991.

Warkentin, John. 'Discovering the Shape of Canada.' *artscanada* 188–9 (Spring 1974): 17–37.

– *The Western Interior of Canada: A Record of Geographical Discovery, 1612–1917.* Toronto: McClelland & Stewart, 1964.

Warwick, Jack. 'Continuity in New Land Themes from New France to the Present.' Chadbourne and Dahlie 27–44.

– *The Long Journey.* Toronto: U Toronto P, 1968.

Watson, Scott. 'Discovering the Defeatured Landscape.' Douglas 247–66.

– 'Race, Wilderness, Territory and the Origins of Modern Canadian Landscape Painting.' *Semiotext(e)* 6.2 (1994): 93–104.

Watson, Sheila. *The Double Hook.* 1959. Toronto: McClelland & Stewart, 1984.

Watson, Wilfred. *Poems Collected/unpublished/new.* Edmonton: Longspoon/ NeWest, 1986.

Watson, Wreford. 'Canadian Regionalism in Life and Letters.' *Geographical Journal* 131.1 (March 1965): 21–33.

Watzke, Beth. 'Writing the West: Regionalism and Western Australia.' *Westerly* 37.1 (Autumn 1992): 21–9.

Wayman, Tom. 'The Ecology of Place.' Daymond and Monkman, 2: 709–10.

Westfall, William. 'On the Concept of Region in Canadian History and Literature.' *Journal of Canadian Studies* 15.2 (1980): 3–15.

Wiebe, Rudy. *My Lovely Enemy.* Toronto: McClelland & Stewart, 1983.

– *Playing Dead: A Contemplation Concerning the Arctic.* Edmonton: NeWest, 1989.

Williams, Glyndwr. 'Myth and Reality: The Theoretical Geography of Northwest America from Cook to Vancouver.' Fisher and Johnston 2–50.

Williams, Raymond. *The Country and the City.* London: Chatto & Windus, 1973.

– *Culture.* London: Fontana, 1981.

– *Keywords.* New York: Oxford UP, 1976.

Willis, Nathaniel Parker. *Canadian Scenery Illustrated,* from drawings by W.H. Bartlett. 2 vols. London: George Virtue, 1842.

Wilson, Ethel. *Swamp Angel.* 1954. Toronto: McClelland & Stewart, 1990.

Winks, Robin W. 'Regionalism in Comparative Perspective.' Robbins, Frank, and Ross 13–36.

Wiseman, Adele. *The Sacrifice.* Toronto: Macmillan, 1956.

Womack, Peter. *Improvement and Romance: Constructing the Myth of the Highlands.* London: Macmillan, 1989.

Wood, Susan. *The Land in Canadian Prose.* Ottawa: Carleton UP, 1988.

Woodcock, George. 'There are no universal landscapes.' *Myth and Landscape* 36–42.

Woodward, David. 'Medieval Mappaemundi.' Harley and Woodward 286–370.

Wordsworth, William. *The Poetical Works of Wordsworth.* Ed. Thomas Hutchinson. Rev. Ed. Ernest de Selincourt. London: Humphrey Miles, Oxford UP, 1942.

Wright, Judith. 'Wilderness and Wasteland.' *Island Magazine* 42.3 (March 1990): 3–7.

Wyatt, Victoria. 'Art and Exploration: The Responses of Northwest Coast Native Artists to Maritime Explorers and Fur Traders.' Fisher and Johnston 176–90.

Wynn, Graeme. 'For the Birds.' *Essays on Canadian Writing* 55 (Spring 1995): 40–50.

– ed. *People, Places, Patterns, Processes: Geographical Perspectives on the Canadian Past.* Toronto: Copp Clark Pitman, 1990.

York, Lorraine M. 'Home Thoughts or Abroad? A Rhetoric of Place in Modern and Postmodern Canadian Political Poetry.' *Essays on Canadian Writing* 51–2 (Winter 1993/Spring 1994): 321–39.

– '"Its Better Nature Lost": The Importance of the Word in Sinclair Ross's *As For Me and My House.*' *Canadian Literature* 103 (Winter 1984): 166–74.

– '"Sublime Desolation": European Art and Jameson's Perception of Canada.' *Mosaic* 19.2 (Spring 1986): 43–56.

Young, Robert J.C. *Colonial Desire: Hybridity in Theory, Culture and Race.* London & New York: Routledge, 1995.

Zaslow, Morris. *Reading the Rocks: The Story of the Geological Survey of Canada, 1842–1972.* Toronto: Macmillan, in assoc. with Dept. of Energy, Mines, & Resources and Information Canada, 1975.

Zeller, Suzanne. *Inventing Canada: Early Victorian Science and the Idea of a Trans-continental Nation.* Toronto: U Toronto P, 1987.

– 'Mapping the Canadian Mind: Reports of the Geological Survey of Canada, 1842–1863.' *Canadian Literature* 131 (Winter 1991): 157–67.

Zukin, Sharon. *Landscapes of Power: From Detroit to Disney.* Berkeley: U California P, 1991.

Index

maleness. *See* masculinity
Mandel, Eli 148, 151–2, 196, 203–4
Manitoba 104, 108–9, 122, 150, 158
Manore, Jean 27
manuscripts, illuminated 9
Maori 72
'Mappemounde' 44
maps, map-making 4, 6, 27, 29, 38,
    44, 47, 55–6, 63, 73–4, 101, 110,
    114, 129, 131, 153, 164, 169, 171–2,
    184, 202, 204, 224; of kinship 220;
    Native mapping 220
Maracle, Brian 221
Maracle, Lee 207
Marakwet 8
margin and centre 7–8, 11, 18, 39,
    103, 104–6, 108, 114–21, 134,
    142–6, 152–6, 172, 200–2
Maritimes 24, 98, 130, 144–5, 152,
    226
Marlatt, Daphne 166–8, 208
Marshall, John 24
Martineau, Harriet 60
Martyrology, The 165
Marxism 10, 228
masculinity, manliness, maleness 3,
    15, 64, 101–2, 104, 109–10, 119,
    123, 126, 152, 166; and empire 87,
    96–100, 114; heroic conventions of
    70, 104, 131, 142–5; conventional
    roles 80, 86, *92,* 96, 171; *see also*
    gender; sexuality
Massey, Doreen 110, 116, 217
Maxwell, D.E.S. 218
McCaffery, Steve 229
McClung, Nellie 108
McGifford, Diane 229
McGrath, Carmelita 226
McGregor, Gaile 163
McKay, Ian 83

McKenna, Katherine 111
McLachlan, Alexander 213
McLuhan, Marshall 218
McMullen, John 82
measurement 63, 72–4, 87, 99, 102,
    106, 112, 114, 145, 148, 158, 161,
    214; *see also* maps; surveyor
Mechanics' Institute 84
media. *See* communications
memory 9–10, 25, 122, 125–6, 164,
    195, 203, 208
'Men Like Summer Snow' 124–5
Mennonites 86
metaphor, metonymy, symbol 3, 6, 8,
    17–19, 30, 38–9, 64, 71, 132, 151,
    155, 165, 178, 186, 211, 215; and
    ethics 96; and real estate 73; meta-
    phors of body 109–11; of camera
    168; of distance 101; of divorce
    109; of economic disparity 112; of
    ice and snow 203; of insider, out-
    sider 116; of land as woman, child
    18; of landscape in motion 114,
    195, 211; of the military 9, 19–20,
    39, 82, 99, 145, 151, 153, 203–4; of
    measurement 99; of property 99;
    of origin 146; of savage wilderness
    18; of sexuality 151; of utility and
    domesticity 18; *see also* imagery
metatextuality, self-reflexivity 3, 149,
    168, 201–2
Metcalf, John 197
Métis 38, 85, 119
metonymy. *See* metaphor
metropolis 158
Mexico 204
Middle West, term defined 147
military images 21, *52; see also* war
mines, mining 6, 74, *88–9,* 107
missionaries 33, *47*

railways 12, 17, 76, 85–6, *90*, 104–6,
112, 128, 194, 207–8
Rainy River 189
Ramusio, Giovanni 55; Italian text
220–1
Raven 35
'Raven and the First Men' 38
Raven Steals the Light, The 37–8, 53–4
Ray, Carl 30, *40*
real estate 6, 20, 73, 208–10
Reaney, James 149, 226
'Reaney's Region' 149
*Red Man Watching White Man Trying
to Fix Hole in Sky 43*
Redbird, Duke 38
Reflections on the French Revolution 63
Regina 157
region 17, 19, 56, 86, 115–60, 167,
201, 203–4; defined 117–18,
146–52; regional idyll 82; *see also*
specific names
Regis, Pamela 35
Reid, Bill 31, 37–8, 53–4, 218
Reid, Jamie 208
Reid, Martine 31
religion 9, 14, 19, 21, 24, 30, 32–7,
42, 54–7, 61, 67, 75–9, 86, 101, 113,
126, 145, 159, 172–4, 176, 199, 202,
212–13; and ecology 31; and American regionalism 147; *see also*
Christ; divine design
Renaissance 4, 21
RePlacing 196
representation 4, 11, 21, 44, 103, 110,
136, 147, 164–5, 180, 189, 192, 208
Reynolds, Sir Joshua 25
Rheingold, Howard 163
rhetoric 9, 29, 32, 54, 64, 78–9, 110,
119, 147, 151, 155, 171, 213, 221; of
science 35, 64

Richard, Jean-Pierre 163
Richler, Mordecai 131, 157
Richmond 210–11
Ridington, Robin 30–2
Ringuet 82, 118–19
Rising Village, The 68, 83
river systems 17, 27, 56, 59, 66–7, 74,
109, 119–22, 128–9, 131, 144–6,
153–4, 191, 195, 207, 210; in Native
tale 53, 61; rivers and music 26
roads, tracks, streets 8, 12, 39, 69, 76,
95, 103, 112–13, 127–8, 162, 186,
191, 196–9, 214
Robber Bride, The 157
Roberts, Sir Charles G.D. 87, 96–100,
114, 142
Rocking Chair, The 119
rocks, crags, outcrops 13, 15, 30, 35,
59, 61, 65–6, 128–9, 145–6, 171–4,
191, 193
Rocky Mountains 12–13, 86, 90, 105,
128, 208
Rogers, Otto *188–9*
romance narrative conventions 70,
96, 98, 106–7, 112, 118, 130, 134,
159; and religion 101
Romeo and Juliet 38
Roper, Edward 190
Rose, Gillian 110
Rosen, Charles 26
Ross, Malcolm 155
Ross, Sinclair 130–1, 155, 157
Roughing It in the Bush 59, 68–71, 75,
171, 212
Roy, Gabrielle 157, 207
Roy, Patricia 107
ruins 26, 35, 61, 100
rural, versions of 25, 61, 82, 84,
122–3, 126, 131, 147, 154–6, 158,
191; rustic 155